D0801531

INVENTING VIETNAM

This book considers the Vietnam War in light of U.S. foreign policy in Vietnam, concluding that the war was a direct result of failed state-building efforts. This U.S. nation-building project began in the mid-1950s with the ambitious goal of creating a new independent, democratic, modern state below the seventeenth parallel. No one involved imagined this effort would lead to a major and devastating war in less than a decade. Carter analyzes how the United States ended up fighting a large-scale war that wrecked the countryside, generated a flood of refugees, and brought about catastrophic economic distortions, results that actually further undermined the larger U.S. goal of building a viable state. Carter argues that well before the Tet Offensive shocked the viewing public in late January 1968, the campaign in southern Vietnam had completely failed and, furthermore, that the program contained the seeds of its own failure from the outset.

James M. Carter obtained his PhD from the University of Houston in 2004 and is currently assistant professor of history at Drew University. His research specialties include U.S. foreign relations, the Vietnam War, and the Cold War. His publications include several articles on nation building in Vietnam and private contractors in both Vietnam and Iraq, in addition to book reviews in *Itinerario*, the *Journal of Military History*, and *Education about Asia*, as well as on H-Diplo. In summer 2007, he was appointed a Fellow of the Summer Military History Seminar at West Point Military Academy.

INVENTING VIETNAM

The United States and State Building, 1954–1968

JAMES M. CARTER
Drew University

CAMBRIDGE
UNIVERSITY PRESS

CAMBRIDGE UNIVERSITY PRESS
Cambridge, New York, Melbourne, Madrid, Cape Town, Singapore, São Paulo, Delhi

Cambridge University Press
32 Avenue of the Americas, New York, NY 10013-2473, USA

www.cambridge.org
Information on this title: www.cambridge.org/9780521716901

© James M. Carter 2008

This publication is in copyright. Subject to statutory exception
and to the provisions of relevant collective licensing agreements,
no reproduction of any part may take place without
the written permission of Cambridge University Press.

First published 2008

Printed in the United States of America

A catalog record for this publication is available from the British Library.

Library of Congress Cataloging in Publication Data

Carter, James M., 1968–
Inventing Vietnam : the United States and State Building, 1954–1968 /
James M. Carter.
p. cm.
Includes bibliographical references and index.
ISBN 978-0-521-88865-3 (hardback) – ISBN 978-0-521-71690-1 (pbk.)
1. Vietnam War, 1961–1975 – United States. 2. United States – Foreign relations –
Vietnam. 3. Vietnam – Foreign relations – United States. 4. United States – Foreign
relations – 1945–1989. 5. Vietnam – Politics and government – 1945–1975. I. Title.
DS558.C38 2008
959.704′32 – dc22 20070454

ISBN 978-0-521-88865-3 hardback
ISBN 978-0-521-71690-1 paperback

Cambridge University Press has no responsibility for
the persistence or accuracy of URLs for external or
third-party Internet Web sites referred to in this publication
and does not guarantee that any content on such
Web sites is, or will remain, accurate or appropriate.

CONTENTS

ACKNOWLEDGMENTS

During the course of research and writing this book, I have accumulated personal and professional debts I can never hope to adequately repay. For now, an acknowledgment and thank-you will have to do.

A number of research aides and archivists have helped me in ways too numerous to mention. At Michigan State University's Archives and Historical Collections Center, I have to thank Jeanine Mazak for her near-constant help during every hour of my time there. She saved me hours of labor and numerous mistakes. I would also like to thank Car Lee, whose detailed understanding of the Vietnam project collection made my work much easier.

At the Lyndon Johnson Presidential Library, John Wilson and Linda Hansen Seelke were always ready to help and willing to share their considerable knowledge and understanding of not only the archives, but also the era of the Johnson presidency. I am also grateful to both the John F. Kennedy and Johnson libraries for their grants in aid of research.

I would like to thank the people at the private corporations that were involved in Vietnam who took the time to help locate documents. Rex Osborne and Kelly Head were very helpful in pinning down what documents remained at the Boise office of Washington Group International (WGI), formerly Morrison-Knudsen. W. Bruce Walters, the Corporate Records Manager at WGI, was also very helpful in finding which of the company's in-house magazine issues pertained to Vietnam. Once I identified them, he simply mailed them all to me. For that I am very grateful. Mary Carter at Boise State University's Albertson's Library was also very helpful in tracking down nearly lost issues of the consortium's Saigon newspaper. I am also eternally indebted to Joe Fleenor at J.A. Jones Construction for not only locating hundreds of documents about to be thrown out, but for then sending all of the originals to me! I owe at least a couple of chapters of this project to him. It is not an exaggeration to say that without these people at the corporations mentioned, I would have been unable to write nearly half of this book.

I would like to thank a couple colleagues at the University of Houston who have tolerated my ignorance and have even played their part in trying to end it. My dissertation committee was very helpful in refining some of the specific arguments and in smoothing out the rough edges of others. My relationship with Martin Melosi, in particular, extends back to my first graduate seminar. He has been a great resource for me and has always been there as editor, critic, colleague, and friend.

Bob Buzzanco has been much more than simply a dissertation advisor. I have known Bob now for nearly eight years. During those years, I have learned more than just history. He and I have made a great team, to borrow from Mark Twain, because he knows everything there is to know and I know the rest. I have learned a great deal about the way history is researched, written, made, and received. I have learned that history is important, that the responsibility of the historian extends well beyond simply writing down the events of the past for posterity. History ought to explain and to make a contribution. Historians ought to tackle large issues and historical problems. And, not simply for the sake of doing it or to satisfy some arcane curiosity, but for the sake of changing the world in which we live. History does not repeat itself, as the shopworn saying suggests. Rather, people repeat poorly understood historical phenomena.

Finally, I have to thank the person who has meant more to me during this process than any other: my wife, Shelli. She began as and has remained a tireless supporter along this journey. It is, in fact, her fault I remained in graduate school. I would have certainly chosen some other path of lesser resistance. She has endured every research junket, every twist and turn, every up and every down with amazing consistency, support, and love. She has read every word, more than once, and has offered valuable insights at every point. I want her to know she has not only contributed mightily to this project, but that she has also kept me sane and focused as well. I love her very much and am forever indebted to her for putting up with me and with this process. For whatever it is worth, I dedicate this work to her.

INTRODUCTION: INVENTING VIETNAM

The country that is more developed industrially only shows, to the less developed, the image of its own future.

– Karl Marx

The great problem from now on out [is] whether we [can] salvage what the Communists had ostensibly left out of their grasp in Indochina.

– Secretary of State John Foster Dulles

I've never seen a situation like this [in southern Vietnam]. It defies imagination.... The government is shaky as all hell. It is being propped up for the moment only with great difficulty. Nothing can help it so much as administrative, economic, and social reforms.... The needs are enormous, the time short.

– Wesley Fishel, 1954

By early 1957,...it became evident the newly created nation [in Vietnam] would survive successfully the series of crises which threatened its existence at the outset.

– Michigan State University Vietnam Advisory Group (MSUG), *Final Report*

Although no MSUG member ever expected to find in newly independent Vietnam all the civil liberties firmly established among older western democracies, some members had misgivings lest the project's technical assistance might serve to strengthen an autocratic regime and retard the development of democratic institutions. Most members...believed our activities were valuable...in creating among the Vietnamese a critical attitude for seeking truth and knowledge through systematic research, promoting the study of social sciences from the western viewpoint, raising the general of educational standards, and implanting in the minds of government officials, police officers and teachers the ideas

of responsibility and responsiveness to the public, individual dignity
and other such concepts, the acceptance of which is a prerequisite for
the eventual evolution of free institutions in Vietnam.

– MSUG *Final Report*, 1962

We are no longer dealing with anyone [in Saigon] who represents any-
body in a political sense. We are simply acting to prevent a collapse of
the Vietnamese military forces which we pay for and supply.

– Senator Mike Mansfield, June 1965

There is no tradition of a national government in Saigon. There are no
roots in the country. . . . I don't think we ought to take this government
seriously. There is no one who can do anything. We have to do what
we think we ought to regardless of what the Saigon government does.

– Henry Cabot Lodge, July 1965

We would be occupying an essentially hostile foreign country.

– General William C. Westmoreland, January 1965, on the
possibility of use of American troops in southern Vietnam

Despite all our public assertions to the contrary, the South Vietnamese
are not – and have never been – a nation.

– General Victor Krulak, U.S. Marines, April 1966

Twelve years have elapsed since we began contributing economic assistance and manpower to . . . Vietnam. Yet, that nation continues to face
political instability, lack a sense of nationhood, and to suffer social,
religious, and regional factionalism and severe economic dislocations.
Inflation continues to mount, medical care remains inadequate, land
reform is virtually nonexistent, agricultural and education[al] advances
are minimal, and the development of an honest, capable, and responsible civil service has hardly begun.

– Representative Donald H. Rumsfeld, 1966

I want to leave the footprints of America in Vietnam. . . . I want them
to say when the Americans come, this is what they leave – schools, not
long cigars. We're going to turn the Mekong into a Tennessee Valley.

– Lyndon B. Johnson, 1966

Vietnam itself is primarily an agricultural country; the only major port is
Saigon. The deployment of large U.S. military forces, and other friendly
forces such as the Korean division, in a country of this sort requires the
construction of new ports, warehouse facilities, access roads, improvements to highways leading to the interior of the country and along the

coasts, troop facilities, hospitals, completely new airfields and major improvements to existing airfields, communications facilities, etc.

– Robert S. McNamara, Secretary of Defense, 1966

The coordinated activities of the Facilities Engineering Command and RMK-BRJ have brought sweeping change to much of the tiny nation's [southern Vietnam] landscape. Hills have been planed down for air bases, and rivers and harbors dredged for ports. Deserted beaches have become busy waterfront depots. Paths have been replaced by highways, new hospitals have been built and old surgical facilities rehabilitated. Billets for tens of thousands of troops have sprung up where little existed before. Today, most of these widely diversified projects serve as support elements vital to the war effort. Tomorrow, many of the developments will help serve South Viet Nam in its peacetime pursuit of national betterment.

– "Viet Nam: Building for Battle, Building for Peace,"
The Em-Kayan, September 1966

How were the U.S. forces...to maintain thousands of miles of roads, hundreds of bridges, and thousands of culverts without stationing engineer units in compounds throughout the length and breadth of Vietnam? How were they to support a complex modern army of half a million men without ports and depots to receive, sort, and store supplies? Where would they house this army and in what kind of structures?...The very nature of the war required a military presence everywhere, and that simply meant dotting the countryside with fire-support bases, maneuver-element base camps, logistics support areas, heliports, and tactical airstrips.... Each base, airfield, and compound had to be joined to its neighbor in an ever-expanding network of primary and secondary roads.

– Lieutenant General Carroll H. Dunn, U.S. Army

The Americans came in like bulldozers.

– Former Ambassador to the United States Bui Diem

It is very clear that in many respects, much of Vietnam is today a nation of refugees.

– Leo Cherne, Chairman, International Rescue Committee

Hell, with half a million men in Vietnam, we are spending twenty-one billion dollars a year, and we're fighting the whole war with Vietnamese watching us; how can you talk about national sovereignty?

– Robert Komer, Special Assistant to the President

It is still not unfair to say that there is no real government in Vietnam. . . .
It is . . . the result of a political structure still so fragmented and weak
that division commanders can choose those orders they intend to obey,
and Ministries can follow their own paths regardless of the desires of
the Prime Minister.

– Richard Holbrooke, Assistant to Robert Komer, 1966

The people I talked to [in Vietnam] didn't seem to have any feeling
about South Vietnam as a country. We fought the war for a separate
South Vietnam, but there wasn't any South and there never was one.

– Paul Warnke, Former General Counsel for the
Defense Department

There are no more pyramids to build. We have just about completed
the largest construction effort in history.

– John B. Kirkpatrick, Former General Manager, RMK-BRJ
Joint Venture Saigon, Vietnam[1]

---

[1] Karl Marx, *Capital: A Critical Analysis of Capitalist Production* (New York: International Publishers, 1967), 1:8–9. Dulles quote is from Foreign Relations of the United States (FRUS), *Memorandum of Discussion at the 207th Meeting of the National Security Council, Thursday, July 22, 1954* (Washington, DC: U.S. Department of State, 1952–4), XIII:1869. Wesley Fishel to Edward Weidner, August 25 and September 4, 1954, Michigan State University Vietnam Advisory Group (MSUG) Papers, Vietnam Project Papers, Correspondence, Edward Weidner, 1954, box 628, folder 101. Next two quotes are from MSUG, *Final Report* (East Lansing: Michigan State University, 1962). Mansfield quoted in George M. Kahin, *Intervention: How America Became Involved in Vietnam* (New York: Anchor Books, 1987), 345. Lodge quote is from FRUS, *Vietnam* (Washington, DC: U.S. Department of State, 1965), 3:193. Westmoreland quoted in Robert Buzzanco, *Masters of War: Military Dissent & Politics in the Vietnam Era* (New York: Cambridge University Press, 1996), 190. Krulak quoted in ibid., 257. Rumsfeld quote is from *An Investigation of the U.S. Economic and Military Assistance Programs in Vietnam, 42nd Report by the Committee on Government Operations, October 12, 1966* (Washington, DC: Committee on Government Operations, 1966), 127. Johnson quoted in Doris Kearns, *Lyndon Johnson and the American Dream* (New York: St. Martin's Press, 1991), 267. McNamara quote is from Senate Committee on Armed Services, *Hearings before the Committee on Armed Services and the Subcommittee on Department of Defense of the Committee on Appropriations*, 89th Cong., 2nd sess., S. Rep, 1966, 12. Dunn quoted from *Base Development in South Vietnam, 1965–1970* (Washington, DC: Department of the Army, 1991), 12. Bui Diem, *In the Jaws of History* (New York: Houghton Mifflin, 1987), 127. Cherne quote is from Senate Subcommittee on Refugees and Escapees of the Committee on the Judiciary, *Refugee Problems in South Vietnam and Laos*, 89th Cong., 1st sess. (1965), 56. Komer quoted in Lloyd Gardner, *Pay Any Price: Lyndon Johnson and the Wars for Vietnam* (Chicago: Ivan R. Dee, 1995), 303. Holbrooke quote is from *Vietnam Trip Report: October 26–November 18, 1966*. Warnke quoted in Christian Appy, *Patriots: The Vietnam War Remembered from All Sides* (New York: Penguin, 2003), 279. Kirkpatrick quote is from "End of Viet Nam Construction Program," *The Em-Kayan*, June 1972.

Early in 2004, the Vietnamese government completed work on the first of a major three-phase highway building program. The highway, when completed in some fifteen years, will run along the route of the famous Ho Chi Minh Trail down the border with Laos. During the period of the American war in Vietnam, *Ho Chi Minh Trail* referred to an elaborate network of arteries that ran the gamut from mere footpaths to large roads able to accommodate heavy truck traffic. The trail ran through Laos, eventually farther south into Cambodia, and crossed the border into Vietnam at a number of strategic points. It was by all accounts an important supply system for the southern insurgency fighting against the Americans and their client regime in Saigon.[2]

This latest road project is to be much greater in scope and will serve a very different purpose. The Vietnamese government hopes the new road, named the Ho Chi Minh Highway, will open up the interior along the border with Laos and allow rural people access to faraway markets. It will also provide important transportation links between the country-side and the cities for a government looking to develop the dilapidated transportation infrastructure of the nation. Sections of the national road Highway 1 have not been updated since the end of the American war some thirty years ago. Near the ancient capital city of Hué, for example, the road shrinks to only one lane, and during the monsoon season, sections of it close completely for days at a time. Much of the rest of the nation's secondary road network also needs updating. The Ho Chi Minh Highway project is an important step in modernizing the nation's roads and in developing the nation's physical infrastructure.

The project has also, however, generated considerable criticism, mainly because the area under construction, in Quang Tri Province, was the most heavily bombed during the Vietnam War, and there remain some 3 million land mines and more than three hundred thousand tons of unexploded ordinance (UXO) littering many square miles of the country. Since 1975, this province alone accounted for more than sixty-seven hundred of the one hundred thousand total wounded and killed by UXO.[3] Building the new highway will, critics argue, unearth some of

---

[2] John Prados, *The Blood Road: The Ho Chi Minh Trail and the Vietnam War* (New York: John Wiley, 1999).

[3] See, e.g., "The Vietnam Veterans Memorial Fund's Project Renew," Vietnam Veterans Memorial Fund, http://vvmf.org/index.cfm?SectionID = 21. David Lamb, "Perils of War Remain in the Soil of Vietnam," *Los Angeles Times*, April 26, 2004.

this long-buried ordinance and place workers, travelers, and the people who live along the proposed roadway in harm's way unnecessarily. Nevertheless, the road building will likely continue. When completed, the Ho Chi Minh Highway will traverse this region and many more areas of the country also littered with UXO. The whole project, couched in terms of economic development, will eventually consist of eight lanes stretching from north to south and covering hundreds of miles of rugged, and mined, terrain. Observers have called it "the most ambitious road project ever in Asia."[4] Whether this claim is true or not, this is certainly not the first time large-scale efforts have been launched to modernize Vietnam.

There is an interesting and insightful juxtaposition in the Vietnamese government developing the nation's system of modern roadways today and the earlier effort by the United States to transform the southern half of that nation through various economic, political, and military development initiatives. That the government is now building those roadways and other infrastructure through heavily bombed regions still scattered with mines and that saw considerable destruction during the Vietnam War also speaks volumes of that earlier effort.

During the period of direct American involvement beginning in 1954, the U.S. mission in Vietnam designed and implemented a range of far-reaching economic, political, and eventually military development projects in one of the most thorough and ambitious state-building efforts in the postwar period. The projects consisted of installing a president; building a civil service and training bureaucrats around him; creating a domestic economy, currency, and an industrial base; building ports and airfields, hospitals, and schools; dredging canals and harbors to create a transportation grid; constructing an elaborate network of modern roadways; establishing a telecommunications system; and training, equipping, and funding a national police force and a military, among others.

Between 1954 and 1960, the United States poured into the southern half of Vietnam nearly US$1.5 billion to pay for its state-building program(s). Despite the enormity of these efforts, the project to build an independent state around Ngo Dinh Diem met with failure. By the early

---

[4] Michael Sullivan, "Analysis: Ho Chi Minh Trail in Vietnam," National Public Radio, April 5, 2004.

1960s, the United States began responding to the project's failings and to a growing chorus in Vietnam opposing the effort with greater levels of military and police force to protect its client regime in Saigon. Ultimately, and almost imperceptibly, U.S. officials glossed over the fact that the state-building project was deeply troubled and failing and instead began justifying greater military involvement and authorizing greater use of force by the regime in order to stamp out the Vietnamese resistance to that effort as well as to mask its deficiencies. At the same time, nearly all American officials began referring to southern Vietnam exclusively as "South Vietnam," as though the state had existed and now compelled defense from outside aggressors bent on conquest. That fiction perpetuated the powerful and politically successful idea that the effort in Vietnam was about combating aggression and that the problem stemmed from North Vietnamese aggression against a putatively independent South Vietnam. In reality, the war in Vietnam resulted not from outside aggression, but from the failure of the six-year effort to build a viable state infrastructure around the regime in Saigon.

Throughout the decade of the 1960s, the United States escalated its presence in Vietnam, began waging a war, expanded its aid program, and launched a military construction effort of unprecedented scale. The war itself brought the most far-reaching changes the region had witnessed so far. Over the course of the fourteen years from 1954, the United States transformed much of the southern half of Vietnam numerous times as part of its effort to build and/or salvage a state below the seventeenth parallel. These transformations were the product of the array of state-building projects, resettlement schemes, commodity/economic aid and cultural transmission, as well as the more obvious effects of military aid, warfare and destruction, and political manipulation. Moreover, the changes brought to Vietnam undulated according to and were a product of the particular agendas of the different American presidential administrations. The differing programs and plans for southern Vietnam are a good barometer of the crisis each administration perceived that it faced in Southeast Asia.[5]

---

[5] The relationship between the war in Vietnam and individual administrations and presidents is an established trend in the historical literature as well. See, inter alia, William Rust, *Kennedy in Vietnam: American Vietnam Policy, 1960–1963* (New York: Charles Scribner's Sons, 1985); Lawrence Freedman, *Kennedy's Wars: Berlin, Lao, Cuba, and Vietnam* (New

The administrations of Dwight D. Eisenhower, John F. Kennedy, and Lyndon B. Johnson, in particular, outlined and implemented an array of short- and long-term policy objectives for Vietnam. Meeting these objectives involved considerable resources from the Central Intelligence Agency (CIA), the U.S. military, the Agency for International Development (AID), Michigan State University (MSU), many private corporations specializing in hundreds of different tasks, religious organizations, private sector economists and bureaucrats, and much more. By the early 1960s, the costs of the project grew to an average of $1 million each day.

Despite this unprecedented effort, the project achieved limited and fleeting success. Oftentimes, failure in one area offsets success in another, such as the public political rehabilitation of Ngo Dinh Diem by the late 1950s, while the resistance to his rule grew into the National Liberation Front by 1960. Efforts to legitimize the regime in Saigon and to spread its influence beyond that city also failed repeatedly, and planners resorted to the use of force simply to keep it in place. In the realm of land reform, industrialization, currency stabilization, encouraging domestic savings, creating a tax base, and opening up the political system to other parties, the overall effort met with unmitigated long-term failure.

Providing evidence of the effort's success, however, received a great deal of emphasis throughout the period. This pressure to demonstrate success in Vietnam (and in the Cold War) led ultimately to the sharp bifurcation between the official story from government sources and the story as told by others on the ground in Vietnam. It also led a majority of U.S. officials to accept, after many years of effort, some of the most important and erroneous assumptions concerning the state of affairs in southern Vietnam. At times, officials both in Washington and in Saigon seemed to will away evidence of failure, excess, waste, fraud, and flawed planning. They did this for a variety of reasons, from individual survival within a particular administration to agency/institutional territoriality, inertia, individual and collective credibility, or some combination of these factors. This is not to suggest that all officials viewed the situation in Vietnam in the same way, nor am I suggesting that their varied criticisms were unimportant. Successive administrations did achieve a

York: Oxford University Press, 2002); Larry Berman, *Lyndon Johnson's War: The Road to Stalemate in Vietnam* (New York: W. W. Norton, 1989); Gardner, *Pay Any Price*; Jeffrey Kimball, *Nixon's Vietnam War* (Lawrence: University Press of Kansas, 1998).

consensus on perhaps the most fundamental issue related to U.S. policy toward southern Vietnam: that there existed an independent, noncommunist state south of the seventeenth parallel that compelled American aid and defense.

This assumption is also reflected, either implicitly or explicitly, in the historical literature on U.S. policy in Vietnam. Historians have not probed what were fundamental problems and obstacles to the achievement of success in Southeast Asia through the lens of this state-building enterprise. This pattern has obscured the tremendous effort, preceding and paralleling the start of major warfare, of building a physical infrastructure in southern Vietnam. The planners who began the effort to build the new state infrastructure clearly recognized that the state as they imagined it did not exist. They saw themselves as building something completely new in southern Vietnam. They then had to rebuild numerous aspects of state infrastructure over again as the objectives and realities in Vietnam shifted. From the outset, American experts and advisors in Vietnam saw themselves engaged in a thoroughgoing campaign to create a modern state out of southern Vietnam. At the same time, security measures such as the creation of a police network, the Vietnamese Bureau of Investigation, and an army paralleled an expanding state-building program carried out by the U.S. Operations Mission (USOM) and specialists from Michigan State University. The two facets of the overall mission, military preparedness and the physical processes of state building, competed for resources and emphasis over the next several years. As the resistance movement grew and security concerns moved front and center, the U.S. mission responded by hurriedly putting in place a vast modern military infrastructure. By the mid-1960s, this military buildup overwhelmed all other efforts in Vietnam. But those efforts did not simply go away; they now took on different meaning and served the purpose of sustaining the wartime economic and political structures that had already been put in place in Saigon. This process of building and rebuilding, of inventing and reinventing, continued over the whole of American involvement from 1954 forward.

The process also disrupted Vietnamese society, created an unstable political environment, and kept the economy in a constant state of shock. As the American role increased dramatically in the 1960s, so too did the level of monetary aid, goods imported into Vietnam, the construction programs, the presence of military personnel, and the pressure on the fragile political structure and economy to accommodate the changes. Meanwhile, the increasing level of warfare turned hundreds of thousands of Vietnamese out as refugees and disrupted Vietnamese rural life and the subsistence agricultural system. A large mobile refugee population and the destruction of warfare also created a grave public health crisis as the urban population swelled and overtaxed an already inadequate public health/medical infrastructure.

The regime in Saigon consistently lacked the ability to mitigate any of these serious problems. It simply did not have the capability (nor, at times, the will) to deal with the needs of the people. It had not been able to reach out to those in the countryside and make itself legitimate during the relative peace of the late 1950s, much less during the full-scale war that existed by the mid-1960s. It also lacked any appreciable means of generating revenue outside the American aid program. It was, as members of the aid mission frankly admitted at the time, singularly dependent upon continued American aid. Its tax base remained tiny and politically sensitive. Its overall decision-making capability was also limited by the realities of war and by the considerable power differential between the regime and the United States. The latter had made a commitment to wage war and defeat the enemy, an increasingly audacious and decades-long revolutionary movement, and had structured the entire aid program toward that end. Vietnamese officials well understood that their own survival also hinged on meeting that objective. Many of them also directly benefited from loopholes and excesses that were a part of the U.S. aid program. Amid growing security concerns and escalating violence and warfare, state building fell out of favor as impractical and untimely. These efforts would have to wait until southern Vietnam could be made secure. Nevertheless, both Vietnamese and American officials continued to assert the existence of "South Vietnam." This assumption papered over considerable failings and future obstacles to progress. These obstacles became further ingrained as the aid program shifted its focus away from ameliorating social misery caused by the war and toward greater energy, money, and other resources for the war effort.

Historians of U.S. involvement in Vietnam have not begun to grapple sufficiently with these matters. In some works the regime in Saigon is recognized as dependent on American aid and an evolving experiment in state building. Historian David Anderson, for example, has written in his study of early U.S. involvement in Vietnam that "there was no

self-sustaining state in the South for the United States to support...
[and] only U.S. military force could maintain the fiction that there
was."[6] And historian George Herring's widely cited general history of
the United States in Vietnam refers to the regime, quoting John Kennedy,
as "our offspring" and recognizes that America's early "nation building" experiment in Vietnam was a "high-risk gamble."[7] Others view the
crafting of the Southeast Asia Treaty Organization (SEATO) as artificial
and as little more than a political tool and see the perpetuation of the
division at the seventeenth parallel beyond 1956 in similar terms.[8]

To be sure, historians have recognized the precarious nature of the
U.S. state-building project and even pointed out its artificiality, particularly in the early years of U.S. involvement. At the same time, others
have accepted "South Vietnam's" existence and, where critical of the
regime, point out its weaknesses and excesses. These studies often discuss the extent to which a variety of shortcomings stood in the way of
ultimate U.S. victory. Many writers believe Ngo Dinh Diem's refusal to
reform his stranglehold on power, for example, posed a serious problem
and, in effect, numbered his days as the leader of the country.[9] Others

---

[6] David Anderson, *Trapped by Success: The Eisenhower Administration and Vietnam, 1953–
1961* (New York: Columbia University Press, 1991), 208–9.

[7] George C. Herring, *America's Longest War: The United States and Vietnam, 1950–1975,*
4th ed. (New York: McGraw-Hill, 2002), 53–54.

[8] Gabriel Kolko deals explicitly with this problem of naming the two geographical entities
created at the Geneva Conference of 1954 and then perpetuated by war. He writes that
the terms used to describe southern Vietnam, such as *RVN* or *GVN*, are "heuristic"
descriptions and have "neither a legal nor a historical basis." See Kolko, *Anatomy of a
War: Vietnam, the United States, and the Modern Historical Experience* (New York: New
Press, 1985), x–xi; George M. Kahin and John W. Lewis, *The United States in Vietnam*
(New York: Delta Press, 1969); Theodore Draper, *Abuse of Power* (New York: Viking
Press, 1966). Writing on the period prior to 1960, a number of widely cited accounts
refer to the precarious and artificial nature of the creation of the regime in Saigon, the
SEATO agreement, and the whole effort in general. See, in addition to the works already
mentioned, Kahin, *Intervention*; Robert D. Schulzinger, *A Time for War: The United States
and Vietnam, 1941–1975* (New York: Oxford University Press, 1997); Stanley Karnow,
Vietnam: A History (New York: Penguin Books, 1991); Marilyn B. Young, *The Vietnam
Wars, 1945–1990* (New York: Harper Collins, 1991); Buzzanco, *Masters of War.*

[9] Philip Catton, *Diem's Final Failure: Prelude to America's War in Vietnam* (Lawrence:
University Press of Kansas, 2002). Ellen Hammer, *A Death in November: America in
Vietnam, 1963* (New York: E. P. Dutton, 1987). Lawrence J. Bassett and Stephen E. Pelz,
"The Failed Search for Victory: Vietnam and the Politics of War," in *Kennedy's Quest
for Victory: American Foreign Policy, 1961–1963,* ed. Thomas G. Paterson (New York:
Oxford University Press, 1989), 223–52. David Halberstam, *The Making of a Quagmire:
America and Vietnam during the Kennedy Era,* rev. ed. (New York: McGraw-Hill, 1988).
Roger Hilsman, *To Move a Nation: The Politics of Foreign Policy in the Administration*

have emphasized the considerable gap in cultural understanding between the Americans and the Vietnamese, which limited the Americans' ability to adequately control and/or influence the government in Saigon.[10] Some have pointed to a pronounced tendency for corruption, waste, and mismanagement in both the American mission and within the Saigon regime.[11] Numerous studies have criticized the American military's approach to the war and/or the politics of the war both in Vietnam and back in Washington. Most of these works, some explicitly and others implicitly, suggest some alternative course might have resulted in victory for the whole project.[12] There has been no lack of critical analysis of the shortcomings of the effort to "win" in Vietnam.

On the other hand, while some historians have made these arguments pointing out the precarious nature of the American experiment in Saigon, particularly during the late 1950s, most do refer back to the regime as a government and to "South Vietnam" as a state when

of *John F. Kennedy* (New York: Doubleday, 1967). David Kaiser, *American Tragedy: Kennedy, Johnson, and the Origins of the Vietnam War* (Cambridge, MA: Harvard University Press, 2000), 186–248. Francis Winters, *The Year of the Hare: America in Vietnam, January 25, 1963–February 15, 1964* (Athens: University of Georgia Press, 1997).

[10] George C. Herring, "'Peoples Quite Apart': Americans, South Vietnamese, and the War in Vietnam," *Diplomatic History* 14 (Winter 1990): 1–23. Neil L. Jamieson, *Understanding Vietnam* (Berkeley: University of California Press, 1993). Francis Fitzgerald, *Fire in the Lake: The Vietnamese and the Americans in Vietnam* (New York: Vintage Books, 1972). Robert Shaplen, *The Lost Revolution: The Story of Twenty Years of Neglected Opportunities in Vietnam and of America's Failure to Foster Democracy There* (New York: Harper & Row, 1966). Loren Baritz, *Backfire: How American Culture Led Us into the Vietnam War and Made Us Fight the Way We Did* (New York: Morrow, 1985).

[11] Of course, there is considerable overlap between these themes and the different historical works. Many of them emphasize these shortcomings and more. Kolko, *Anatomy of a War*, esp. chap. 18. Bernard Fall, *The Two Viet-Nams: A Political and Military Analysis* (New York: Praeger, 1964). Two dated but still very useful works are Robert Scigliano, *South Vietnam: Nation under Stress* (Boston: Houghton Mifflin, 1963), and Scigliano and Guy Fox, *Technical Assistance in Vietnam: The Michigan State University Experience* (New York: Praeger, 1965).

[12] Eric Bergureud, *The Dynamics of Defeat: The Vietnam War in Hau Nghia Province* (Boulder, CO: Westview Press, 1991). Douglas Blaufarb, *The Counterinsurgency Era: U.S. Doctrine and Performance* (New York: Free Press, 1977). Buzzanco, *Masters of War*. Larry Cable, *Unholy Grail: The US and the Wars in Vietnam, 1965–8* (New York: Routledge, 1991). Bruce Palmer, *The Twenty-five Year War: America's Military Role in Vietnam* (Lexington: University Press of Kentucky, 1984). Neil Sheehan, *A Bright Shining Lie: John Paul Vann and America in Vietnam* (New York: Random House, 1988). Harry G. Summers, *On Strategy: A Critical Analysis of the Vietnam War* (Novato, CA: Presidio Press, 1982). For much more detail on these and other works, see Gary R. Hess, "The Unending Debate: Historians and the Vietnam War," *Diplomatic History* 18 (Spring 1994): 239–64.

discussing the later years around the mid-1960s. Though historians have pointed out the initial state-building efforts, they have not stayed on that course and delved deeply into the evolution (or devolution) and consequences of those efforts beyond the late 1950s. In reality, "South Vietnam," to the extent that it came into being at all, was a failed American invention. And although historians have pointed out the shortcomings of the American effort to prop up the Saigon regime beginning in 1954, none have pursued the implications and larger meanings of this failure of state building and resulting war into the late 1960s.

At least one of the results of this pattern in the historiography has been the near-total neglect of the state-building efforts that began in 1954 and continued through the Americanization of the effort and large-scale warfare of the mid- and late 1960s. When these efforts to create the economy, industrialize rapidly, educate and train a civil service, create a military and police system, and build a network of deep-draft ports and airfields and primary and secondary road networks are examined as critical features of the U.S. role in Vietnam, it becomes clear that the war in Vietnam resulted from the failure of the state-building experiment and the related refusal to recognize that failure. At no point in all the years of American involvement there did the Saigon experiment become a viable, independent state capable of standing on its own without substantial American aid. Moreover, the large and ineluctable U.S. aid program failed to contribute to the development of an independent state and actually worked at cross purposes to that outcome. The heavy emphasis on security and military preparedness, justifiable or not, also undermined the development of an independent modern, democratic, and liberal state, the supposed objective of the early state-building program.

Though objectives always centered on the creation of a noncommunist bastion in southern Vietnam, those objectives shifted numerous times across the span of some fourteen years beginning in 1954. The early state-building program designed and carried out by USOM and the MSU group was eclipsed by a more thoroughly military set of solutions by the early 1960s that witnessed the triumph of so-called counterinsurgency tactics and the strategic hamlet program. These essentially military features of U.S. policy finally triumphed in total by the mid-1960s and were manifest in hundreds of thousands of troops and major warfare. Amid these changes in U.S. policy and the ebb and flow of state building and modernization/development programs and military initiatives, the transformation of southern Vietnam continued apace. As will be clear in the chapters that follow, the results were often far from what planners had envisioned.

I should explain my use of specific terms and phrases in the pages that follow for the sake of greater clarity and understanding. First of all, throughout these chapters, I use the phrase *state building* to describe these processes over many years to create something new and different and useful to U.S. interests in southern Vietnam. I use the phrase in a specific way, to connote something more than simply an economic or military aid program or even the two combined. The aid program and the U.S. mission to Vietnam went well beyond the scope of simply aiding a state either to fend off its enemies or to rebuild following the devastation of war. It was an attempt to create a new state infrastructure starting from scratch, to build something akin to what one historian has termed a *proto-state* in southern Vietnam. The project involved the building and piecing together of all the features of a modern state to create a new whole: a composite, really, of other, western and modern states. It also involved many large-scale infrastructure projects aimed at reshaping the social, economic, and political landscape of Vietnam. These large building projects, while also sharing much with similar initiatives under traditional colonialism, served as symbols of America's technological prowess and as reminders of U.S. power.[13] In the pages that follow I discuss many of these projects in detail and am purposefully dealing with the physical rather than the ideational processes of state building. My objective here is to tell the story of the many efforts to physically transform southern Vietnam and build the state of South Vietnam and to tell that story from the perspectives of those attempting to bring off this transformation. They were, numerous times over the years, inventing a new Vietnam.

In the larger sense, state building became a quite common feature of the Cold War rivalry. Although the Vietnam example stands out for its enormous scale, the United States was not alone in this kind of

---

[13] James C. Scott, *Seeing Like a State: How Certain Schemes to Improve the Human Condition Have Failed* (New Haven, CT: Yale University Press, 1998), esp. chap. 3. Michael Adas, *Dominance by Design: Technological Imperatives and America's Civilizing Mission* (Cambridge, MA: Harvard University Press, 2006), esp. chap. 5.

enterprise. In the aftermath of World War II, dozens of former colonies emerged from the ashes of that system and began groping about for not only independence, but developmental aid and assistance. The colonial system continued its collapse begun during the war right on into the 1960s. Between 1957 and 1962 alone, twenty-five new states declared independence. These emerging states were in dire need of large-scale aid to overcome the ravages of colonialism with its attendant lack of infrastructure, education, and economy. The Cold War added urgency to the problems of what came to be termed the *third world*. The rising global competition between the Soviet Union and the United States (and the British, French, and Chinese as well) sparked a fierce battle for influence and control of the former colonial areas of the world. The prevalence of illiteracy, poverty, and general underdevelopment became obstacles to be overcome in the pursuit of Cold War aims. Consequently, the dominant Cold War states took on many state-building projects in Asia, the Middle East, Latin America, and Africa. These projects ranged broadly in terms of success and failure, external versus internal control, infrastructure development, and level of disruption through civil war or revolutionary or counterrevolutionary violence. Many of these states lacked a modern physical infrastructure, native political-economic institutions, or an independent economic base, all of which significantly impacted the particular features of the state-building enterprise.[14] For at least two decades following World War II, a string of new states struggled against considerable historical obstacles as well as daunting Cold War limitations in their quest for sovereignty. This is the global context for the initiation of the U.S. state-building campaign in southern Vietnam beginning in 1954.

To refer to the American-led effort below the seventeenth parallel in Vietnam as the invention of a state is, I believe, a more precise and historically useful phrasing than the numerous alternatives. Describing an invented Vietnam is a compromise among terms such as *imported state*, *proto-state*, *dependency*, or *client state*.[15] Certainly there are elements

---

[14] Adas, *Dominance by Design*, esp. chap. 5.

[15] On *dependency*, see Anthony Brewer, esp. chap. 8, *Marxist Theories of Imperialism: A Critical Survey*, 2nd ed. (New York: Routledge Press, 1980), 161–199. See also Adas, *Dominance by Design*, chap. 5, "Imposing Modernity." Odd Arne Westad, *The Global Cold War: Third World Interventions and the Making of Our Times* (New York: Cambridge University Press, 2005), 76, 90.

of these types present at various junctures in Vietnam. Their use, however, cannot be productively sustained over the years from 1954 to 1968.
The shifting aims, objectives, and realities of U.S. policy and of circumstances on the ground in southern Vietnam defy this kind of categorization. Furthermore, the United States and its Cold War rivals committed
considerable resources of time, money, and energy to rapidly create
something useful for themselves out of the collapse of the old colonial
system in the two decades following 1945. Oftentimes, those efforts
ignored the on-the-ground realities of host societies. In some cases these
realities were perceived as obstacles, "traditional" and "backward,"
to be swept aside in the name of modernization and to clear the path
for "development." At times, too, this developmentalist rhetoric was
used to mask rather conventional uses of power and coercion. Seen in
this way, the many state-building efforts during the period were as much
invention as anything else. There is little that one might objectively term
natural about these efforts. Nor is there one pattern for the process, and
the success or failure of these many efforts is anything but clear from
the outset. My description of the U.S. effort in Vietnam as an invention
is intended to place that experience alongside the numbers of others in
this larger global context. This phenomenon and how it led to greater
U.S. involvement in Southeast Asia is the focus of Chapter 1.

In Vietnam, the United States brought to the project economic
aid, educational and construction programs, technological initiatives,
humanitarian relief aid, and innumerable cultural transmissions and
involved the resources of the government, military, private corporations, and nongovernmental organizations. Alongside what might be
considered more traditional nation-building initiatives and programs,
I also include military aid and the massive military construction program inaugurated in the mid-1960s in my discussion of state building
in Vietnam. The point in doing so is that one cannot understand the
project in Vietnam and its transformative impact, or its failure, if these
omnipresent features of U.S. policy are left out. Humanitarian, economic, cultural, political, and social features of the U.S. mission worked
right alongside, if ultimately subordinate to, military features. This odd
marriage led to what I later refer to as "the paradox of construction
and destruction," borrowing a phrase from an observer in Vietnam at
the time. The result was certainly not what the early U.S. state builders
of the late 1950s had in mind when they confidently went to work on

transforming southern Vietnam. It was not even what later planners and policy makers had hoped for, and more importantly, it was not a new, modern, independent, democratic state below the seventeenth parallel.

Challenging the view that the United States acted in defense of the state of "South Vietnam" in going to war in the 1960s, I argue, based on substantial new evidence, that the United States had from the start attempted to build a new state out of the southern half of Vietnam and that, judged on it own terms, it failed completely. Coincident with this writing, there has emerged a full-throated revision of the United States in Vietnam and of the war there in general. A key element of this latest revisionism is the rehabilitation of Ngo Dinh Diem and thus the ennobling of the American effort in Vietnam. As anyone who reads the literature on the United States in Vietnam knows, the subject has remained controversial and often ideologically charged since at least the 1960s. Veterans, politicians, academics, and a host of others have, over the years, revisited the Vietnam War with an eye toward rehabilitating the American role there and the war in general. Lately, this revisionism has become much more strident and explicit through the writings of scholars such as Mark Moyar and Keith Taylor. Among other things, both suggest a war in Vietnam that was being won and that was a noble cause, but that was ultimately undermined by "self-loathing" Americans back at home and "liberal" journalists who opposed the war. Much of what academics had for decades taken for granted as settled on that episode is now being questioned. Was it really a mistake for the United States to make such a commitment to Vietnam? Was Ngo Dinh Diem really such a bad guy? Why did the United States lose; *did* it lose? Who is to blame? Robert Buzzanco responded to some of these arguments and charges in a brief 2005 essay published by *Counterpunch*, a political newsletter. Soon, something called the *Buzzanco-Taylor debate* emerged, which once again brought some very basic assumptions regarding American involvement in Vietnam to the fore.[16]

---

[16] What actually emerged was really not a debate at all since Buzzanco and Taylor never actually met to debate anything. Robert Buzzanco, "Fear and (Self) Loathing in Lubbock, Texas, or How I Learned to Quit Worrying and Love Vietnam and Iraq," *Passport*, December 2005. Edward Miller, "War Stories: The Taylor-Buzzanco Debate and How We Think about the Vietnam War," *Journal of Vietnamese Studies* 1, no. 1–2 (February/August 2006): 453–484. See also Mark Moyar, *Triumph Forsaken: The Vietnam War, 1954–1965* (New York: Cambridge University Press, 2006).

My own work bears directly on this discussion. My research shows clearly that American planners, policy makers, and experts understood that they were building something that did not exist and also that they understood the reasons behind the failings of the project to build the new state below the seventeenth parallel. They understood the reasons for the failings even as they steadfastly refused to consider the implications or alternatives. The resulting failure was very much of their own making and had been built into the program during the early years of involvement.

Planners launched large-scale efforts to transform Vietnam's agricultural sector, create an industrial base, build a bureaucracy and police force, and buttress all this with hundreds of millions in economic aid. After years of effort with little long-term success, U.S. policy evolved slowly into a military defense of a piece of real estate in Southeast Asia. Rather than admit the failure of the state-building experiment, the United States chose the use of force to maintain what was by all accounts a precarious foothold in southern Vietnam. I argue throughout these pages that at least by the mid-1960s, the state building of the early years had been supplanted by a massive campaign to turn southern Vietnam into militarily defensible territory by putting in place a modern, integrated military infrastructure of unprecedented scale. The consequence of this incremental policy shift was that the regime in Saigon only grew more and more dependent on American aid, and the increased level of warfare and related destruction further sealed the fate of the entire project. At the same time, planners and policy makers invented and reinvented what they were doing in southern Vietnam to suit their immediate needs and to respond to faltering conditions on the ground.

By 1968, not coincidentally, the year of the Tet Offensive and the end of this study, the United States presided over a strange creation in southern Vietnam. Well over one-half million U.S. troops combined with another one-half-million-strong Vietnamese army, tens of thousands of police and other paramilitary forces, an aid program annually pouring nearly US$2 billion in military, commodity, and currency aid into the effort, several million Vietnamese refugees fleeing the war and swelling the cities, and a concomitant hemorrhaging economy all illustrated the unmitigated failure to build a state that could survive an American withdrawal. Though southern Vietnam had been made militarily defensible, the project was no closer to an independent, modern, democratic state than it had been all those years earlier. To be sure, there were a number of other factors that contributed ultimately to the American failure in Vietnam such as a powerful, organized insurgent revolutionary movement; aid for that resistance from Hanoi (and China and Russia as well); profound misunderstandings between the Vietnamese and the Americans; and a Cold War climate precluding deeper and more nuanced understanding of obstacles to a peaceful outcome. From the moment the United States opted to begin its state-building project, however, the fact that a separate, independent state below the seventeenth parallel did not exist was the most pressing problem in 1954 and remained so throughout all the years of American involvement in southern Vietnam.

2

THE COLD WAR, COLONIALISM, AND THE ORIGINS OF THE AMERICAN COMMITMENT TO VIETNAM, 1945–1954

In February 1950, when the Truman administration extended formal recognition to the State of Vietnam and material aid to the French effort to reestablish a crumbling empire, American officials never imagined the quarter-century-long Vietnam War would be the ultimate result. The French had, for several years, been attempting to beat back Vietnamese nationalists led by Ho Chi Minh and his Viet Minh fighters and to reimpose colonial rule in Vietnam. Significant American military intervention remained relatively far off. The United States had only recently begun to formulate any policy toward Southeast Asia. Vietnam, alongside Laos and Cambodia, remained primarily a French problem that compelled U.S. monetary aid. Direct American interest in Southeast Asia was only very slowly developing. In just a few short years, however, global conditions had changed dramatically. French ambitions in Vietnam had been thwarted by 1954. Japan had been substantially rebuilt and needed regional trade partners. From Guatemala and the Congo to Egypt and Indonesia, a global cold war and the end of colonialism brought greater instability and the threat of independent nationalist leaders around the world bent on pursuing neutralist foreign policy and nationalist domestic policy agendas. In the United States, intellectuals, policy makers, and others had begun to refine and implement ideas for controlling what they perceived to be the most undesirable and dangerous aspects of this unstable global environment through economic aid and modernization in former colonial areas. In this changed context, aid to Vietnam had mushroomed, and objectives shifted from the restoration of colonialism.

Ultimately, the United States decided to stay on following the defeat of the French for reasons having more to do with global instability and the Cold War than the Vietnamese. Through myriad economic development initiatives and with the modernization paradigm as the rationale, the United States began the effort to invent a new Vietnam below the seventeenth parallel.

THE END OF COLONIALISM, THE COLD WAR, AND VIETNAM

Following World War II, the U.S. government had to somewhat grudgingly accept that the French would restore stability and order to Southeast Asia. Notwithstanding U.S. admonition of colonialism and advocacy of a trusteeship period for former colonies, emerging global economic concerns and Cold War politics convinced American officials that a French colonial revival was preferable to an extension of communist influence.[1] The Soviet Union and, following 1949, the People's Republic of China (PRC) seemed poised to extend power around South and Southeast Asia and close the latter's doors to trade with a revitalized Japan. Policy makers had come to view the advance of communism in the region as threatening to the economic rebuilding and revitalization that planners had counted on. Just as in Europe, any potential for postwar recovery depended on the restoration of substantial regional trade and commercial intercourse. Policy toward East Asia, then, had less to do with Vietnam and much more to do with larger, regional and global interests and concerns. The United States, and Great Britain and France as well, sought to hasten global economic recovery. This objective, as historian Andrew Rotter has written, laid "the path to Vietnam" for the United States.[2]

Over the course of the few years from 1950 to 1954, the United States adopted the French effort in Indochina as its own, if for very different reasons. During the war years, Vietnam stood alongside a number of other colonies in the region whose particular circumstances

---

[1] U.S. Department of State, "Problem Paper Prepared by a Working Group in the Department of State," in *Foreign Relations of the United States* (Washington, DC: GPO, 1950), VI:711–15; hereinafter *FRUS*.

[2] Andrew J. Rotter, *The Path to Vietnam: Origins of the American Commitment to Southeast Asia* (Ithaca, NY: Cornell University Press, 1987). *The Pentagon Papers: The Defense Department History of Decisionmaking on Vietnam*, Senator Gravel ed. (Boston: Beacon Press, 1971), I:34–42.

and yearnings counted for relatively little in the larger calculus of post-war planning. First and foremost, American planners considered the problems that hounded their European allies. Among them, a war-torn economy, political strife, a growing activism on the political left, and a related, nascent Soviet threat loomed large.[3] Marshall Plan aid alongside political and military containment began to turn around Western Europe by the late 1940s. To be sure, some postwar problems persisted, not least of which concerned a significant British trade debt within its Sterling bloc and a similar lackluster recovery on the part of the French. Prior to the war, both of these nations had relied heavily on their colonies in Southeast Asia for raw materials and dollar earnings. Following the establishment of the PRC in 1949, a number of influential figures began to suggest that rebuilding this old and war-torn network in Southeast Asia be given much greater emphasis. According to some, an Asian Marshall Plan might even be necessary.[4]

With the dreamed-of China market now effectively unrealizable, policy makers began to consider the implications of this loss of China for the recovery of Japan and for the restoration and liberalization of Asian regional trade. Prior to the war, Japan had relied heavily on regional trade for export of its manufactured goods and for the importation of raw materials and foodstuffs in quantities it did not produce. Following a U.S. embargo on oil imports in 1940, for example, the Japanese quickly moved into other areas of Southeast Asia, such as Malaya, Burma, Indonesia, and Vietnam, to make up for shortfalls. Alongside this Southeast Asian trade, China had been Japan's largest regional trading partner before the war. When the United States refused to recognize the PRC, it made clear that Japanese trade with China would be limited as well.

U.S. policy makers considered Chinese influence upon Japan too great a danger. Consequently, as Secretary of State Dean Acheson pointed out in 1949, "the only hope for the kind of Japanese recovery envisioned by the United States now must involve substantial trade links between that

---

[3] Gabriel Kolko, *The Politics of War: The World and United States Foreign Policy, 1943–1945* (New York: Random House, 1968). Melvyn P. Leffler and David S. Painter, *Origins of the Cold War: An International History* (New York: Routledge, 1994).

[4] "State Department Memo on Far Eastern Marshall Plan," in William Appleman Williams et al., *America in Vietnam: A Documentary History* (New York: Anchor Books, 1985), 66–67.

nation and Southeast Asia." Later that same year, U. Alexis Johnson, deputy director of the State Department's Office of Northeast Asian Affairs, elaborated: "With regard to Japanese trade with south and Southeast Asia the problem involves the maximizing of the food and raw materials production in those areas, thereby enabling the acquisition of foodstuffs and raw materials by Japan in exchange for industrial products." Johnson explicitly recognized that Japanese recovery absolutely relied upon such imports from Southeast Asia.[5] In a detailed estimate of Japan's potential trade with the nations of Southeast Asia written in early 1950, the Economic and Scientific Section of the American occupational government concluded that Japan's exports to these countries could reach a level of approximately $700 million by 1955 and that these exports would easily exceed 50 percent of its total projected export trade.[6] Thus political and economic stability became vital for the recovery of the region's economy as well as that of France and Great Britain.

The restoration of French rule in Indochina presented the path of least resistance to achieving U.S. goals for the region, while at the same time allaying French (as well as British) concerns over American intentions for its European allies and their global interests. Abandoning the trusteeship scheme for developing the third world was perhaps a bitter pill insofar as it challenged the liberal trade agenda, which called for an end of colonialism and protectionist state policies and sought free access for commercial exchange. However, the United States could avoid the taint of imperialism by playing only a supporting role. It could accomplish its larger regional and global goals of revitalizing its European friends and integrating Southeast Asia into a modern liberal capitalist network in the long run by bringing the French into a Western military alliance, the North Atlantic Treaty Organization. Aid to the French effort in Indochina began in 1950 with $10 million and the establishment of a U.S. Military Assistance Advisory Group in Saigon to oversee this and continued investments. Over the next few years, American aid to the French steadily mounted. By 1954, the year of French defeat, the United States subsidized nearly 80 percent of the costs of what had become a

---

[5] Rotter, *Path to Vietnam*, 45–47.
[6] "Japan's Export Potential with Specific Reference to the Economic Development of the Countries of South and Southeast Asia," in Williams et al., *America in Vietnam*, 86–87.

quagmire for French forces. Despite millions in military aid, including $385 million for 1954 alone, the Vietnamese handed the French a decisive defeat in the spring of that year, and the Second Indochina War came to an end. Simultaneously, the Geneva Conference took up the Indochina developments and imposed regroupment zones north and south of the seventeenth parallel. Free elections were to follow in 1956 to reflect the will of the people and unify the country of Vietnam.[7] It seemed to many in Vietnam that the long Vietnamese struggle for national independence had come to a triumphant end.

MAKING THE WORLD SAFE THROUGH DEVELOPMENT

Following the Geneva Conference, Ho Chi Minh and the Vietnamese Communist Party moved to consolidate its position as the government of an independent Vietnam, initially proclaimed in 1945. Almost assuredly, the party would become the government of a unified Vietnam in the scheduled national elections of 1956, as mandated by the conference. At this point, the stakes for American policy makers had grown considerably, and the global dynamic between the Western democratic capitalist world and the Eastern socialist world had changed profoundly. Following the 1948 Berlin crisis, the United States and the Soviet Union reached a kind of stalemate in Europe, with the latter retaining a high degree of influence in Eastern Europe. In October 1949, the Chinese Communists triumphed in that nation's civil war, thus ending any hope of insuring an important role for the Guomindang and Jiang Jieshi. Nationalist forces threatened American aims the world over: in Egypt in 1952, Gamal Abdul Nasser led a revolt among military officers that removed the king and began a nationalist reform program to eliminate heavy British influence and assert the nation's independence. The next year, the Central Intelligence Agency (CIA) promptly moved to overthrow the regime of nationalist Mohammed Mossadegh, who attempted to nationalize Iranian oil and reform the Iranian political system. In Indonesia, Sukarno appeared committed to a neutralist foreign policy, something Secretary of State John Foster Dulles viewed as "immoral and shortsighted." In America's own backyard, Guatemala's Jacobo Arbenz also

---

[7] "Final Declaration of the Geneva Conference (July 21, 1954)," in FRUS, 1952–1954, XVI:1540–42.

began a nationalist program of political and land reform that directly threatened the interests of the American corporation the United Fruit Company.[8] Indeed, the global balance of power constantly shifted during these tumultuous years. Southeast Asia was no exception.

The French suffered defeat there in 1954 at the battle of Dien Bien Phu, and this event seemed to portend an end to Western presence and influence in that part of the world. Almost immediately, however, the United States scrambled to piece together a reliably noncommunist state below the seventeenth parallel in Vietnam. As Secretary Dulles explained one day after the Final Declaration of the Geneva Conference at a National Security Council meeting, "the great problem from now on out [is] whether we [can] salvage what the Communists had ostensibly left out of their grasp in Indochina."[9] The Cold War effectively meant a divided world, with little room for nationalist and neutralist distinctions. The West had to act swiftly if the rest of Asia was to be kept within the capitalist orbit and out of the communist one. As one country fell under the influence of the communists, its neighbor was all the more likely to do so in short order. This so-called domino theory did not require substantial justification and seemed to thrive instead from a lack of subtlety and nuance. Nevertheless, the goal was quite clear: stem the tide of communism in Asia or watch as all of Southeast Asia, and eventually Japan, falls.

There was yet another equally important dynamic at work during these years. The continued collapse of formal colonialism contributed to the global instability that so alarmed officials in the west. Dozens of former colonies now demanded independence, and the forces of nationalism quickly became important and unavoidable. Across the globe, and in Europe as well, parties from the political left were in the ascendancy.

---

[8] Peter L. Hahn, *The United States, Great Britain, and Egypt, 1945–1956: Strategy and Diplomacy in the Early Cold War* (Chapel Hill: University of North Carolina Press, 1991). Mary Ann Heiss, *Empire and Nationhood: The United States, Great Britain, and Iranian Oil, 1950–1954* (New York: Columbia University Press, 1997). George Kahin and Audrey Kahin, *Subversion as Foreign Policy: The Secret Eisenhower and Dulles Debacle in Indonesia* (New York: Free Press, 1995). Richard Immerman, *The CIA in Guatemala: The Foreign Policy of Intervention* (Austin: University of Texas Press, 1982). W. Michael Weis, *Cold Warriors & Coup D'etat: Brazilian-American Relations, 1945–1964* (Albuquerque: University of New Mexico Press, 1993). Dulles quote is in *Department of State Bulletin* XXXIV (June 18, 1956): 1000.

[9] Memorandum of Discussion at the 207th Meeting of the National Security Council, Thursday, July 22, 1954, *FRUS*, 1952–1954, XIII:1867–71; quote is on 1869.

Nationalist leaders, Vietnam's Ho Chi Minh among them, promised an end to the years of hardship, untold suffering, and undue foreign influence and control over national resources that had accompanied colonialism.[10] The United States and, somewhat belatedly, the Soviet Union began to compete to ensure the allegiance of third world countries to one or the other political economic system. Indeed, the Cold War added greater urgency to issues of development regarding Latin America, Africa, the Middle East, and Asia. As the Cold War shifted geographically away from Europe and toward these areas of the world in the decade following World War II, colonialism's legacy of poverty, lack of infrastructure, lack of political-economic institutions, and general underdevelopment presented enormous problems that would have to be overcome.[11]

For its part, the Soviet Union had, since the 1917 revolution, sought to hasten and guide development within the colonial world. The very founding ideology of the Bolshevik Revolution and the Soviet system was predicated on development and required the uplift of the world's downtrodden. The Bolsheviks had promised, through the Comintern, established in 1919, support for revolutions against colonialism around the world. They offered direct aid and training for those revolutions and, subsequently, offered a developmental model of the new state.[12] In the postcolonial context, Marx's dictum that "the country that is more developed industrially only shows, to the less developed, the image of

---

[10] David Schmitz, *Thank God They're on Our Side: The United States & Right-Wing Dictatorships, 1921–1965* (Chapel Hill: University of North Carolina Press, 1999). Melvyn P. Leffler, *A Preponderance of Power: National Security, the Truman Administration, and the Cold War* (Stanford, CA: Stanford University Press, 1992), 3–9. Thomas G. Paterson, *On Every Front: The Making of the Cold War* (New York: W. W. Norton, 1979), 26–27.

[11] On the generally increased concern over these issues following World War II, see Center for International Studies, *The Objectives of United States Economic Assistance Programs* (Cambridge: Massachusetts Institute of Technology, January 1957). H. W. Arndt, *Economic Development: The History of an Idea* (Chicago: University of Chicago Press, 1989), introduction.

[12] For an analysis of the complexities and contradictions of Russian revolutionary utopianism, see Richard Stites, *Revolutionary Dreams: Utopian Vision and Experimental Life in the Russian Revolution* (New York: Oxford University Press, 1989). Historian Michael Adas, *Dominance by Design: Technological Imperatives and America's Civilizing Mission* (Cambridge, MA: Harvard University Press, 2006), 247, has argued recently for greater "convergence" between the U.S. and Soviet versions of the modernization and economic development formula, writing, "The advocates of market capitalism and command communism deployed remarkably similar strategies for providing development assistance to emerging nations."

its own future" took on even greater importance. Following a period of years during which Stalinism actually seemed to undermine Soviet aims in the third world, the Soviet Union took much greater interest in the emergence of nationalist leaders and parties attempting to create the new states. During his famous 1956 speech denouncing Stalin's cruelties, the new Soviet premier Nikita Khrushchev also announced renewed Soviet support in the third world and assured nationalist leaders that "they now have no need to go begging to their former oppressors for modern equipment. They can obtain such equipment in the socialist countries."[13]

In most cases, nationalist leaders took the lead in organizing and struggling for their own independence. Within a decade following the end of World War II, many of them had come to see the Cold War rivalry between the United States and the Soviet Union as an impediment to their own development and fraught with danger. There was a striking ambivalence among third world leaders about the proper course to development, the nature and the role of the state, and the international relationships best suited to a particular developmental course. These sentiments culminated in the 1955 Bandung Conference, attended by delegates from some twenty-nine developing countries representing more than half of the world's population. Indonesia's Sukarno delivered an impassioned opening speech welcoming those attending and lauding the "undying, indomitable spirit" of the people in the countries represented. Looking toward a new day of unity and cooperation, with this conference as a starting point, the Indonesian nationalist articulated his hope that "this Conference will give *guidance* to mankind, will point out to mankind the way which it must take to attain safety and peace."[14] The conference really represented the collective declaration by the former colonial areas of an independent, or neutralist, course in the Cold War.

For their part, the Americans believed many of these former colonial areas incapable of self-rule and viewed neutralism with derision

---

[13] Khrushchev quoted in Odd Arne Westad, *The Global Cold War: Third World Interventions and the Making of Our Times* (New York: Cambridge University Press, 2005), 51 and chap. 2. Marx, *Capital: A Critical Analysis of Capitalist Production*, (New York: International Publishers, 1967), 1:8–9.

[14] Jussi M. Hanhimaki and Odd Arne Westad, *The Cold War: A History in Documents and Eyewitness Accounts* (New York: Oxford University Press, 2003), 350–51. Westad, *Global Cold War*, chap. 3.

and consternation. American postwar planners had earlier decided that they must somehow be, under supervision, modernized and then integrated into a broader, liberal capitalist system. Their understanding of the relationship between the industrialized countries and the former colonial areas had been demonstrated earlier at the 1944 conference in Bretton Woods, New Hampshire. This gathering of delegates from forty-four nations around the world, which economist John Maynard Keynes derisively referred to as "a monstrous monkey house," agreed to the Bretton Woods economic arrangement, the International Bank of Relief and Recovery (World Bank), and the International Monetary Fund (IMF).[15] The conferees understood that this Bretton Woods "system" would help both the European powers and the former colonial areas. Each of these structures had in mind the restoration and/or establishment of a stable, liberal capitalist economic system. The Bretton Woods currency regime pegged the world's currencies to the value of the U.S. dollar at an effective rate of thirty-five dollars per ounce of gold, fully convertible. The IMF and the World Bank were designed to oversee continued buttressing of weaker economies through infusions of capital and loans for development projects. Barely two years later, announcement of the Truman Doctrine and aid to Greece and Turkey, designed to "contain" communism, reinforced the American commitment to the world. Planners hoped that this combined system would begin to bring order out of the chaos of the crumbling imperial system. No one dared risk a return to the kind of economic depression visited on Europe and the United States in the years prior to the outbreak of the Second World War. However, with colonialism itself now a victim of war, the industrialized countries of the West were forced to deal with these new nations and peoples, if not as equals, at least as critical to the establishment of the new world order. Though the measures crafted at Bretton Woods would no doubt help, much more would have to be done to modernize and develop the former colonial world.

Rarely referred to prior to World War II, the postwar global environment now drew greater attention to the problems of the economic

---

[15] Quoted in Richard Peet, with Elaine Hartwick, *Theories of Development* (New York: Guilford Press, 1999), 40. Robert Skidelsky, *John Maynard Keynes: Fighting for Freedom, 1937–1946* (New York: Penguin Books, 2002), 343–60.

development of undeveloped areas.[16] While this perpetual lack of development served colonialism well, it now stood in the way of quick integration. Former colonies, in a sense, needed to be caught up with other modern states to protect continued access to the raw materials and labor they provided, to modernize their physical infrastructure, and to guard against the spread of communism's influence. Economic development became the watchword of economists and others concerned with issues of global raw materials production, finance and trade, technical aid, trade discrimination, labor, and general poverty.[17] In its 1948 *World Economic Report*, the United Nations spoke of "the urgent problem of the economic development of under-developed countries."[18] Over the next couple of years, the global economy experienced inflation, an impending shortage of goods, and a trade deficit, all of which were only exasperated by the start of the Korean War. In its report issued in 1951, the United Nations still believed that "the economic development of the under-developed countries remains the most important single long-run economic problem confronting the world" and that the sustained and systemic recovery of the world economy depended upon international efforts to close the gap between rich and poor countries by encouraging, and even sponsoring, economic development within the latter.[19]

The idea of a large economic aid program for the far-flung areas of the world came only slowly to American policy makers. A program of such scope was without precedent in the nation's foreign policy. The

---

[16] Although, during the war, some began to explicitly recognize the serious consequences of the end of colonialism and the general undeveloped nature of much of the former colonial world. One economist wrote just before the war's end, "If we want to ensure a stable and prosperous peace, we have to provide for some international action to improve the living conditions of those peoples who missed the industrialization 'bus' in the nineteenth century." See P. N. Rosenstein-Rodan, "The International Development of Economically Backward Areas," *International Affairs* 20, no. 2 (1944): 157–65; quote is on 158.

[17] William Adams Brown Jr. and Opie Redvers, *American Foreign Assistance* (Washington, DC: Brookings Institution, 1953), 383–88.

[18] Department of Economic Affairs, *World Economic Report, 1948* (Lake Success, NY: United Nations, 1949), 251. See also Department of Economic Affairs, *Economic Development in Selected Countries: Plans, Programmes and Agencies* (New York: United Nations, 1947).

[19] Department of Economic Affairs, *World Economic Report, 1949–1950* (Lake Success, NY: United Nations, 1951), 1–10. Of course, there was considerable division among the experts over the most effective specific measures to bring about the desired economic development. See Peet, *Theories of Development*, 40–47.

overwhelming success of the Marshall Plan for Europe, begun in 1948, however, suggested the possibilities for the rest of the world, which was in even greater need of economic aid and assistance. The Marshall Plan's $14 billion had primed the European economic pump and kept up demand for U.S. manufactures very effectively. That this might also be accomplished for the undeveloped nations seemed at least worthy of consideration. President Truman eventually announced just such a program in his inaugural speech in January 1949, saying the United States "must embark on a bold new program for making the benefits of our scientific advances and industrial progress available for the improvement and growth of underdeveloped areas."[20] Far from being a one-way street, the president later wrote of the plan that "the development of these countries would keep our own industrial plant in business for untold generations." The announcement, though vague and hastily conceived, called for "a continuing and self-perpetuating program of technical assistance to the underdeveloped nations of the world," according to the president's memoirs. A perpetual global aid plan as a permanent feature of American foreign policy distinguished this new "Point Four" plan from others such as the Marshall Plan.[21] The plan was ahead of its time. Opposition emerged from a skeptical Congress, a reluctant private investment community, a wary State Department, and even an apparently surprised Dean Acheson. The Point Four aid plan remained logjammed in Congress and eventually emerged as Title IV of the Aid for International Development Act in 1950, funded at well below what administration officials considered the minimum needed.[22] Nevertheless, it seems economic development as a tool of foreign policy was an idea whose time had come. Within a handful of years, U.S. foreign aid to the rest of the world grew dramatically at the same time as aid to Europe diminished.

[20] Public Papers of the Presidents, Harry S. Truman, 1949, Inaugural Address, January 20, 1949, 114.

[21] Harry S. Truman, Years of Trial and Hope (New York: Doubleday, 1956), 269, 266, respectively. Dean Acheson, Present at the Creation: My Years in the State Department (New York: W. W. Norton, 1969), 264–66.

[22] Truman, Years of Trial and Hope, 271–72. For a contemporary analysis of the process of funding Point IV, see Brown and Redvers, American Foreign Assistance, 388–99. See also "Transcription of Extemporaneous Remarks by Secretary of State Dean Acheson, Concerning Point 4 of the President's Inaugural Address, January 26, 1949," FRUS, 1949, I:758–59. For an explanation of some of the obstacles to Point IV, see "Editorial Note," FRUS, 1950, I:851–52. Rotter, Path to Vietnam, 18–22.

Many experts and elected officials in the United States, Europe, and elsewhere came to realize their own economic recovery depended on improving and supporting the economies of the rest of the world. To ignore this important connection invited potentially profound economic disorder, not to mention the loss of prestige in the world. Officials on the National Security Council Planning Board offered the following assessment of the importance of the undeveloped world in 1953:

Despite the Soviet threat, many nations and societies outside the Soviet bloc...are so unsure of their national interests...that they are presently unwilling to align themselves with the United States and its allies. Although largely underdeveloped, their vast manpower, their essential raw materials and their potential for growth are such that their absorption within the Soviet system would greatly, perhaps decisively, alter the world balance of power to our detriment. Conversely, their orderly development into more stable and responsible nations, able and willing to participate in defense of the free world, can increasingly add to its strength.[23]

The balance of power had shifted and become much more diffuse, even if some remained reluctant to accept it. The United States, as well as the other major capitalist nations, believed that if poverty, misery, and general backwardness persisted, then many former colonial countries would more easily succumb to communist influence. Under these circumstances, access to markets, raw materials, sources of labor, and other strategic interests would be sharply limited. By the early 1950s, the Cold War, the prevalence of nationalist leaders bent on neutralism and national independence, and growing concerns over the stability of the economic system created a political rationale for increasing American aid to the non-European world.[24] Foreign aid soon became a far greater element of U.S. foreign policy than had been the case at any time during the country's past. During the years from 1949 to 1952, nearly three-fourths of all American economic aid went to European

[23] National Security Council 162/1, a report to the NSC by the NSC Planning Board, "Review of Basic National Security Policy," October 1953, quoted in Irene Gendzier, *Managing Political Change: Social Scientists and the Third World* (Boulder, CO: Westview Press, 1985), 23.

[24] Special Senate Committee to Study the Foreign Aid Program, *The Objectives of the United States Economic Assistance Programs*, by the Center for International Studies, Massachusetts Institute of Technology, 85th Cong., 1st sess., 1957, 11–13. Dudley Sears, "The Birth, Life and Death of Development Economics," *Development and Change* 10 (1979): 707–19.

countries.[25] During the next five years, that same percentage, a greater volume in dollar terms, of American aid went to third world or developing countries. By 1962, 90 percent of all U.S. aid went to underdeveloped countries.

Much of this aid went into security and military preparedness, to be sure. However, an increasing share of foreign aid was channeled into specific projects and schemes to bring about economic development aimed at creating modern nations within a relatively brief span of years. By 1960–1961, development assistance combined with food aid surpassed all worldwide military aid given by the United States.[26] Much of the increased foreign aid aimed to rebuild and modernize large areas of the undeveloped world to protect against revolutionary nationalism and communism. This mammoth task of building new, independent states out of traditional and/or former colonial societies also coincided with the recent growth of an academic, intellectual body of work articulating and promoting greater development and technical aid to solve the myriad problems associated with forced national development. Sociologists, political scientists, economists, and others took up these complex problems and began to formulate solutions. Economic development ideas quickly became pervasive within both academic and policy-making circles during the 1950s and into the 1960s.[27] Academic intellectuals and their ideas seduced government officials in search of a countervailing force or framework to revolutionary nationalism. The question was how to oppose revolutionary nationalism, appear progressive and committed to an end of colonialism, and win over the support of and maintain some control over developments within the former colonial world.

INTELLECTUALS, MODERNIZATION, AND THE THIRD WORLD

Soon, ideas poured forth in books, articles, conference papers, research projects, and innumerable case studies. Specialists analyzed every

---

[25] For a detailed breakdown of U.S. foreign aid for these years, see "Statistical Survey of United States Government Postwar Foreign Aid," *FRUS*, 1950, I:810–14.

[26] Doug Bandow, "Economic and Military Aid," in *Intervention into the 1990s: U.S. Foreign Policy in the Third World*, 2nd ed., ed. Peter J. Schraeder (Boulder, CO: Lynne Rienner, 1992), 79, 81, 83.

[27] For a discussion of the early, prewar literature, see Arndt, *Economic Development*, chap. 2.

feature of so-called traditional societies, compared them with industrial societies, and compared them with each other; they investigated birthrates, mobility patterns, rates of illiteracy, the role of the church and of superstition, climate, geography, per capita income, and the savings rate and political structures.[28] On the basis of these investigations, experts offered modernization as the solution to what were seen as problems and limitations that kept these peoples and societies from participating in the fruits of a modern world. One of the most popular of this genre was Daniel Lerner's aptly titled *The Passing of Traditional Society* and subtitled *Modernizing the Middle East* (1958). In this study, Lerner, a sociologist at the Massachusetts Institute of Technology, analyzed some 1,600 interviews conducted by the U.S. government in half a dozen Middle Eastern countries and drew the conclusion that contact with the developed Western world would benefit the third world by bringing it modernity and by creating among the people a desire for a better life. People outside the Western world would have to be changed, made into what the sociologist termed "mobile personalities" capable of "empathy," to replicate the Western experience of modernization in just a few short years. This kind of person, Lerner found, adapted quickly to new circumstances, a trait vital to the modernization process, and readily learned an appreciation for others within modern society that made the whole coherent and functional.[29] Traditional people would, in a sense, have to reject and cut themselves off from their cultural, historical, societal pasts and quickly adapt to newer forms, as articulated and demonstrated by Western experts and technicians.[30] Western and modern nations could, through a kind of demonstration effect, thus hasten the passage from traditional to modern, the presumed goal of peoples and societies everywhere.

---

[28] Arturo Escobar, "Power and Visibility: Development and the Invention and Management of the Third World," *Cultural Anthropology* 3, no. 4 (1988): 428–43.

[29] Daniel Lerner, *The Passing of Traditional Society: Modernizing the Middle East* (London: Free Press of Glencoe, 1958), 47–50, 79–81.

[30] The United Nations determined in 1951 that the process also meant that "ancient philosophies have to be scrapped; old social institutions have to disintegrate; bonds of caste, creed and race have to be burst; and large numbers of persons who cannot keep up with progress have to have their expectations of a comfortable life frustrated. Very few communities are willing to pay the full price of rapid economic progress." United Nations, *Measures for the Economic Development of Under-Developed Countries*, 1951, quoted in a Brookings Institution study of a few years later. See Brown and Redvers, *American Foreign Assistance*, 386.

Other influential texts in this genre included Talcott Parsons and Edward Shils's *Toward a General Theory of Action* (1951), Walt W. Rostow's *The Process of Economic Growth* (1952), Lucian Pye's *Guerilla Communism in Malaya* (1956), Max Millikan and Walt W. Rostow's *A Proposal: Key to an Effective Foreign Policy* (1957), S. N. Eisenstadt's "Sociological Aspects of Political Development in Underdeveloped Countries," and what was perhaps the seminal economics text offering an explanation of historical national development, Walt W. Rostow's *The Stages of Economic Growth: A Non-communist Manifesto* (1960).[31] Taken together, these works and the academic production behind them brought together considerable intellectual energies from the fields of political science, economics, and sociology to offer solutions to immensely complex problems. The combined efforts of scholars working in these academic disciplines really represented a unified theory of society and an explanation of the process from traditional to modern. In short, their findings made the former colonial world understandable and its problems and limitations, at least as the experts in the West saw them, solvable in a way that directly benefited U.S. foreign policy.[32]

Those studying the former colonial world often discovered nations that lacked exactly those features that made the United States, and the Western world more generally, modern. Thus the sharp demarcation between modern and traditional really differentiated Western industrial nations from other parts of the world and elevated the former as the model to be copied.[33] As academics and other experts laid plans to

---

[31] Talcott Parsons and Edward Shils, *Toward a General Theory of Action* (Cambridge, MA: Harvard University Press, 1951). Walt W. Rostow, *The Process of Economic Growth* (New York: W. W. Norton, 1952). Lucian Pye, *Guerilla Communism in Malaya: Its Social and Political Meaning* (Princeton, NJ: Princeton University Press, 1956). Max Millikan and Walt W. Rostow, *A Proposal: Key to an Effective Foreign Policy* (New York: Harper & Brothers, 1957). S. N. Eisenstadt, "Sociological Aspects of Political Development in Underdeveloped Countries," *Economic Development and Cultural Change* 5, no. 4 (1957): 289–98. Walt W. Rostow, *The Stages of Economic Growth: A Non-communist Manifesto* (New York: Cambridge University Press, 1960).

[32] Michael Latham, "Ideology, Social Science, and Destiny: Modernization and the Kennedy Era Alliance for Progress," *Diplomatic History* 22 (Spring 1998): 199–229. Gendzier, *Managing Political Change*, chap. 2. Arndt, *Economic Development*, chap. 3. Peet, *Theories of Development*.

[33] As cultural studies professor C. Douglas Lummis, *Radical Democracy* (Ithaca, NY: Cornell University Press, 1996), 63, has written, "Underdevelopment . . . is a truly remarkable concept. It succeeds in placing the vast majority of the world's cultures into a single

modernize the numerous traditional societies around the world, they necessarily moved to alter or eliminate those features that kept them traditional.[34] *Traditional* usually referred to a lack of infrastructure, a high rate of illiteracy, an absence of an urban workforce, an absence of a favorable trade balance, no or limited capacity to exploit natural resources, an ineffective transportation and communication system, and decentralized family and/or clan rule over political affairs, among other limitations.[35] An important underlying assumption of this theory of economic development suggested that each nation would naturally evolve from a traditional into a developed state. The path from one to the other was viewed as linear in that no matter the specific context, all nations would ultimately arrive at the same end point; that is, they would all eventually replicate the Western national historical experience. Economic development and modernization theories necessarily promoted the notion that societies could be measured according to a set of static, universal standards of measure, which separated the modern from the traditional. Societies became variables, independent units whose own position along the path toward universal development was often determined using a few discernable, often material, factors.[36]

The efficacy of economic development was taken on faith and assumed to provide the most logical solution to the problems of poverty, political instability, and conflict around the world. Believing it was precisely this lack of development on which communism thrived, advocates of economic development, or modernization, rationalized intervention as benevolent and justified the system of which they were a part as the model of the development process. It is worth recognizing how these ideas dovetailed with the decades-long effort on the part of

---

category the sole characteristic of which is the absence of certain characteristics of the industrialized countries."

[34] For a useful recent essay on the history of the ideas around economic development and modernization in the postwar period, see Nick Cullather, "Development? Its History," *Diplomatic History* 24 (Fall 2000): 641–53.

[35] Rostow defined a traditional society as one in which "a ceiling existed on the level of attainable output per head. This ceiling resulted from the fact that the potentialities which flow from modern science and technology were either not available or not regularly and systematically applied." Rostow, *Process of Economic Growth*, 311; Rostow, *Stages of Economic Growth*, 4–7.

[36] Nick Cullather, "Development," 643–46. Rostow, *Stages of Economic Growth*. Peet, *Theories of Development*, 76–79.

the United States to break the back of colonialism dating at least from the Open Door Notes of the turn of the century. This missionary zeal and promise of betterment had long justified U.S. forays into the non-European world. If the former colonial world could be developed in a controlled, purposeful way, this would assuredly yield positive results not only within the Cold War context, but for the U.S. role in the world. As these new states were modernized, they would be integrated into the global political economy being put in place by American policy makers at the time. Experts and specialists in various academic fields, imbued with an unshakable faith in science and technology, went about making this hope a reality. Economic development ideas permeated official thinking from 1945 into the 1960s.

From the 1950s forward, dozens of American universities and research institutions committed substantial resources to analyzing how best to develop a traditional society. Not surprisingly, these groups also became the recipients of government aid and attention as development ideas abounded and seemed to many self-explanatory.[37] Because researchers began with a problem (lack of development), they necessarily arrived at a solution (development) that accorded with the aims of American foreign relations.[38] As the development mantra spread, so too did the number of studies, research projects, institutes, and think tanks engaged in legitimizing its claims.[39] Economic development and modernization experts within and on the payroll of the U.S. government launched a global effort to speed up and control the development of modern societies around the underdeveloped world. The increased attention to these nations and peoples, the rise in foreign aid, and the emergence of modernization/economic development ideas as remedies for revolutionary nationalism all came together in Vietnam to launch a comprehensive state-building project beginning in 1954.

---

[37] For example, see the series of essays, several of them personal accounts, of the relationship between the state and the university contained in Noam Chomsky et al., *The Cold War and the University: Toward an Intellectual History of the Postwar Years* (New York: New Press, 1996). Sigmund Diamond, *Compromised Campus: The Collaboration of Universities with the Intelligence Community, 1945–1955* (New York: Oxford University Press, 1992).

[38] Christopher Simpson, *Universities and Empire: Money and Politics in the Social Sciences during the Cold War* (New York: Free Press, 1999), xiv.

[39] Bruce Cumings, "Boundary Displacement: Area Studies and International Studies during and after the Cold War," in Simpson, *Universities and Empire*, 159–88.

THE STATE OF VIETNAM: HISTORY, GEOGRAPHY, AND IMPERIALISM

Regrettably, American policy makers knew frightfully little of Vietnam's history, culture, politics, or physical infrastructure. During the interwar years, according to one historian, American perceptions of Asians and of Southeast Asia in general were shaped by a very limited reportage literature, accounts of Vietnamese people filtered through the French lens, and an abiding faith in a racially hierarchical world.[40] Consequently, American officials viewed the Vietnamese as incapable of self-government and unable to resist outside influence from China and the Soviet Union. If left to their own devices, the Vietnamese people would become an appendage of one or both of their two more powerful and expansive neighbors. As one historian has written, "Southeast Asians have been reduced to roles as mere bit players, too weak to do more than reflect the brilliance of other civilizations."[41] These ideas shaped how the United States perceived its role in the region following French defeat. Vietnam became a kind of test case to demonstrate the capacity of American power to create noncommunist allies among former colonies and win influence in the Cold War. Part of the flaw in this logic stemmed from a misunderstanding of what exactly had been inherited from the French.

It is precisely the diminution of Southeast Asians as creators of their own destiny that has served Western nations so well during the past two centuries. Vietnam, of course, did not emerge suddenly following World War II and begin groping about for guidance. Rather, the country had its own rich and deep history extending back millennia prior to direct French involvement in the late nineteenth century. It must be noted that despite the considerable influence of larger and more powerful Indian and Chinese neighbors, cultural and political institutions of the whole of Southeast Asia developed in distinct ways. Geographically, the peninsula is isolated enough from these two nations to afford at least a modicum of autonomy. In reality, this area of the world has encountered a greater

---

[40] Mark Philip Bradley, *Imaging Vietnam and America: The Making of Postcolonial Vietnam, 1919–1950* (Chapel Hill: University of North Carolina Press, 2000). Michael H. Hunt, *Ideology and U.S. Foreign Policy* (New Haven, CT: Yale University Press, 1987), chap. 3.

[41] David Joel Steinberg, ed., *In Search of Southeast Asia: A Modern History*, rev. ed. (Honolulu: University of Hawaii Press, 1987), 1.

diversity of cultural influences than perhaps any other place and yet has managed to incorporate those aspects found useful and desirable and reject those found impractical and undesirable. The result has been the evolution of distinct cultures and political institutions long before the arrival of Europeans bent on colonization.[42]

Around the middle of the nineteenth century, the Europeans came to this part of the world in search of raw materials, expanded trade routes, and goods. The British and the French had by mid-century imposed upon China the treaty system granting them most favored nation status as well as access to at least a dozen ports.[43] As early as the 1860s, the French had begun to coerce concessions of land and power from a number of Vietnamese who were either disenchanted with the imperial government and/or were receptive to payoffs in the form of land grants. The French confiscated tens of thousands of hectares of land in Cochinchina (southern Vietnam) and gave it over in huge concessions to French citizens to encourage settlement. These concessions also included a number of Vietnamese, as long as they met the requirements of the *assimlé* status.[44] Those who had their land expropriated, in many instances, became tenant farmers on land they formerly owned, paying rent to their French and Vietnamese absentee landlords.[45] The French maintained control over what are today Vietnam, Cambodia, and Laos (French Indochina) through a combination of quiescence and force from the late nineteenth century until World War II.

During those years, Vietnam was the object of French design more than the other regions under French suzerainty. The colonials squeezed from Vietnam, particularly the southern region around the rich Mekong

---

[42] Steinberg, *In Search*. Nicholas Tarling, ed., *The Cambridge History of Southeast Asia*, vol. 2, *The Nineteenth and Twentieth Centuries* (New York: Cambridge University Press, 1992). Keith W. Taylor, *The Birth of Vietnam* (Berkeley: University of California Press, 1983). Joseph Buttinger, *Vietnam: A Political History* (New York: Praeger, 1968).

[43] Warren I. Cohen, *America's Response to China: A History of Sino-American Relations*, 4th ed. (New York: Columbia University Press, 2000), chap. 1.

[44] The French colonial system, enveloping all of what are today Vietnam, Laos, and Cambodia, nevertheless recognized the three culturally, politically, socially, and historically varied regions of Vietnam: Cochinchina in the south, Annam in the middle, and Tonkin in the north. French rule was eventually extended to all three by 1884. Martin J. Murray, *The Development of Capitalism in Colonial Indochina, 1870–1940* (Berkeley: University of California Press, 1980), 55.

[45] Ngô Vĩnh Long, *Before the Revolution: The Vietnamese Peasants under the French* (New York: Columbia University Press, 1973), 11–15.

Delta, enormous productivity. Employing a system of forced (corveé) labor, the colonizers were able to turn Vietnam (or Cochinchina, the southern rice-producing region) into the second leading rice producer in the world in the mid-1930s. Efforts at industrial production paled by comparison: cement, ceramics, wood, paints, vegetable oil, fireworks and explosives, leather and rubber products, and a few other commodities employed a combined total of only 85,000 to 150,000 persons in a country of approximately 30 million. Another comparison is illustrative: during peak years in the 1930s, coal and rubber exports (almost all of both commodities were exported) never amounted to more than about 4 and 5.5 percent, respectively, of total exports. Exports of rice and maize, on the other hand, accounted for the rest. Tonkin rice exports amounted to two hundred thousand metric tons per year. Cochinchina rice exports rose to more than one million tons per year. Rice and rice by-products accounted for 65 percent of all exports from the whole of Indochina during the decades prior to the Second World War.[46]

Indochina's industrial infrastructure, or lack thereof, is consistent with the aims of the colonial relationship. An export economy based on raw materials benefits the colonizers and perpetuates the need to retard the development of a modern industrial sector. At the same time, 58 percent of all imports went to the maintenance and defense of the system and to the small numbers of elite who ruled (European, Vietnamese, and Chinese). The vast majority of Vietnamese peasants remained in the countryside and tied to the land. During the immediate postconquest period, the amount of land cultivated skyrocketed, while at the same time, the French further increased the output and the prevalence of resident tenant farmers and sharecroppers.[47] Consequently, rice exports, particularly in Cochinchina but elsewhere as well, grew dramatically. However, the amount of land held communally by villages steadily decreased, particularly in Cochinchina, where it reached a low of 2.5 percent of all cultivable land by the 1930 high point of French domination. The figures for Annam and Tonkin were 25 and 20 percent, respectively.[48] As late as 1960, 2 percent of the population owned

---

[46] Charles Robequain, *The Economic Development of French Indochina* (London: Oxford University Press, 1944), 308–11, 363.

[47] Ibid., 220.

[48] Communal lands had continued to expand over many years as an outgrowth of a village custom in Vietnam. Land did not pass to one's family following one's death. Instead, it

45 percent of the cultivable land below the seventeenth parallel.[49] The land held by these largely absentee landlords, either French or Vietnamese collaborators, increased dramatically, reducing Vietnamese farmers to tenants and sharecroppers on lands they had used communally for many years.

In addition to a near-total lack of industry, Vietnam also lacked any appreciable transportation or communication infrastructure by the Second World War. The French had constructed a number of main and secondary roads, railroad lines, dredged canals for navigation, and so on to facilitate export of commodities and control over the region. By 1936, only about seventeen thousand miles of roads connected all of Indochina.[50] For the area below the seventeenth parallel in Vietnam, road mileage is estimated at approximately thirty-seven hundred, including national and provincial roads. Estimates are necessarily crude, and it must be noted that much of this road system became impassable during certain parts of the year and generally lacked routine maintenance. During the First Indochina War (1946–1954), much of this already limited infrastructure was badly damaged or completely destroyed. For example, over seven hundred miles of national roads had been damaged, with much of it rendered unusable. Greater than one-third of the 860 miles of railroad track was destroyed. Hundreds of bridges and canals had been either badly damaged or fell into disrepair during the conflict.[51] Only by the early 1970s had the United States rebuilt most of the transportation system. By the 1950s, this lack of infrastructure coincided with a growing insurgency that came to control large sections of the southern half of Vietnam and rendered much of the countryside inaccessible. Hundreds of thousands of hectares of

became communally owned. Thus, as villages aged, the amount of land held communally tended to increase. Long, *Before the Revolution*, 102–3. Murray, *Development of Capitalism*, 51, 58–61.

[49] Bernard Fall, *The Two Viet-Nams: A Political and Military Analysis* (New York: Praeger, 1963), 309.

[50] Robequain, *Economic Development*, 98–105.

[51] USOM, *Vietnam Moves Ahead: Annual Report for Fiscal Year 1960* (Washington, DC: U.S. Operations Mission to Viet Nam, 1961), 8–12. Robert Scigliano, *South Vietnam: Nation under Stress* (Boston: Houghton Mifflin, 1963), 105. According to Charles Robequain's earlier study, the French had managed to expand railway to a peak of around 1,800 miles by the eve of World War II. Robequain, *Economic Development*, 93–94.

cultivable lands were simply abandoned to the jungle or the Viet Minh by absentee landlords unable or unwilling to venture out into the countryside. What infrastructure remained by 1954, the year the United States effectively replaced the French, consisted of a decaying colonial apparatus that, until the end, had attempted to thwart the development of national political, social, and economic institutions.

One of the tools used by the French to maintain effective control involved the careful meting out of educational opportunities. For example, while the quality of education provided by the French was high, the numbers allowed to participate remained quite small. As the Second World War began, colonial high schools permitted the enrollment of a scant five thousand students for all of Indochina. At the University of Hanoi, the only university serving the Indochinese Union, only seven hundred students attended. The number of students in lower-level education totaled approximately one-half million. As David Marr points out in his study of the transformation of Vietnam during the interwar period, at no point were even 10 percent of school-age children actually going to school.[52]

Not surprisingly, Vietnamese intellectuals began to react in ways not anticipated by the French, as nationalist resistance to colonial rule mounted. The intelligentsia assumed ownership of *quoc ngu*, the Romanized script used by Western missionaries many years earlier, and made it the vernacular to disseminate ideas on a wider scale. *Quoc ngu*, in effect, became the language of the people. The Vietnamese launched a massive literacy campaign between 1920 and 1940, publishing eighty-eight different language primers in 364 editions totaling approximately 3.7 million copies. The Vietnamese had seized upon language as an important tool in opposing French rule, and when the Viet Minh were run out of Hanoi in 1946, they took the printing presses with them.

In the mid- to late 1920s, as revolutionary nationalist Phan Boi Chau was sentenced to life in prison and longtime nationalist friend and namesake Phan Chu Trinh succumbed to tuberculosis, less than 10 percent of

---

[52] David G. Marr, *Vietnamese Tradition on Trial, 1920–1945* (Berkeley: University of California Press, 1981), 35. Similarly, William J. Duiker, *Sacred War: Nationalism and Revolution in a Divided Vietnam* (New York: McGraw-Hill, 1995), 15, writes that "during the 1930s, only about 1 percent of the school-age population in Vietnam was enrolled in a school above the elementary level."

the Vietnamese populace could read in any language. Yet a literacy campaign launched during that period more than reversed those numbers. The intelligentsia began to rethink Vietnam's place in the scheme of things and to formulate answers to new questions. They questioned the relationship between ruler and ruled, the role of women in society, the assumed superiority of the West, the meaning of history, and the efficacy of revolution, among other things. The August Revolution of 1945 was, in many ways, the culmination of those efforts. Though the French colonizers had very purposefully prevented the economic development and establishment of a physical infrastructure in Vietnam, they had also, if unwittingly, contributed to the development of a vital and dynamic Vietnamese nationalism that, internal differences notwithstanding, called for the removal of outside influence and the restoration of national independence.[53]

By the time the United States began to carry the burden of the French effort to recapture its colony, Vietnam was a nation in great flux. Struggling to free itself from colonial rule, Vietnam also struggled to define itself and to do so without outside interference. It is somewhat ironic, and tragic, that when the U.S. mission to Vietnam entered the country's southern half bent on creating a new and modern state below the seventeenth parallel, Vietnamese nationalists were themselves doing just that and had long before put these important issues on the national agenda.[54]

INVENTING VIETNAM: THE UNITED STATES AND STATE BUILDING

While the battle between the Vietnamese and French at Dien Bien Phu raged, CIA operative Colonel Edward G. Lansdale and the Saigon Military Mission (SMM) carried out covert operations aimed at weakening the Viet Minh (Vietnamese Communists) through psychological warfare, disinformation, propaganda, and assassination. The group spread rumors of Chinese perfidy among the Vietnamese, buried weapons in

---

[53] Marr, *Vietnamese Tradition*, esp. chap. 4. Duiker, *Sacred War*, 21.

[54] For an interesting recent study of Vietnamese print culture and an examination of some of these issues based on Vietnamese sources, see Shawn McHale, *Print and Power: Confucianism, Communism, and Buddhism in the Making of Modern Vietnam* (Honolulu: University of Hawaii Press, 2004).

Hanoi cemeteries to be used later by saboteurs being trained at Clark Air Field, tainted Hanoi's oil supply with acid, and generally spread the story of gloom and doom that would follow a Communist victory. In a cable to General J. Lawton Collins, U.S. special representative in Vietnam, Lansdale simultaneously argued for making an increased commitment to the effort because to lose or withdraw, however gracefully, would "encourage politically powerful people in other Asian nations to question America's role in the world." Lansdale then asked rhetorically, "What will it take to win?" Answering his own question, the colonel suggested continued aid, "but not so much as to make the Vietnamese dependent upon us, but to build the muscularity of national abilities."[55] The ambitious effort in Vietnam required not only the efforts of the SMM, but a much larger commitment on the part of the U.S. government as well. A month following the arrival of Lansdale, the successor to Emperor Boa Dai, Ngo Dinh Diem, arrived in Saigon. A handful of U.S. officials chose Diem, with Lansdale among his most ardent supporters, because he possessed a modicum of nationalism buttressed by a fierce anticommunism. He retained a certain legitimacy that his predecessor lacked.[56] He was, nevertheless, a Catholic in an overwhelmingly Buddhist country, and his credibility remained a crucial question until his overthrow in late 1963. The United States steadfastly supported Diem as the best hope below the seventeenth parallel, and he was put in place as president of the new state by the summer of 1954. Diem went on to trounce Bao Dai in a farcical referendum in 1955.[57] The United States had now effectively taken over the French role and embarked on a building project all its own in Southeast Asia.

In deciding to stay on in Vietnam, the United States assumed from the French a traditional society, with the added burden of its having

[55] Memorandum from the Chief of the National Security Division, Training Relations Instruction Mission (Lansdale) to the Special Representative in Vietnam (Collins), January 3, 1955, *FRUS*, 1955–1957, I:3–8.

[56] Even though officials settled upon Diem, he was by no means the clear choice. Following a meeting between Diem and American embassy officers in Paris, one ambassador noted wryly, "On balance we were favorably impressed but only in the realization that we are prepared to accept the seemingly ridiculous prospect that this Yogi-like mystic could assume the charge he is apparently about to undertake only because the standard set by his predecessors is so low." *FRUS*, 1952–1954, XIII:1609.

[57] Despatch from the Ambassador in Vietnam (Reinhart) to the Department of State, November 29, 1955, *FRUS*, 1955–1957, I:589. See also Fall, *Two Viet-Nams*, 257.

been a colony for almost one hundred years. As mentioned, the French sought to curtail the development of national institutions to as great an extent as possible in Vietnam. Historically, imperial powers constructed a relationship between the home country and the colony that kept the former in a position of overall dominance. That meant, among other things, restricting a colony's market options through trading blocks, protectionism in the form of tariffs and, if needed, military force, and encouraging development only to the extent that the colonizer benefited from the comparative advantage of the colony. It was this basic relationship that the United States explicitly challenged following World War II. As advocates of a trusteeship period for former colonies, a number of American officials (most notably President Franklin D. Roosevelt) insisted on a liberal, free-trade world order, which, as it happened, dovetailed in the postwar environment with the growth of economic development/modernization ideas to deal with the thorny problems of former colonies. Following French defeat in Vietnam, the United States chose to stay on and to prevent the reunification of that nation by Ho Chi Minh. An American mission began, instead, to invent a new Vietnam.

From the outset the project involved transforming, or inventing, Vietnam to produce a modern state that could then be integrated into a much larger regional, and even global, capitalist system. The program inaugurated by Michigan State University in 1955 to study how best to develop Vietnam exercised considerable influence within policy-making circles. The project, known as the Michigan State University Vietnam Advisory Group, concerned itself with establishing in the southern half of Vietnam the accouterments of a viable state, with Ngo Dinh Diem at its head. During the long course of the Vietnam War, the United States launched numerous efforts to invent Vietnam that involved the energies of a staggering array of people and institutions: American universities, the military, American religious groups, elected officials, private foundations, governmental groups, the CIA, the U.S. military, the American Friends of Vietnam, and others. Indeed, it is somewhat perplexing that most discussions of American policy toward Vietnam center on the military escalation following 1964. In some ways, the very escalation that has come to symbolize the entirety of the American effort represents instead the failure of this earlier effort. During the 1950s, the United States saw an opportunity in Southeast Asia to replicate the American historical experience of national development, stabilize the region, and, simultaneously, prevent the growth in influence of the communist world. A small group of scholars specializing in civic programs, economics, police administration, and development in general, in conjunction with overt military measures, was at the forefront of this effort.

3

"THE NEEDS ARE ENORMOUS, THE TIME SHORT": MICHIGAN STATE UNIVERSITY, THE U.S. OPERATIONS MISSION, STATE BUILDING, AND VIETNAM

Before the French suffered defeat at Dien Bien Phu in spring 1954, the United States had dispatched the Central Intelligence Agency's (CIA) Edward G. Lansdale to Vietnam to assist in counterguerrilla actions and training, just as he had in the Philippines. American officials had already begun to plan for an eventual French withdrawal. In the interim, the United States desired its own people on the ground in Southeast Asia, rather than channeling aid through French representatives.[1] However, the specific and long-term purpose of this transition remained somewhat unclear. In late October, President Dwight Eisenhower tapped General J. Lawton Collins as "the best qualified" American to orchestrate the new role in Vietnam. Collins thus became the president's special representative in Vietnam, with the rank of ambassador. Several months earlier, Ngo Dinh Diem emerged as the figure preferred by the Americans to lead what would soon be a state-building effort. Diem quickly surrounded himself with a number of consultants who might aid in his consolidation of power. One of his most trusted advisors and friends was a relatively obscure political scientist from Michigan

---

[1] Edward G. Lansdale, *In the Midst of Wars: An American's Mission to Southeast Asia* (New York: Fordham University Press, 1991), 126–27.

1. Wesley Fishel (left) and Ngo Dinh Diem in Saigon.

State University (MSU), whom he had met in Japan a few years earlier: Wesley R. Fishel. Fishel immediately made plans to go to Saigon and to the aid of Diem, who he termed his "very dear friend."[2] In remarkably rapid succession, the French left Vietnam, only to be replaced by a group of Americans with considerable ambition, resources, and energy, all designed to whip southern Vietnam into a separate, developed, independent state.

The seemingly extraordinary uniformity in pursuit of the goals in southern Vietnam may not have appeared quite so extraordinary at the time. However coordinated the academy, the military, the government, and various groups seemed, consensus on how best to proceed in developing Vietnam was not the order of the day. The military split regarding the abilities of Ngo Dinh Diem and debated internally the efficacy of increased involvement, the U.S. government struggled to articulate a policy that both considered the restrictions of the Geneva Accords

---

[2] U.S. Congress, *The U.S. Government and the Vietnam War: Executive and Legislative Roles and Relationships, Part I: 1945–1961* (Washington, DC: U.S. GPO, 1984), 287–88.

47

and the limitations Congress might place on new ventures, and various academics promoted some development theories and dismissed others.[3] Each guarded territory and pursued institutional and individual interests. Despite at times rancorous divisions over tactics, however, the overall mission to invent a new Vietnam moved ahead.

Within the Eisenhower administration, a number of officials, notably Secretary of State John Foster Dulles, explicitly recognized both the danger and the opportunity in the region. For example, the "loss" of China blamed on President Harry Truman had been a bitter blow and a direct challenge to a significant American role in Asia. Consequently, there existed the danger of collapsing dominoes under pressure from the Chinese, which could then seriously threaten the American gains in Japan.[4] On the other hand, the administration had also remained officially distant from the proceedings at the Geneva Conference during the spring and summer of 1954 and was thus largely unencumbered by its dictates, as was Diem. Opportunity lay in the possibility of piecing together a collective security agreement within the region and building up what Lansdale termed the "muscularity" of the southern half of Vietnam in time to side-step the 1956 national elections called for in the Final Declaration of Geneva in July. Although recognizing formidable difficulties domestically, internationally, and internally in Vietnam, the Eisenhower administration moved ahead to shore up a most precarious toehold in Southeast Asia.

---

[3] Robert Buzzanco, *Masters of War: Military Dissent & Politics in the Vietnam Era* (New York: Cambridge University Press, 1996). David L. Anderson, *Trapped by Success: The Eisenhower Administration and Vietnam, 1953–1961* (New York: Columbia University Press, 1991). John Ernst, *Forging a Fateful Alliance: Michigan State University and the Vietnam War* (East Lansing: Michigan State University Press, 1998). On various development schemes, Jefferson P. Marquis of the RAND Corporation writes that for the duration of the war in Vietnam, "American social scientists never reached a consensus on the question of how to transform an alien, fragmented, and war-torn region into a viable nation-state and reliable non-Communist ally." See his "The Other Warriors: American Social Science and Nation Building in Vietnam," *Diplomatic History* 24 (Winter 2000): 79–105, quote on 104.

[4] For an analysis of the historical literature on the Eisenhower presidency and an assessment of the revisionists, see Robert J. McMahon, "Eisenhower and Third World Nationalism: A Critique of the Revisionists," *Political Science Quarterly* 101 (1986): 453–73; Richard H. Immerman, "Confessions of an Eisenhower Revisionist: An Agonizing Reappraisal," *Diplomatic History* 14 (Summer 1990): 319–42; Stephen G. Rabe, "Eisenhower Revisionism: The Scholarly Debate," in *America in the World: The Historiography of American Foreign Relations Since 1941*, ed. Michael J. Hogan (Cambridge: Cambridge University Press, 1995), 300–25.

As for the American military, many ranking officers looked warily upon any venture into Southeast Asia and had since at least 1950. By the mid- to late 1950s, a number of officers tempered their skepticism with the realities of operating within a political environment. As historian Robert Buzzanco has written, "despite their increasing awareness of Diem's repression, the ARVN's [Army of the Republic of South Vietnam] weaknesses, the Viet Minh's strengths, and politico-military constraints at home, U.S. service leaders kept insisting that they could build a credible military establishment in the south and contain communism in Vietnam."[5] To a large extent, politics determined the parameters of policy and action in Vietnam. Over the course of the next several years, during which the United States made increasingly deep and wide-ranging commitments to Southeast Asia, politics continued to shape the decisions of not only the military, but every other facet of involvement as well.

For his part, Wesley Fishel eagerly assumed the role of presidential advisor to his friend Ngo Dinh Diem. Secretary Dulles had even phoned Fishel's boss at Michigan State, president John Hannah, to ask that he come on board as an advisor to Diem while at Geneva, but ultimately working under General Collins in Vietnam. The relationship between Saigon leaders and MSU solidified quickly, and by spring 1955, Fishel and a number of other MSU specialists were working closely with a few Vietnamese to develop fledgling or nonexistent elements of a separate state. Specialists from the university were to provide assistance in public administration, police administration, public information, and public finance and economics. Fishel, together with university president John Hannah, created the Michigan State University Vietnam Advisory Group (MSUG) in 1955 to facilitate this effort. Despite numerous difficulties involving internal security, a war-torn countryside, lack of political legitimacy, and seriously damaged or nonexistent transportation and communications infrastructure, the program to build a new Vietnam below the seventeenth parallel moved ahead.

COLLECTIVE SECURITY AND CRAFTING CONSENSUS

Shortly following the conference at Geneva in 1954, the United States embarked on an ambitious project to transform at least a part of

---

[5] Buzzanco, *Masters of War*, 66.

2. The Michigan State Group, Fall 1954 (left to right): Charles Killingsworth (Economics), Arthur Brandstatter (Police Administration), Edward W. Weidner (Governmental Research Bureau), Ambassador Donald Heath, Wesley R. Fishel, and James Denison (special assistant to university president John Hannah).

Vietnam by rebuilding it along Western political-economic lines. Recognizing that southern Vietnam lacked a stable and reliable political leadership, the United States moved to prop up its effort with the establishment of a regional security agreement that would prevent further Communist gains until leadership could be found and its power consolidated. From the days of the Dien Bien Phu crisis, the Eisenhower administration, and particularly Secretary Dulles, envisioned an increased role in Southeast Asia. Both men believed that the very survival of Japan depended upon access to the mainland for exports and raw materials. For this reason, the Americans remained notably standoffish during the proceedings at Geneva in the late spring and summer of 1954. Dulles himself has received attention for refusing to shake hands with Chinese foreign minister Chou En-lai or even to sit at the same table with Communist leaders. As George Herring has pointed out, however, focusing on Dulles's stubborn attitude misses the point. His "major objective throughout these months was to establish a collective security mechanism for the future defense of Southeast Asia."[6] The Americans wanted a presence at Geneva, but they also wanted not to be bound by any arrangements that recognized the Vietnamese Communists or tied the hands of the United States in the future. Thus the secretary's behavior was part of a much larger set of goals related to retaining influence in the region through an arrangement to which those gathered in Geneva might not agree.

Ultimately, the United States, France, and Great Britain reached an agreement around a set of principles allowing for the independence of Laos, Cambodia, and southern Vietnam.[7] The arrangement also prescribed noncommunist governments and the maintenance of military forces, and permitted foreign military aid and advisors from other nations.[8] Even though the United States had, for all intent and purpose, conceded northern Vietnam to Ho Chi Minh and the Communists, Dulles considered the deal a victory. In part, the details of the deal brokered at Geneva mattered little since the United States did not officially participate. Dulles gave assurances that his government would not attempt to subvert the provisions of the Final Declaration and proceeded immediately to craft the collective security structure for the region that had been his object for months.

Results came in the form of the Manila Pact (Southeast Asia Treaty Organization, or SEATO) signed on September 8, 1954, and ratified by the U.S. Congress early the following year. From the start the pact proved vague, its provisions highly elastic, and its membership list limited. The agreement, for example, did not compel signatories to take any action in response to aggression. Instead, it called only for "consultations" among member nations, each of whom could then take action in accord

[6] George C. Herring, "'A Good Stout Effort': John Foster Dulles and the Indochina Crisis, 1954–1955," in *John Foster Dulles and the Diplomacy of the Cold War*, eds. Richard H. Immerman et al. (Princeton, NJ: Princeton University Press, 1990), 213–34, quote is on 227.

[7] For the details of this agreement, see *Foreign Relations of the United States* (Washington, DC: GPO, 1952–1954), XIII:1828–34; hereinafter *FRUS*.

[8] Memorandum from Paris to Secretary of State (Dulles), July 14, 1954, in *The Pentagon Papers: The Defense Department History of United States Decisionmaking on Vietnam*, Senator Gravel ed. (Boston: Beacon Press, 1971), I:554–56; hereinafter *PP*.

with their own "constitutional processes."[9] Due to Geneva's restrictions, Cambodia, Laos, and Vietnam did not become signatories. Burma, Indonesia, and India refused participation. The United States could count on membership from the Philippines, Thailand, and Pakistan but could not depend on these fortuitous allies to vigorously defend the Cold War objectives of the Eisenhower administration. The pact did, however, assuage skepticism that had threatened the effort within the U.S. Congress.[10] Congressional leaders, Democrats and Republicans who had both been critical of what had been "lost" at Geneva, welcomed the pact because it avoided the old go-it-alone approach, did not obligate American servicemen to the defense of Asians, did not threaten spiraling defense expenditures for far-flung adventures, and yet managed to construct a Cold War multilateral arrangement to protect Western interests in Asia. Gradually, too, the United States provided the French with an out and took over its role in Vietnam. To be sure, the brash Americans did serious damage in their relations with European allies. Those alliances, however, remained intact.[11]

More importantly, despite the ambiguous language that seemed to render the pact meaningless, it came to provide the legal foundation and rationale for vastly increased American involvement in the region, the subversion of the Geneva restrictions on outside interference, and the sidestepping of national elections. The pact maneuvered around Geneva's restrictions on participation by Cambodia, Laos, and the southern half of Vietnam by extending an "umbrella of protection" that involved the former two and the latter as "the free territory under the jurisdiction of the State of Vietnam."[12] With this stroke, a state of "South Vietnam" now compelled defense, protection, and, more importantly, development. The three were thus brought into the arrangement, though none of them could officially be signatories. In effect, the Manila Pact provided for a permanent division of the country of Vietnam and paved the way for the United States to consolidate the power of

---

[9] Southeast Asia Treaty Organization, *FRUS*, 1952–1954, XII; also reprinted in William Appleman Williams, Thomas McCormick, Lloyd Gardner, and Walter LaFeber, *America in Vietnam: A Documentary History* (New York: W.W. Norton, 1989), 174–77.

[10] Herring, "A Good Stout Effort," 226–28. Robert A. Divine, *Eisenhower and the Cold War* (New York: Oxford University Press, 1981), 53–55.

[11] Herring, "A Good Stout Effort," 233.

[12] Protocol to the Treaty, September 8, 1954, see note 10.

Ngo Dinh Diem and to begin to piece together a new state in southern Vietnam.[13]

"THE NEEDS ARE ENORMOUS, THE TIME SHORT": MICHIGAN STATE UNIVERSITY IN VIETNAM

The situation in Vietnam had not improved over the course of these policy developments. If anything, many within the military remained as skeptical as ever. The problem was easy to identify but very difficult to remedy: the state being cobbled together by the Eisenhower-Dulles team south of the seventeenth parallel did not really exist. As the French prepared to move out of Vietnam, the American contingent, or country team, prepared to move in and begin constructing one. In early September, Diem embarked on a tour of refugee camps housing a sudden influx of Catholics from northern Vietnam. In his absence, Dr. Fishel was charged with "reorganizing the office of the president."[14] The MSU professor had been in Vietnam only a short time but enjoyed considerable support from and influence on President Diem. Despite an alarming lack of governmental infrastructure and the admittedly narrow base of support for Diem (limited to the Catholic refugees ferried into Saigon), Fishel and others remained optimistic that a state infrastructure could be built around his leadership. They had their work cut out for them.

In 1954, the southern half of Vietnam as well as other areas of the country suffered from years of war, neglect, dislocation, and political chaos.[15] These obstacles to U.S. policy were explicitly recognized by some within intelligence and military circles immediately. A frank intelligence estimate and general survey of the situation in Indochina in August 1954 concluded that while the Viet Minh would shortly consolidate its base north of the seventeenth parallel, the prospect for the French and their Vietnamese allies to the south "for this development are poor." The situation, according to this report, was "likely to continue

---

[13] Less than two years later, Secretary Dulles, responding to a query from the president, ensured him that SEATO authorized the U.S. to intervene in Southeast Asia within a matter of a few hours without consulting Congress, though the secretary pointed out congressional approval would be useful. See *FRUS, 1955–1957*, I:701–2.

[14] *FRUS, 1952–1954*, XIII:2006.

[15] Bernard B. Fall, *The Two Viet-Nams: A Political and Military Analysis*, rev. ed. (New York: Praeger, 1964), chaps. 13 and 14.

to deteriorate progressively over the next year" and result in elements of the Saigon regime "seek[ing] unification with the North even at the expense of Communist domination. If the scheduled national elections are held...the Viet Minh will almost certainly win."[16]

Officials within the administration, the military, and Congress also recognized this. The dilemma for the United States centered on what could be created in the southern half of Vietnam to stymie "the popularity and prevalence" of Ho Chi Minh. In a major speech before the U.S. Senate in April 1954, a young John Kennedy outlined the only clear policy for the United States: the French must grant independence to Vietnam prior to any commitment on the part of America. "I am frankly of the opinion that no amount of American military assistance in Indochina can conquer an enemy which is everywhere and at the same time nowhere...which has the sympathy and covert support of the people." Vietnam would not be able to develop an effective fighting force unless and until the achievement of independence, the establishment of a stable and legitimate government, and an end to French domination of the economic, social, and political life of the people took place. Senator Kennedy sharply criticized the facts that the French still controlled "nearly 100 percent" of the export economy, "66 percent of the rice export trade," and overwhelmingly dominated landholding.[17] Senator Mike Mansfield added punch to Kennedy's critique of the situation and of France's handling of the war. The situation was indeed dangerous for the United States as long as the French retained overwhelming influence. Mansfield pointed out that despite several hundred thousand troops, the French actually seemed to be losing ground.[18] Under present circumstances, American intervention seemed doomed as well. Those speaking in the Senate, from Senators Mansfield and Kennedy to John Stennis (D-MS) and William Knowland (R-CA), were keenly aware of the talks about to convene at Geneva. Over the course of 1954, the removal of the French became a very important piece of the overall formula for "saving Southeast Asia." As long as the French stayed on, the whole effort suffered the taint of a colonial war. Furthermore, and more

---

[16] National Intelligence Estimate, "Post-Geneva Outlook in Indochina," August 3, 1954, *FRUS, 1952–1954*, XIII:1905–6.

[17] "Senator John Kennedy speech to the Senate, April 6, 1954," 83rd Cong., 2nd sess., *Congressional Record* 100, Part 4 (April 1, 1954–April 28, 1954), S 4673.

[18] *Congressional Record* 100, Part 4 (April 6, 1954), S 4677.

bothersome, the French would also want to retain considerable influence. Although not immediately, the French would have to be removed for the United States to carry out its program.[19]

Senator Mansfield outlined these problems in a caustic and candid report written upon his return from a visit to Laos, Cambodia, and Vietnam during August and September. The senator was alarmed at what he saw in southern Vietnam. "The most explosive single problem in Vietnam revolves about the current political crisis in south Vietnam.... Even before 1956, south Vietnam could give way to complete internal chaos." In short, Mansfield concluded that no base existed for the establishment of a reliable noncommunist government. The indigenous forces and actors were far more concerned with petty rivalries, individual gain, and graft than about creating a government "of the Vietnamese people." The capital city of Saigon "seethed with intrigue and counter-intrigue, with rumors and counter rumors. The political plotting goes on in army circles, government circles, foreign circles, in party headquarters, in police headquarters, and even in the demimonde of ill-disguised gangsters, pirates, and extortionists." Indeed, the political situation in Saigon was "devious and complex," and the senator found it "virtually impossible" to determine "responsibility for the crisis" that gripped the city. Diem had almost no tangible support. Numerous actors plotted against him and were themselves plotted against. The atmosphere proved dangerous enough that "Diem [had] become a virtual prisoner in his residence." Senator Mansfield, himself a Catholic and ardent supporter of Diem, advocated not removal from Vietnam based on these findings, but continued aid. The report effectively communicated a palpable sense of urgency. Only a brief window of opportunity existed to shore up Diem and a "free and independent Vietnam." Should his government fall, aid should be immediately suspended. In short, the report concluded that Diem was the only hope in a hopeless situation.[20] The senator's zeal for the project in part blinded him to the reality in southern Vietnam – but only partly. He clearly recognized

[19] *PP*, I:213.

[20] U.S. Congress. Senate. *Report on Indochina: Report of Senator Mike Mansfield on a Study Mission to Vietnam, Cambodia, Laos* (Washington, DC: GPO, 1954), 9. On the threat to Diem from religious sects and the military, see *PP*, I:219–20; and for details on chaotic situation in Saigon, see "Lansdale Team's Report on Covert Saigon Mission in 1954 and 1955," in *PP*, I:573–83.

that no basis existed for the creation of a new state, that internal chaos prevailed, and that the actors on the ground there did not constitute a government.

In addition to political difficulties, the physical infrastructure and economy of southern Vietnam remained undeveloped, damaged, and/or abandoned following years of war. The political division of the country at the seventeenth parallel further aggravated the situation. Most of Vietnam's natural resources lay north of that line, and so too did much of the nation's industry. Southerners had, prior to 1954, relied on the north for imports of cement, glass, coal, chemicals for rubber production, and textiles. The south exported its rice surplus to, in effect, subsidize these imports, not unlike the American South prior to the 1860s. Coupled with an influx of close to a million (largely Catholic) refugees and the departure of the French Expeditionary Corps as a major source of foreign capital and job creation, the southern economy quickly disintegrated.[21] A flood of foreign aid only masked serious problems. As dire as circumstances seemed, to those who promoted economic development schemes for integrating the third world, there could scarcely be a better place and time to build a new state.

While various military and governmental officials worked out the policy of increased American involvement and the removal of the French, Saigon became a veritable laboratory for development initiatives. MSU's Wesley Fishel went to work immediately upon arriving in Saigon in August. Fishel also communicated his shock at the situation in a letter to a colleague: "I've never seen a situation like this. It defies imagination. . . . The government is shaky as all hell. It is being propped up for the moment only with great difficulty. Nothing can help it so much as administrative, economic, and social reforms. . . . The needs are enormous, the time short."[22] Despite the difficulty involved, Fishel remained optimistic. He, like a number of intellectuals during the era, committed

---

[21] "The Economic Consequences of the Partition into Two Vietnams," excerpt from Buu Hoan, University of Washington, MSc thesis, London School of Economics. Michigan State University, Fishel Papers, Vietnam Project, Aid to Vietnam, box 1209, folder 21; hereinafter *MSUG Papers*, followed by specific collection information. Robert Scigliano, *South Vietnam: Nation under Stress* (Boston: Houghton Mifflin, 1963), 101–2, points out that by the time the French had pulled out in 1956, approximately eighty-five thousand Vietnamese lost jobs associated with that presence.

[22] Fishel letter to Edward Weidner, August 25 and September 4, 1954, *MSUG Papers*, Vietnam Project Papers, Correspondence, Edward Weidner, 1954, box 628, folder 101.

himself to the proposition that the underdeveloped world needed only development. Once developed, these new states, most of them formerly colonies, could be integrated into the global liberal capitalist system.

MSU had already taken up this mission, signing contracts with the federal government to aid in development projects in Latin American countries such as Colombia and Brazil. MSU was not alone. Princeton, Harvard, Columbia, American University, the Massachusetts Institute of Technology, and numerous other campuses took part in this project to shore up large parts of the globe through political and economic development. Enthusiastic students took part in an explosion of "area studies" to learn of the economies, cultures, politics, languages, and religions of the world on the way to becoming "experts."[23] The relationship between these area studies programs or development projects and the Federal Bureau of Investigation and CIA was thorough and the funding plentiful.[24] Aid to Vietnam represented a far larger task but one that MSU eagerly accepted, "in the context of the public service philosophy," according to an explanation offered by Fishel.[25] University president John Hannah came to see involvement in Southeast Asia as an opportunity to enhance the prestige of himself and MSU. Hannah held the position of president for nearly three decades, during which time he vastly expanded the size of MSU, its enrollment, and its prestige around the state and among potential faculty around the nation by offering higher pay and housing. Hannah's successor, Walter Adams, believed that he "converted a sleepy cow college...into a megaversity."[26] He

[23] By 1969, American colleges educated over sixty-five thousand graduates and over two hundred twenty-seven thousand undergraduates in a wide range of area studies programs, offering 8,890 courses. See Immanuel Wallerstein, "The Unintended Consequences of Cold War Area Studies," in *The Cold War and the University: Toward an Intellectual History of the Postwar Years*, eds. Noam Chomsky et al. (New York: New Press, 1996), 209.

[24] Bruce Cumings, "Boundary Displacement: Area Studies and International Studies during and after the Cold War," in *Universities and Empire: Money and Politics in the Social Sciences during the Cold War*, ed. Christopher Simpson (New York: New Press, 1999), 159–188. Sigmund Diamond, *Compromised Campus: The Collaboration of Universities with the Intelligence Community, 1945–1955* (New York: Oxford University Press, 1992).

[25] "The Role of the Michigan State University Group in Vietnam," by Dr. Wesley Fishel, speech delivered September 1957, *MSUG Papers*, Fishel Papers, Publications, box 1200, folder 74.

[26] For more detail on Hannah's role during his long tenure at MSU, see John Ernst, *Forging a Fateful Alliance: Michigan State University and the Vietnam War* (East Lansing: Michigan

had given the university national clout. A large development project like that being requested by Ngo Dinh Diem likewise contributed.

Wesley Fishel was uniquely positioned to influence events because of his personal relationship with Ngo Dinh Diem. Hannah and others encouraged the relationship. Ed Weidner, chief advisor of the MSUG, recognized Fishel's importance to the whole program when he arrived in Vietnam in early October. Cabling Hannah, Weidner explained that "the situation here is extremely serious" and that according to the "highest authority ... Professor Wesley R. Fishel is quite essential to American policy as long as Diem stays in power."[27] Fishel, too, viewed his role as critical, writing to Weidner a couple of weeks earlier,

I go in and out of the palace so often these days I'm treated as one of his [Diem's] staff by the guards. Yesterday I was there for 15 hours, and on Saturday for 19 hours. Today is abnormal. I was only with him for two hours this morning, and I've not been in the place for five whole hours now. But as soon as I seal this letter, off I'll go again.[28]

The otherwise obscure college professor seemed to be especially proud of his relationship with a foreign head of state and of his responsibility for making the fiction a reality. By October, a team, or "mission," of specialists from the university gathered around a nascent government in Saigon. The American mission spent that fall essentially plugging holes in a leaky governmental boat.[29] This mission included Fishel, already in Vietnam, Weidner (another political scientist and department head back at MSU), Arthur Brandstatter as a specialist on police administration, James Denison as a public relations specialist, and economics professor Charles Killingsworth. Of the group, only Fishel was an "Asia expert."

State University Press, 1998), chap. 1. Quoted material is from 5. Hannah also served the government as a member of the International Development Advisory Board of Point Four (1950–1952) under President Truman, served as Eisenhower's assistant secretary of defense for manpower and personnel, won the Medal of Freedom, chaired the Civil Rights Commission (1957), and later became head of the Agency for International Development (1969).

[27] Letter to John Hannah from Ed Weidner, October 6, 1954, *MSUG Papers*, Weidner Correspondence, 1954, box 628, folder 101.

[28] Letter from Wesley Fishel to Ed Weidner, September 20, 1954, *MSUG Papers*, ibid.

[29] See, e.g., prefatory remarks in "Final Report Covering Activities of the Michigan State University Vietnam Advisory Group" for the period May 20, 1955–June 30, 1962, *MSUG Papers*, Fishel Papers, Vietnam Project, Aid to Vietnam, box 1209, folder 27.

The rest read what they could at MSU and en route to Vietnam. The team conducted a very brief survey in two weeks and began to piece together an aid program based on their findings. The report, submitted in October, recommended emergency measures in public and police administration and efforts to shore up the economy.[30] Officially under contract with the U.S. government's Foreign Operations Administration, predecessor to the Agency for International Development, the MSU project divided duties with government economists and others already in-country. With the aid of Fishel and other MSU faculty, Diem and other Saigon leaders quickly began a crash program to install a political structure that could ensure control over and development of the southern half of Vietnam.

From 1954 to 1955, Diem, with much foreign aid and advice, survived a number of serious challenges to his position. Almost immediately, threats emerged from within the regime being cobbled together. When Diem swore in his government on July 7, 1954, for example, it contained almost none of the sizable political opposition parties/groups. Religious sects, such as the Cao Dai or the Hoa Hoa, and the powerful band of gangsters, the Binh Xuyen, remained conspicuously absent.[31] Most governmental positions went, in fact, to either the Catholic minority that now ringed Saigon as recent refugees and/or the Ngo family. Of his six-member cabinet, three of the appointees belonged to the Ngo family. Madame Nhu, Diem's outspoken and controversial sister-in-law, later started her own women's brigade and became a lightning rod for controversy. Her father became ambassador to Washington. Diem's youngest brother, Ngo Dinh Luyen, became ambassador to Great Britain. Another brother, Archbishop Ngo Dinh Thuc, was the eldest and became an influential advisor, though he held no official post. Ngo Dinh Can, another brother, also held no official post but held sway over central Vietnam as a kind of personal fiefdom. The most important and written about of Diem's influential family was his brother Ngo Dinh

---

[30] For details of this report, see "First Report of the Michigan State University Vietnam Team in Public Administration," August 19, 1955, *MSUG Papers*, Fishel Papers, Vietnam Project, Public Administration, box 1206, folder 51.

[31] Anderson, *Trapped by Success*, 76–77; Bernard Fall, *Viet Nam Witness: 1953–1966* (New York: Praeger, 1966), chap. 11. As an example of the power of these groups, Fall writes that the Hoa Hoa had membership of 1.5 million spread out over Vietnam, 149.

Nhu. He served as the president's political counselor, and according to contemporaries, his power exceeded even that of Diem.

The plots and schemes to overthrow Diem and remove his family were numerous and complex, with many overlapping loyalties and deceptions. The French and General Nguyen Van Hinh maneuvered Buu Hoi, Emperor Bao Dai's cousin living in Paris, to replace Diem as prime minister. Former prime ministers Tran Van Huu, Nguyen Van Tam, and Buu Loc maneuvered for position. Various sect leaders also worked behind the scenes for a share of the political and economic pie, notably, the leaders of the Binh Xuyen, who reportedly paid Bao Dai a large sum of money for gambling and prostitution rings and control of the police. The most serious threat came from General Hinh, chief of staff of the Vietnamese National Army. Hinh, like many others in the officer corps, became disenchanted over the role played by Diem's family in the government. Hinh had bragged that he could, at any time, take power from Diem. He enjoyed the loyalty of the armed forces and certainly had the means. Hinh and a number of others had demanded that Diem dismiss his brother Ngo Dinh Nhu and broaden the government. Diem refused. Late in 1954, Hinh made it clear that a coup was imminent. He obtained the cooperation of the various sects, the armed forces, and various political figures. The American ambassador, Donald Heath, worked feverishly, as did Lansdale, to thwart such a coup. Lansdale spirited key opposition leaders out of the country on some spurious mission. Heath maintained contacts with Hinh and the opposition, making clear that the U.S. administration desired stability above all else. The decisive move came, however, when the ambassador made it clear to the plotters that should such a coup take place, all aid would be cut off. Hinh himself later admitted, "The Americans let me know that if that happened [a coup], dollar help would be cut off . . . but the country cannot survive without American help."[32] By early 1955, this episode had come to a close with the removal of Hinh and other leaders of the plot. These events cast in relief serious problems with the Diem experiment. Certain American officials, Eisenhower's own representative J. Lawton

---

[32] *FRUS, 1952–1954,* XIII (part II):1995–96; *PP,* I:219–20. There are a number of accounts of these events. See Anderson, *Trapped by Success,* 78–79; Fall, *Viet Nam Witness,* chap. 11. Hinh quote is from George M. Kahin, *Intervention: How America Became Involved in Vietnam* (New York: Anchor Books, 1987), 82–83.

Collins and Ambassador Donald Heath, remained highly critical of his capacity to lead and to solve these problems.[33]

The MSU mission also had to reassess earlier findings of 1954. In a "comprehensive" report written sometime in 1955, the authors noted, "At the time of the original survey and report [October 1954], it was not apparent that it would be necessary to develop as extensive an internal security force as is now proposed." The new plan called for increased police capacity over the whole of southern Vietnam. A national police force of twenty-five thousand (shortly increased to forty-five thousand) would be a necessary start. This force would combat "subversion," and its members would need to "popularize" themselves with the peasants, among whom they would live. As the rural Vietnamese did not support the Saigon regime, this force could bridge that gap only if its members could enjoy "the confidence of the citizens they serve."[34] The report also recommended the creation of a Vietnamese Bureau of Investigation (VBI) made up of around four thousand officers. Its responsibilities "will generally be the same as those of our F.B.I."[35] The third piece of the security triumvirate would be the expansion of an already extant municipal police force in incorporated areas and large cities.[36] The three should share knowledge and training and should, above all, emphasize the nonmilitary, civilian nature of police enforcement as a tool to win over the people of Vietnam to a government based in Saigon. The MSU people would coordinate this increased police activity by adding twenty-three persons to the mission the first year and another sixteen the next year, at a cost of nearly $1.4 million.[37] At about the same time, MSU signed a contract with both the U.S. government and the Saigon regime, effectively creating the MSUG and cementing the relationship

---

[33] For Collins, see "Telegram to State Department," March 31, 1955, *FRUS*, 1955–1957, I:168, and Memorandum from the Director of the Office of Philippine and Southeast Asian Affairs (Young) to the Assistant Secretary of State for Far Eastern Affairs (Robertson), April 30, 1955, ibid., 337.

[34] "Report of Comprehensive Work Plan to USOM and Vietnamese Government," *MSUG Papers*, Vietnam Project, Correspondence, Ed Weidner, 1954, box 628, folder 102. See also "Telegram from the Ambassador in Vietnam (Reinhardt) to the Department of State," August 25, 1955, *FRUS*, 1955–1957, I:527.

[35] The VBI eventually involved over seventy-five hundred agents. Ibid., 5.

[36] Letter to Arthur Brandstatter (Head, Department of Police Administration) from Howard Hoyt (Deputy Advisor, Police), July 5, 1955, *MSUG Papers*, Vietnam Project, Police Administration, Arthur Brandstatter Correspondence, 1957–1961, box 681, folder 10.

[37] Ibid., Appendix I.

between the three.[38] By May, additional MSU personnel began arriving in Saigon.

The spring of 1955 was indeed a propitious time for the Diem experiment. By mid- to late March, relations between Diem and the various sects had gone from bad to worse. Following the removal of Hinh, the prime minister tightened the screws on other opposition groups. Some among the sects had formed a loose coalition opposing his leadership. The Binh Xuyen, considered the most dangerous of the opposition, controlled the Saigon police and the Sûreté and used this authority to seize key parts of the city.[39] In late March, fighting began with Binh Xuyen forces attacking police headquarters to oust the National Army (Diem's) forces. At the same time, Binh Xuyen fighters launched mortar shells into the president's palace. These attacks and a couple of others resulted in approximately fifteen killed and over seventy wounded.[40] Although these actions proved relatively minor in the scheme of things, they brought the friction to a head and proved that Diem was not about to share power.

Against the advice of many, and following the advice of his brother Nhu, Diem aggressively went after and defeated this coalition of Cao Dai, Hoa Hoa, and Binh Xuyen, or at least those the CIA had not been able to pay off.[41] In late April, he unleashed his National Army troops and, along with American backing and at least French quiescence, routed the opposition.[42] These groups remained the most significant opposition to Diem. Rather than broaden the government to allow

---

[38] See, e.g., "Agreement between the Government of the United States represented by the Foreign Operations Administration and Michigan State University," April 19, 1955, *MSUG Papers*, Vietnam Project, Contract, MSU-ICA, box 627, folder, 80.

[39] For the Binh Xuyen takeover of the Sûreté, or national police, see "Brief History of the Sûreté in Indo-China," *MSUG Papers*, Vietnam Project, Police Administration, Municipal Police Section, box 684, folder 33. For a detailed synopsis on Binh Xuyen activities see *PP*, I:293.

[40] Telegram from the Special Representative in Vietnam (Collins) to the Department of State, March 30, 1955, *FRUS*, 1955–1957, I:163.

[41] One of those counseling against the forced removal of the Binh Xuyen was General J. Lawton Collins. See his Telegram from the Special Representative in Vietnam (Collins) to the Department of State of March 15 and March 21, 1955, *FRUS*, 1955–1957, I:125–28, 137–40, respectively. Apparently, Gen. Lansdale had been busily spreading money around as an inducement to Cao Dai and Hoa Hoa members to jump ship and fight on behalf of Diem. Tens of thousands of them did. Bernard Fall, *Two Viet-Nams*, 246, estimated that as much as $12 million in bribes was handed out during March and April.

[42] *PP*, I:229–34.

them representation, something this "United Front" insisted upon, Diem sought to eliminate them, incorporate the remnants of their armed forces, and do so while he had American financing and support. Diem's retention of power required the elimination of native and popular leadership. He was not about to incorporate elements over which he could not exercise full control. Furthermore, to broaden his government also meant broadening the base of opinion regarding America's role and American aid – something the Americans were loathe to contemplate. As a result of his triumph over his rivals to power, U.S. officials suddenly rallied around him. Skepticism began to quickly ebb. As George M. Kahin has written, "Overnight, in the eyes of most American officials and much of the U.S. press, Diem was metamorphosed from a stubborn, narrow, politically maladroit failure into a wise and clever hero."[43]

To some extent, this metamorphosis resulted from wishful thinking on the part of American officials. American prestige had become linked to the Diem experiment. Abandoning him, even under the most justifiable circumstances, besmirched the nation's credibility, something Secretary Dulles considered when General Collins repeatedly insisted on replacing Diem. At the same time, a small but influential group of individuals had by this time organized themselves into the American Friends of Vietnam (AFV). While Dulles considered the U.S. government's options in Southeast Asia, he also had to consider Senator Mike Mansfield as Congress dealt with the Mutual Security bill and other appropriations. Mansfield, a prominent member of the AFV and an ardent supporter of Diem, made clear that Congress would frown upon appropriations for a regime in Saigon without Diem as its leader.[44] Not to put too fine a point on it, the AFV were just that, Diem's American friends. They did not create policy, although they undoubtedly influenced the creation of policy. To Eisenhower and Dulles, however, credibility and national prestige were likely the critical factors, and the role of the AFV should not be overstated. The U.S. government had linked itself firmly with Diem and now recognized the danger in withdrawing support for arguably the only credible nationalist force ready to play the right role.[45] The AFV was, in many instances, preaching to the choir. In

[43] Kahin, *Intervention*, 83–84.
[44] *PP*, I:232.
[45] Telegram from the Secretary of State to the Embassy in Vietnam, April 9, 1955, *FRUS*, 1955–1957, Vietnam, I:231–35.

fact, the administration waited for and desired a solution that involved Diem, and following the events of April 1955, that solution came.[46]

In May, the MSU group began its work in the immediate aftermath of Diem's apparent triumph. Diem had surprised his critics with a show of force and provided a justification for continued and increased U.S. support. Nevertheless, if the effort was to survive the Geneva-mandated national elections of 1956, the MSUG, the military, U.S. Operations Mission (USOM), and whoever else might be brought on board would need to quickly stabilize, popularize, and legitimize Diem's rule. The project had heretofore involved, regrettably, plugging holes and waiting to see if the chosen vessel of the United States could survive. Now those involved took the offensive in aggressively promoting Diem, while, at the same time, rapidly building an infrastructure around him.

The MSUG worked alongside a number of other U.S. personnel belonging to organizations with their own agendas. As a consequence, the earlier and more ambitious objectives set out by the four-man study team were sharply curtailed. Supported by USOM, Ambassador Collins, and the State Department, these cutbacks guarded territory, prevented overlapping responsibilities between the various groups building Vietnam, and limited the MSUG essentially to two fields: police administration and public administration.[47] A sharper focus on these two fields also reflected the emergency state of affairs in Vietnam. A number of other projects had to be placed on indefinite hold until some modicum of security could be brought to Vietnam and the regime's power consolidated.[48] MSU's School of Police Administration and Public Safety,

---

[46] This short period between April and early May is complex and full of intrigue. For example, the Eisenhower administration sent out cables in effect sanctioning the removal of Diem and the transition to another figure. Once the news of the fighting and of the triumph of Diem's NVA poured in, the United States did an abrupt about-face and scuttled the earlier cables. Diem, by a narrow miss, remained the American choice for leader of the whole experiment. See *FRUS*, 1955–1957, Vietnam, v. I:277–80, 291–92. As late as April 27 (the day the heavy fighting broke out in Vietnam), the United States sent off cables calling for a transition in government; see telegrams 3828 on p. 294 and 3829 on p. 297 in ibid. Also, Anderson, *Trapped by Success*, chap. 5, discusses the events very clearly.

[47] Ernst, *Forging a Fateful Alliance*, 13.

[48] See Letter from Edward W. Weidner (Chief Advisor) to Leland Barrows (Director, USOM), August 10, 1955, *MSUG Papers*, Vietnam Project, Correspondence, Ed Weidner, 1954, box 628, folder 103.

the oldest in the nation, brought together a team of specialists in April. Headed by MSU's Arthur Brandstatter, as department head in East Lansing, and Howard Hoyt, as his deputy, headed up the effort to build a layered police apparatus for their client.[49]

Vietnam in the 1950s was not without a police force. Far from it, the Vietnamese inherited the French Sûreté. The French had established this organization some seventy years earlier to police their far-flung empire of Indochina, which they divided into five "states": Tonkin, Annam, Cochin China, Laos, and Cambodia. A relatively small force prior to World War I, the French expanded it from around six hundred to around five thousand in response to increased "anti-French" activity, or Vietnamese nationalism. As the Sûreté expanded, the presence of Vietnamese in it increased dramatically, to about 80 percent by 1939, although these positions were always lower echelon and poorly paid relative to the French. The system remained a French one, and French officers occupied the top 7 percent of the force and made all the decisions. The French also began construction of numerous prisons spread out over their colony, arresting an increasing number of people each year.[50] These conditions changed dramatically during and following World War II and the defeat and occupation of France by Germany. The French, at least marginally, lost control of the Sûreté during Japanese occupation of Indochina, and then, following the war, during their own struggle to retake Vietnam. Consequently, well-placed Vietnamese moved into this vacuum and took over the French police system. In the early 1950s, the Binh Xuyen obtained control of the police force from an apparently pliant Boa Dai. The Binh Xuyen gradually replaced all top positions with their own people, took over the selling of certain trade licenses and permits, organized the trafficking of opium from Laos, and controlled the lucrative gambling and prostitution houses in

---

[49] Ralph Turner, "Law Enforcement in South Viet Nam," January 1, 1958, *MSUG Papers*, Vietnam Project, Police Administration, Publications, box 682, folder 11. For list of Police Administration members and background, see *American Staff Members, Police Administration Division, MSUG*, box 679, folder 2.

[50] Approximately 80 percent of those arrested were "for purely political reasons." See "Brief History of the Surete in Indo-China," January 10, 1956, *MSUG Papers*, Vietnam Project, Police Administration, Municipal Police Section, box 684, folder, 33, 4. See also Peter Zinoman, *The Colonial Bastille: A History of Imprisonment in Vietnam, 1862–1940* (Los Angeles: University of California Press, 2001), 48, 64.

the Saigon-Cholon area.[51] Following Diem's rout of the Binh Xuyen, the latter bolted the force with vehicles, weapons, ammunition, and numerous dossiers gathered on various personalities in Vietnam. The Sûreté, now containing about sixty-five hundred personnel, came to be nominally controlled by Saigon. The system, however, defied rigid control and coordination.

The MSUG found the current police system lacking proper authority, organization, trained personnel, and buildings and equipment.[52] In addition to building a new national police force of some forty-five thousand, excluding the municipal forces and the VBI,[53] Howard Hoyt recommended to Brandstatter in July that the MSU program scrap "everything else," such as the Gendarmerie, Sûreté, "and all other various enforcement agencies." He believed they were all "going around in circles, stepping on one another's toes," and that the MSUG "should at least set the example" of how a police system ought to work.[54] The security apparatus needed far more than a fresh coat of paint, and the chief advisor, Weidner, worried "about the future of democracy in Vietnam" because of the degree of insecurity and the inability of Saigon's leadership to address the problems.[55] Reorganizing, training, and equipping a police force occupied much of the group's energy over the course of the next couple of years.

By late fall 1955, the MSUG established a National Police Academy in Saigon. A year later, the school had graduated over six hundred

---

[51] See ibid., 5–6. See also Ralph Turner, "Law Enforcement in South Viet Nam," *MSUG Papers*, Vietnam Project, Police Administration, Publications, box 682, folder 11.

[52] "Report on the Proposed Organization of the Law Enforcement Agencies of the Republic of Vietnam," Michigan State University Police Advisory Staff, April 1956, *MSUG Papers*, Fishel Papers, Vietnam Project, Education Department, Law Enforcement, box 1206, folder 40.

[53] The VBI basically evolved out of the old Sûreté structure (although the documentary record repeatedly uses the terms interchangeably) and replaced it as the national police force, also garnering an inordinate share of the funding and equipment. The Civil Guard comprised Provincial Guards, Communal Police, and Northern National Guards and was created in April 1955 for the purpose of policing the provinces. For details on the evolution of the various levels of police enforcement, see "Special Report on Police," March 5, 1956, *MSUG Papers*, Vietnam Project, Police Administration, Municipal Police Section, box 684, folder 7.

[54] Howard Hoyt to Arthur Brandstatter, July 5, 1955, *MSUG Papers*, Vietnam Project, Police Administration, Brandstatter Correspondence, 1957–1961, box 681, folder 10. Letter from Hoyt to Brandstatter, July 25, 1955, in ibid.

[55] Letter to Wesley Fishel from Ed Weidner, November 9, 1955, *MSUG Papers*, Fishel Biographical Files, Correspondence, 1953–1955, box 1184, folder 15.

officers from all over Vietnam. The MSUG also created a training program for the Civil Guard that had trained over eleven thousand police in areas such as riot control, traffic management, equipment and weapon maintenance and use, radio repair and maintenance, and criminal investigation, while a contingent of CIA agents conducted counterespionage training.[56] MSU advisors skimmed potential instructors from the classes through the use of a sixth-grade-level examination of forty arithmetic and one hundred language questions plucked from a Vietnamese language *Reader's Digest*.[57] MSU advisors went on to almost completely rebuild the police structure, updating equipment, importing modern fingerprinting methods and training, providing funding for the construction of facilities such as vehicle garages, barracks, interrogation centers, detention centers, and crime laboratories, and training in various police tactics and weaponry. In 1956, the group further centralized the system by moving the VBI to a former French facility in Saigon. Indeed, the VBI became a kind of showpiece for the project, receiving much of the attention and funding of the police program.[58] Once up and running, Diem used the agency as a tool to ferret out and eliminate his political opponents. With little oversight and continued American advice and funding, the Diem regime used the rapidly developing police capabilities to arrest and imprison more than twenty thousand people by 1956.

More than once did the police advisors complain of the terrorist nature of police activities. Differences over the role of various police organizations became, in fact, very serious during the late 1950s and into the 1960s. The MSUG wanted the Civil Guard to act as a typical U.S. civil police force. Advisors pushed to reduce Civil Guard numbers

---

[56] "Special Report on Michigan State University Group," September 14, 1956, *MSUG Papers*, Vietnam Project, Reports, box 658, folder 81.

[57] Ernst, *Forging a Fateful Alliance*, 68–69. Also useful, although clinical in its description, is the MSUG's *Final Report*, 45–51.

[58] According to budget estimates for CY 1956, the Civil Guard received the lion's share of funding; approximately VN$4.3 billion (piasters) compared to approximately VN$2.83 billion for the VBI. See "Special Report on Police," March 5, 1956, *MSUG Papers*, Vietnam Project, Police Administration, Municipal Police Section, box 684, folder 7. Also, according to a MSUG report on the "duties and responsibilities" of the VBI, it shouldered much of the responsibility for law enforcement as well, including customs and immigration, the postal system, subversive activities, collection of intelligence information, pure food and drug laws, banking, national labor laws, national taxes and revenues, and civil aeronautics authority, among others. See "Report on the Proposed Organization of the Law Enforcement Agencies of the Republic of Vietnam," in note 60.

and remove the "over-age, physically unfit and the more illiterate members." The Diem regime wanted a paramilitary force able to fight low-intensity warfare. The Military Assistance Advisory Group (MAAG) as well as Lansdale, not surprisingly, agreed with Diem. Ultimately, the system served the regime's basic purpose of eliminating the opposition.[59] The VBI, for example, became rather notorious for its tactics in snaring "subversives" and imparting fear. In the summer of 1956, an American officer parked across the street from the VBI headquarters witnessed an escaped "prisoner" run away from the building. The American watched as agents "rush[ed] this prisoner and sh[ot] him down in cold blood. The prisoner had a rock in his hand." People quite naturally refused to testify in such cases for fear of reprisal.[60] Almost certainly, the police aimed for this level of control, despite what was said publicly. As the police, both VBI and Civil Guard, were spread out across the whole of southern Vietnam, visits to outposts were infrequent (and announced), and communications, transportation, and equipment remained obsolete or nonexistent. On a trip from Saigon to the seventeenth parallel in early November 1955, MSU police advisors reported a lack of transportation and communications equipment for the VBI agents patrolling the "borderline." One hundred five men patrolled less than half of the line, covering a distance of approximately thirty kilometers. They communicated by running from one to another. The team wrote that because of the "unbelievable" lack of proper equipment and supplies, such as paper to file reports and even food to feed prisoners and cells to hold them, they were therefore "eliminated after interrogation."[61] Proximity, however, was not the determinant factor in police

[59] See "Report of Comprehensive Work Plan to USOM and Vietnamese Government," *MSUG Papers*, box 628, folder 102, and "Monthly Report Requested by CPD–ICA-Washington," March 6, 1957, 3, *MSUG Papers*, Vietnam Project, Police Administration, box 679, folder 29; Memorandum of a Conversation, Saigon, November 7, 1955, and Letter from the Chief of the Military Assistance Advisory Group in Vietnam (Williams) to the Commander in Chief, Pacific (Stump), October 18, 1957, *FRUS*, 1955–1957, I:571–72, 850–53, respectively; George Herring, *America's Longest War: The United States and Vietnam, 1950–1975* (New York: John Wiley, 1979), 58–59. Ernst, *Forging a Fateful Alliance*, chap. 4.

[60] Letter from Howard Hoyt (Chief of Police Program), October 31, 1956, *MSUG Papers*, Police Administration, VBI Criminal Field Reports, box 684, folder 24.

[61] "Reconnaissance Trip to the 17th Parallel on November 3–6, 1955," November 21, 1955, *MSUG Papers*, Vietnam Project, Police Administration, VBI Criminal Field Trip Reports, box 684, folder 23. This is a very useful report, containing detailed information on road

behavior. In September 1956, a USOM field officer reported that the wife of his driver had become involved in a scuffle in the local market one morning. When the police arrived, she apparently inadvertently tore one of the officer's uniforms. They beat her so badly, she had to be hospitalized. They later forcibly took her from the hospital, jailed her, and no one, including her lawyer, had been able to get her out.[62] This incident occurred in Da Lat, one of three cities where the VBI had central offices.[63]

Diem used the police system and other products of American aid to bolster his own position throughout 1955 and into 1956, and after November 1955, the Civil Guard came under his direct control. He understood that the Americans viewed him as the only hope for their objective of establishing a reliable noncommunist state below the seventeenth parallel. Diem reorganized the military, removing those who he feared might oppose him. He and brother Nhu tightly controlled and censored the press, permitting no opposition editorials or advertising from political opponents. The regime finally removed the last significant obstacle to its unfettered power through a political referendum in October 1955. Given the choice between Diem and the establishment of a "democratic regime" and Bao Dai and the continuation of the monarchy, Diem ran away with a resounding 98.2 percent of the vote. In several instances he won tens of thousands more votes than there were voters. Even though his American backers, including the ever-present Lansdale, assured him that something like 60 percent would be sufficient, Diem balked and demanded a higher percentage of the vote. Despite its comic excesses, the vote was heralded as legitimizing the government.[64] Upon winning the referendum, Diem quickly disbanded the "Revolutionary Committee" that had been so active on his behalf, for fear of future opposition from its members. He and the ruling family continued during 1956 in the establishment of, in effect, a police state. Diem issued a Presidential Ordinance in early 1956 expanding the scope of

conditions on Highway 1, levels of traffic, problems with flooding, as well as information on critical shortages at virtually every stop along the way.

[62] Letter from Howard Hoyt Chief of Police Program, October 31, 1956, see note 67.

[63] The others were Hué and, of course, Saigon.

[64] Despatch from the Ambassador in Vietnam (Reinhardt) to the Department of State, November 25, 1955, *FRUS, 1955–1957*, I:589–94; Scigliano, *South Vietnam*, 23–24; Kahin, *Intervention*, 95; Fall, *Two Viet-Nams*, 257–58.

the Anti-Communist Campaign, launched the previous summer. Despite the name, this campaign meant far more to ordinary peasants as anyone who might threaten the government was to be arrested, jailed, placed in camps for political indoctrination, or some combination of these. Though exact numbers are impossible to obtain, by 1960, thousands had been killed, almost fifty thousand jailed, and into the hundreds of thousands "re-educated" in the numerous reeducation or concentration camps set up by the regime.[65]

Diem used the Civil Guard and made that force more amenable by loading it with Army of the Republic of (South) Vietnam (ARVN) officers. MSU's monthly report for September 1957 outlined the problem as they saw it. Civil Guard operations for the month included nineteen enemy killed, three wounded, and the arrest of almost two hundred Viet Cong suspects. Six Civil Guard were killed and six wounded in these operations. MSU advisors continued to believe that the force ought to be a civil police force. Its paramilitary activities clearly indicated that Diem and the MAAG had won out. ARVN officers occupied many of the upper ranks. Rank accrued to them first, passing over Civil Guard officers and affecting morale. In August, 2,870 guards deserted the force. A year earlier, desertions amounted to about three or four per month.[66] Differences between the government and the MSUG mounted until, in late 1957, the latter suspended aid to the Civil Guard "pending...agreement between the Vietnamese Government and American authorities with respect to the future status of the Civil Guard."[67] Aid to the Civil Guard resumed only when the USOM created its own Public Safety Division and took over the project two years later.[68] Larger forces than MSUG were at play, and aid continued, as it continued over numerous years into the 1960s, despite a flourishing dictatorship in Saigon.

Besides the police project, the MSUG also spent considerable effort and resources on public administration. A broad net, public

[65] *PP*, I:311–12.

[66] "September Monthly Report," October 9, 1957, *MSUG Papers*, Vietnam Project, Police Administration, box 679, folder 29.

[67] "Monthly Report of the Michigan State University Group," December 10, 1957, *MSUG Papers*, Vietnam Project, MSU Group Monthly Reports, box 1206, folder 54.

[68] United States Operations Mission, "Review and Observation of Civil Police Administration and Improvement of Municipal Police and Surete," May 20, 1960, *MSUG Papers*, Vietnam Project, Police Administration, Brandstatter Correspondence, 1957–1961, box 681, folder 10. Ernst, *Forging a Fateful Alliance*, 79.

administration involved formal advice and training for the people who were to become the bureaucrats of the new state. In August 1955, the MSUG and Diem created the National Institute of Administration (NIA) for the purpose of training civil servants to further develop a state and ensure that Vietnam could "keep pace with global modernizing trends."[69] Part of the program involved training in Vietnam at this school in fields such as comparative administration, fiscal and budgetary problems, elements of political science, introduction to public administration, comparative governments, management of private enterprise, and others. Another part of the program involved foreign training in places like the Philippines, Malaya, Hong Kong, and particularly, the United States. Additionally, around 325 foreign-educated Vietnamese returned to Vietnam following Diem's ascension to power and began to fill in positions in the civil service. As one MSUG member pointed out, however, the main "external source of trained civil servants is the study programs financed by the American government."[70]

Officially known as the Participant Program, MSUG and USOM sought out exceptional students, who were then sponsored to continue their education in the United States. The MSUG, responding to a request from Diem, also sought out Vietnamese students already in the United States to provide instruction at the NIA.[71] Ideally, upon completion of their studies, these students would return to Vietnam and become part of the Saigon government. As MSUG advisor Stanley Sheinbaum described it, "this is primarily a technical assistance program not a cultural exchange."[72] The program should avoid those students who would not later be active participants in the process. Estimates of the number of participants vary greatly, in part due to sponsorship from separate bureaucracies. The MSUG's *Final Report* indicates, for example, that its participant program sponsored 179 Vietnamese for training, 116 of those in the United States, from 1955 to 1961. The USOM, from 1954

[69] "Final Report Covering the Activities of MSUG," *MSUG Papers*, 22.

[70] Scigliano, *South Vietnam*, 64–65.

[71] "Work Plan, Degree or Certificate Program," August 25, 1955, *MSUG Papers*, Fishel Papers, Vietnam Project, Correspondence, 1955–1960, box 1206, folder 32. Letter from Weidner to Diem, July 8, 1955, *MSUG Papers*, Vietnam Project, Weidner Correspondence, 1954, box 628, folder 102. Letter from Weidner to Fishel, July 8, 1955, *MSUG Papers*, ibid.

[72] Letter from Stanley K. Sheinbaum to Edward Weidner, February 16, 1956, *MSUG Papers*, Vietnam Project, Correspondence, Stanley Sheinbaum, 1956, box 628, folder 98.

to 1961, sponsored 1,705 students, 1,037 of those in the United States. MSUG advisor Robert Scigliano has pointed out that these numbers are only a fraction of the actual number of Vietnamese trained in the United States during the period.[73] In any event, the NIA facilities in Vietnam trained a much larger number of students, enrolling between two hundred and three hundred per term (and about five hundred per term in the evening school) and training thousands more through an in-service program.[74]

Some MSUG members viewed the training project as only marginally successful. Advisors and instructors grew frustrated over the reluctance of the Vietnamese to take their advice and establish a school on the basis of the American system. Some Vietnamese, for example, relied on the old French system of teaching, which emphasized lecture and little or no classroom interaction. MSUG personnel later complained that, while understandable, Vietnamese were "unwilling to sit in on classes taught by MSUG professors, and almost equally reluctant to offer courses jointly with them."[75] The problems extended to more than just matters of style. There were also obvious cultural differences aggravated by language barriers that complicated the relationship. Furthermore, as in a number of other instances, the Diem regime insisted on very close personal scrutiny of the program and of potential candidates. Diem, or someone close to him, demanded ultimate oversight, thus involving bureaucratic channels that created a logjam and increased the time required to fund the program, approve travel, train personnel, and fill positions in the government. As MSUG advisor Robert Scigliano wrote shortly after the program had expired, the system was handicapped "by the government's insistence upon furnishing it with weak leadership, using its faculty positions as a convenient dumping place for civil servants not wanted elsewhere." Consequently, the NIA did not "enjoy a high reputation among high government officials and intellectuals

73 "Final Report Covering Activities of MSUG," 60; USOM, *Vietnam Meets Its Challenge, Annual Report for Fiscal Year 1961*, 67; Scigliano, *South Vietnam*, 65.
74 "Fourth Report of the Michigan State University Viet Nam Advisory Group in Public Administration to the Government of Viet Nam," submitted by Wesley R. Fishel, Chief Advisor, December 31, 1956, 15, *MSUG Papers*, Fishel Papers, Vietnam Project, Public Administration, box, 1206, folder 51. "Final Report Covering Activities of MSUG," 29.
75 Ernst, *Forging a Fateful Alliance*, 51.

generally."[76] Despite the difficulties, the institute ultimately trained tens of thousands of people in conjunction with the in-service, participant, and others types of formal training.

Over the course of the multiple specific programs inaugurated in 1955 until 1957, the aid project involving MSU, USOM, and others created enough of a government to be relatively sanguine in progress reports. For the MSUG public administration effort, the NIA English-language catalogue had just been published, outlining new course offerings. The student body had almost doubled. A night school program offering eight courses commenced. Eleven new public administration candidates had been chosen, and their training in the English language would soon begin. Diem approved an in-service training program and simultaneously increased its status. Hundreds of new books arrived to bring the institute's library collection to six thousand total. Long-awaited equipment began to arrive.[77] The Police Administration also continued to train tens of thousands of new police, from VBI agents to municipal officers, despite the fact that MSU suspended aid to the Civil Guard in 1957. Overall personnel on the MSUG staff increased to a high of 182, excluding those employed directly by USOM.[78] Indeed, the program expanded considerably, and events, despite occasional setbacks, seemed to justify increased effort.

At the same time, Diem had quelled much of the opposition that so challenged his tenuous hold on power and clouded his relations with various Americans. By 1957, certain of the more serious obstacles seemed

---

[76] Scigliano, *South Vietnam*, 65. The USOM also was "not convinced that the results obtained from the expensive participant training program . . . merit a continuation of this type of training." After $500,000 and eighty-seven participants, barely half of them had returned to Vietnam, and the MSUG had not conducted a systematic study to determine whether or not even these were now of benefit to the Saigon regime. See USOM, "Review and Observation of Civil Police Administration and Improvement of Municipal Police and Surete," May 20, 1960, 27, *MSUG Papers*, Vietnam Project, Police Administration, USOM Audit of Police, box 681, folder 21.

[77] "Evaluation of NIA Progress and Problems," November 15, 1957, *MSUG Papers*, Fishel Papers, Vietnam Project, Aid to Vietnam, box 1209, folder 21.

[78] Up from one hundred forty-nine the previous month, the staff consisted of fifty Americans, five under "piaster contract," one hundred twenty-five Vietnamese, and two consultants. The above data are from "Monthly Report of the Michigan State University Group," October, 8 and December 10, 1957, *MSUG Papers*, Fishel Papers, Vietnam Project, Monthly Reports, box 1206, folder 54. Details on the training of the police forces contained in USOM, "Review and Observation," 24.

at least diminished in degree. The October 1955 referendum effectively removed Bao Dai. Diem seated his National Assembly early the following spring with similar pomp and circumstance and little substance.[79] Of the 123 members, Diem approved and/or handpicked 90 of them to ensure passage of a constitution drafted by him and his coterie of advisors.[80] With the support of the United States, Diem was building all the accouterments of a government, while retaining ultimate control. Almost incidentally, the date for the Geneva-mandated national unification elections came and went during 1956. Neither the United States nor Diem had any plans to comply with free national elections that the Communists would almost surely win. Rather, Saigon leaders cited conditions preventing the possibility of free elections and simply scuttled the mandate. American officials, although concerned about international and domestic criticism, agreed that conditions prevented such elections. Consequently, the scheduled elections for reunification of Vietnam were not held in 1956 or any other year. The United States and the Saigon regime desired a way out, for whatever strength the Diem government possessed, neither believed it could overcome Ho Chi Minh and the Communists in an election. The Geneva Accords for Indochina became what Secretary Dulles envisioned in 1954: a stop-gap measure to buy time to develop a U.S.-friendly regime below the seventeenth parallel. Once sufficiently in place, the restrictions imposed at Geneva became at least a nuisance and at worse a serious threat to the entire project.

The experiment below the seventeenth parallel also required a substantial aid program. The MSUG had been an important part of that program. From its harried survey in 1955, its members developed a wide-ranging series of training and advising projects to build a state. The MSUG, however, was only part of a much larger U.S. mission. Vietnam remained a traditional society in many respects, and the country contained little of what those advisors considered "developed" infrastructure such as communications, transportation, industry, and so on. Additionally, the Vietnamese economy, such that it was following a

---

[79] At least part of the calculation behind Diem seating a national assembly involved buttressing his government to sidestep the Geneva national elections scheduled for 1956. See telegram from the Charge in Vietnam (Anderson) to the Department of State, September 20, 1955, *FRUS*, 1955–1957, I:540–42.

[80] Anderson, *Trapped by Success*, 129.

brutal occupation and war, could not sustain the barrage of aid, which amounted, on average, to $220 million–$250 million annually. This influx quickly overwhelmed this traditional society. The task before MSUG, USOM, and the Eisenhower administration revolved around this problem. Large-scale aid created little incentive for the Saigon leaders to foster internal growth, and at the same time, it threatened spiraling inflation and a loss in standard of living for those who might otherwise support Diem. However, Diem could not remain in place to carry out U.S. objectives without this arrangement, as many officials recognized.

In part to alleviate the resulting problems, the United States, in 1955, inaugurated an import-subsidization program, through which it channeled the lion's share of the total aid. The so-called Commodity Import Program (CIP) served a number of purposes for both the United States and the Diem regime. First, it allowed for the infusion of massive aid, most of it military, without spiking inflation and making conditions unlivable for the small middle class that supported Diem. The program also provided opportunities for importers who could secure a license from Saigon and get in the aid pipeline themselves. Many reaped windfall profits before importing or exporting anything because of the nature of the published and unpublished exchange rates. Finally, the CIP also provided Diem a source of revenue that freed him from having to tax the population heavily, which translated into continued political support. Through the CIP, over $1 billion in goods of various kinds entered Vietnam between 1955 and 1959. American aid paid for 85 percent of the total imports during 1958 alone, leaving the Saigon government with a $177 million trade deficit.[81] This deficit was also subsidized by the United States. In part, the program, by design, paid the costs associated with massive U.S. aid. However, it was also designed to generate internal economic growth that would allow for a gradual weaning of the Saigon regime (and indeed of the new state) from continued aid, at least on such a grand scale.

---

[81] Imports amounted to $232 million, while exports for the year were worth $55 million. USOM, *Vietnam Moves Ahead, Annual Report for Fiscal Year 1960*, 31. The Saigon government continued to run large trade deficits in every year from 1956 through 1974 of no less than $150 million and highs of over $800 million. See Milton C. Taylor, "South Viet-Nam: Lavish Aid, Limited Progress," *Pacific Affairs* 34, no. 23 (1961), 244; Douglas Dacy, *Foreign Aid, War, and Economic Development: South Vietnam, 1955–1975* (New York: Cambridge University Press, 1986), 82.

A critical aspect of the CIP was the counterpart fund. This fund consisted of monies paid out by Vietnamese importers who wished to buy foreign goods, usually American, but others as well. These importers obtained a license via Saigon to do business. Once they determined what commodities to import and received approval, they simply paid for the goods in piasters to the regime at a fixed rate of exchange.[82] That money went into the counterpart fund, which was then used by the regime to pay the costs of its military, police, civil service, foreign travel for students, various training programs, and so on. At the same time, the American aid program paid the exporter for the value of the goods to be shipped. In this way, the American aid mission directly subsidized most of the goods imported into Vietnam.[83] The objective was twofold: to provide Saigon with money to pay for its needs and operating costs and provide consumer goods to promote economic development and maintain a relatively high standard of living.[84] Without such a system in place, the level of aid and the concomitant influx of wealth would surely have wiped out the value of domestic currency and prevented all but the most local of home production. Rampant inflation and disincentives to home production could threaten the very objectives of state building: an economically, socially, and politically developed independent South Vietnam.

In practice, the program operated differently than drawn up on paper. It did not generate internal economic development, as some had hoped. Rather, during the years from 1956 until 1960, nearly 80 percent of the total aid given went into the military budget to include defense, communications, and transportation infrastructure as well as equipment and training. Excluding the aid generated by the counterpart fund for the moment, the International Cooperation Agency (ICA) reported that "project aid" during 1955–1960 was disbursed as follows: 45 percent for transportation, 15 percent for public administration, 9 percent for industry and mining, 9 percent for agriculture, 6 percent for health and sanitation, 5 percent for education, 4 percent for welfare, and the remaining 7 percent for miscellany, for a total of approximately

---

[82] The official rate of exchange was fixed at thirty-five piasters to the U.S. dollar until 1961.

[83] "United States Economic Assistance to South Vietnam, 1954–1975," Agency for International Development, II:431–32. Scigliano, *South Vietnam*, 113.

[84] Taylor, "South Viet-Nam," 246.

$166 million.[85] Of these funds, the 45 percent for transportation involved highway and bridge construction for the purpose of defense. To put the numbers in perspective, project aid accounted for 13 percent of the total aid flow. The CIP accounted for 87 percent. The regime allocated 43 percent of its public expenditures to the military, monies supplied via the CIP. To cite one example, a twenty-mile stretch of highway running northwest from Saigon to Bien Hoa deemed "suitable for military traffic" cost more than was spent on labor, community development, social welfare, health, housing, and education combined for the period 1954–1961.[86] The American aid program provided southern Vietnam with a distinctly military form of modernization.

Charges of corruption also plagued the system almost from its inception. For example, the licensing program became, in some cases, a tool to reward the regime's favored friends.[87] The Saigon authorities awarded some twenty thousand of these much sought after import licenses during 1955. And although the number issued decreased in later years due to pressures to consolidate, they remained a key determinant of support for the regime. The relative few importers who obtained them understood their value both in political terms as well as in economic terms. So long as the system operated in this way, the aid flowed. Once disrupted, as in late 1963, the relationship between Diem and the business leaders quickly eroded. Importers profited through the fixed exchange rate and the regime's continual refusal to devalue.[88] At the same time, unofficial or black market rates held out even greater potential. Saigon profited simply by the exchange rate. It earned thirty-five piasters for every dollar's worth of goods imported. Additionally, officials skimmed

---

[85] USOM, *Vietnam Moves Ahead*, 5.

[86] Scigliano, *South Vietnam*, 113–15.

[87] U.S. Congress, *Improper Practices, Commodity Import Program, U.S. Foreign Aid, Vietnam, Hearings before the Committee on Government Operations*, 90th Cong., 1st sess., April 25–27, 1967. See also U.S. Congress, *Situation in Vietnam, Hearings before the Committee on Foreign Relations*, 86th Cong., 1st sess., July 30–31, 1959.

[88] During a Washington meeting in May 1957, Diem explained to those gathered, including Secretary of State Dulles, Ambassador Elbridge Durbrow, and others, that devaluation was simply not possible. Diem recognized that such a move would set off "a panic in Viet-Nam." Diem stated, "Devaluation was possible only for a country with a very high level of production," and such was not the case in his Vietnam. When asked about the difference between the official rate of exchange and the unofficial that was perhaps double, Vietnamese officials present explained that "this difference was responsible for the improved Vietnamese standard of living." See Memorandum of Conversation, Blair House, Washington, May 10, 1957, *FRUS, 1955–1957*, I:812–16, quotes are on 815–16.

a further eighteen piasters per dollar through customs duties on the same goods, already paid for.[89] So abundant was the aid flow that the regime in Saigon piled up a cash reserve of around $216 million.

The American aid program accomplished part of its objective, if only in the short term. First, it facilitated the expansion of a defense network extending out from Saigon into rural areas, through which Diem exerted some control. Second, the CIP promoted the importation of numerous consumer and luxury items, such as automobiles, refrigerators, cigarettes, wristwatches, and various textiles, which created a sense of middle- and upper-class prosperity in the urban environments. The import data for fiscal year 1957 show that a significant portion of imports involved consumer goods.[90] MSUG consultant Milton Taylor concluded in 1961 that "at least three-fourths of American aid [CIP] has been used for the importation of either consumption goods or raw materials for the production of consumer goods."[91] Such estimates reflect the nature of the aid package. For example, the USOM reported under the category "Imports of Industrial Equipment" a total of $110,714,000 for 1957–1959. These commodities, which included industrial electrical equipment, engines and turbines, mining equipment, and machine tools, were aimed at economic development, as outlined. However, under the "All Other Commodities" category, such items as clothes, food products, pharmaceuticals, transportation vehicles, books, watch parts, and paper products accounted for $215,412,000 for the same period. The latter category excluded other consumer items such as tobacco and newsprint. In 1959, the CIP facilitated the importation of close to the same amount of clothing ($24 million) as all industrial equipment and machinery ($28 million), which explained "why the people of Saigon appear so well-clothed."[92] Visitors to Saigon commented on its cleanliness, on the numerous and modern shops, on the new cars and scooters, on the continual construction projects, and on the availability of a wide

---

[89] Kahin, *Intervention*, 86; John Montgomery, *The Politics of Foreign Aid: American Experience in Southeast Asia* (New York: Praeger, 1962), 91–93; while the official exchange rate was thirty-five piasters to the dollar, the black market rate could be as high as one hundred to the dollar. See Anderson, *Trapped by Success*, 157.

[90] USOM, *Vietnam Moves Ahead*, 32–33.

[91] Taylor, "South Viet-Nam," 247.

[92] Data are from USOM, *Vietnam Moves Ahead*, 32–33; quote is from Taylor, "South Viet-Nam," 247.

range of consumer goods.[93] It is clear that by 1957, aid financed increasing defensive readiness and an artificially high standard of living, while keeping inflation at bay. Though not a permanent solution to much deeper problems with the project, such manifestations of American aid provided a basis for the belief that a state had been created and made secure and legitimate south of the seventeenth parallel.[94]

CONCLUSION

The southern half of Vietnam witnessed significant change between 1954 and 1957. A war-torn, divided, and economically ruined place in 1954, the United States had, by 1957, helped to fund and train a national police force, educate tens of thousands of Vietnamese in the affairs of government, modernize elements of a national infrastructure, rebuild roads and bridges, schools, and hospitals, deliver a staggering amount of aid that spread across the whole of southern Vietnam, and create an artificial economy that sustained a much higher standard of living for a few than would have otherwise been possible. Over fifteen hundred strong by the late 1950s, the Americans in southern Vietnam made up the largest state-building project anywhere in the world.[95] The diverse, sometimes divergent groups that made up this effort had, in effect, invented a Vietnam below the seventeenth parallel that had never existed.

Equally as important, Ngo Dinh Diem himself had been transformed. In late 1954, many officials looked warily on the project to build a state around him. Nationalist though he was, he was also mercurial, stubborn, autocratic, too politically rigid, and excessively clannish. He nevertheless became the chosen instrument of American foreign policy in Vietnam. Grudgingly, Diem's critics either came around or muted their criticism. Particularly following his triumph over other rivals for power in early and mid-1955, he seemed to mute some of the criticism himself by demonstrating that he could in fact use force successfully

---

[93] Scigliano, *South Vietnam*, 115.

[94] These much deeper problems surfaced in later years and threatened the entire effort. They included less than 10 percent private investment in the economy – the amount considered necessary to develop underdeveloped countries. Additionally, approximately 25 percent of the workers were unemployed as late as 1961. Despite these deficiencies, the standard of living actually rose due to the enormity of aid. See Scigliano, *South Vietnam*, 116.

[95] Herring, *America's Longest War*, 56.

to retain power. In short order, officials dropped plans to remove him and seek a replacement. Though criticism of him did not go away, it now became muted by changed parameters. Diem was, after all, anti-communist beyond criticism. If he committed some excesses along the way to ensuring that the tide of communism did not sweep all of Asia and threaten American interests, these would be tolerated. As some explained at the time, democracy as Americans saw it appeared alien to the Vietnamese and simply was not applicable in this context.[96] A number of similar justifications transformed Diem into a brave and besieged defender of the free world.

Word of his successes moved beyond the American mission and stale governmental meetings and field reports. It moved into the pages of the nation's leading newspapers and magazines. The inveterate *Life* magazine dubbed Diem "the tough miracle man of Vietnam."[97] In a state visit carefully orchestrated by the administration, John Hannah, and Diem's own American public relations firm, he came to embody the very noble and necessary global struggle against tyranny. The Eisenhower administration also desired this visit to promote relations with third world leaders and enhance American influence.[98] The embassy of Viet-Nam in Washington released a short "biography" in anticipation of the visit. In it, Diem was hailed as a "most brilliant" administrator and "a living symbol of uncompromising integrity and patriotism." The brief informed readers that he had "saved" a Vietnam "infested" with "vicelords . . . warlords . . . defeatists and communist agents everywhere!"[99] Traveling aboard President Eisenhower's personal plane, Diem met with the AFV, the National Press Club, the State Department, and both the governor of New York and the mayor of New York City; he addressed the Far-East American Council of Commerce and Industry at the Waldorf-Astoria, the Council on Foreign Relations, and a joint session of the U.S. Congress; he was given an honorary degree at Seton Hall University and made his way to MSU, saying upon disembarking

---

[96] Wesley Fishel, "Vietnam's Democratic One-Man Rule," *The New Leader* 42 (November 1959): 10–13.

[97] John Osborne, "The Tough Miracle Man of Vietnam," *Life*, May 13, 1957, 156–76.

[98] On Diem's request for a state visit, see *FRUS*, 1955–1957, I:762–63. On Eisenhower's tendency toward improving relations with other world leaders, see Anderson, *Trapped by Success*, 161.

[99] "Short Biography of President Ngo Dinh Diem," May 1, 1957, *MSUG Papers*, Vietnam Project, Ngo Dinh Diem Visit to U.S., 1957, box 672, folder 62.

the plane, "Why, it's like coming home."[100] MSU rolled out the carpet as well, arranging a string trio and the "State Singers"; inviting distinguished guests, including the governor and MSU president Hannah; and bestowing upon the Vietnamese president another honorary degree.[101] Diem relished the visit[102] and exploited the opportunity to ask for further aid, referred to acidly as "a heavy shopping list."[103]

Diem's rehabilitation lasted only a short while. By 1959, conditions in Vietnam changed dramatically. Unrest in the countryside spread. A plan to pacify the population backfired, alienating many rural Vietnamese. By the following year, a highly organized and widespread insurgency formed itself into the National Front for the Liberation of Vietnam to oppose Diem and his American backers. In the cities, too, Vietnamese within and without the government opposed the regime. Several MSU personnel became disenchanted with lack of progress and resistance to reform from Saigon. The MAAG, USOM, and MSUG continued to part ways regarding the basic mission in Vietnam. Although both Saigon and MSU readily agreed to renew their contract in 1957, by 1960, the relationship had soured. This led to the lapse of the contract in 1962, the removal of MSU, and the rapid militarization of the effort. Looking back from 1957, however, many believed that while there were certainly problems requiring more aid and advice, they had achieved substantial gains in putting together the pieces of a modern state.

---

[100] Letter to John Hannah from Wesley Fishel, June 1, 1957, box 672, folder 62. Diem's address before the U.S. Congress as well as all major speeches delivered during this visit are contained in Bernard Fall Papers, box PR-9, folder "VN-1," JFKL.

[101] Letter to Diem from John Hannah, April 12, 1957; Cable from Saigon, April 23, 1957; Letter from Paul D. Bagwell to Vice President Hamilton, April 26, 1957; Letter to Stanley Sheinbaum from Wesley Fishel, May 6, 1957, *MSUG Papers*, box 672, folder 62.

[102] Diem apparently spoke fondly of the visit back in Vietnam to anyone who would listen. See Fishel letter to Hannah, June 1, 1957, and Diem letter to Hannah, box 672, folder 62; also Sheinbaum letter to Hannah, June 3, 1957, box 628, folder 93.

[103] Anderson, *Trapped by Success*, 163.

4

SURVIVING THE CRISES: SOUTHERN VIETNAM, 1958–1960

In January 1958, Michigan State University Vietnam Advisory Group (MSUG) police advisors George Kimball and Carl Rumf left Saigon on a routine field trip to Da Nang and Hué. They met with the chiefs of police in both cities. Both men asked for further assistance from the MSUG in the form of training and films. Phan Dinh Ly, the chief of police in Da Nang, was well liked and affable, according to American opinion. Le Xuan Nhuan, chief of police at Hué, was a former student in the Participant Program the previous year and seemed eager to carry out his training. Once the MSUG located the needed equipment, a team scheduled another trip to check on its delivery and installation and to perhaps oversee a demonstration. They submitted the necessary forms and forwarded the necessary requests for such a visit to forewarn the Vietnamese officials in Hué and Da Nang. On the trip in early March, the MSUG team found conditions had changed. Chief Ly had an "entirely different attitude" and was "cold and to the point" with the advisors. He told them he had no prior knowledge of the trip. When they phoned the Sûreté officials in Hué, they, too, claimed no prior knowledge of the visit and "could not understand what our mission was and what we had made the trip for." After an "unofficial" and face-saving patrol around the city, the team made arrangements for their prompt return to Saigon, having accomplished little on the trip. Once in Saigon, Rumf discovered that both Hué and Da Nang had been sent telegrams informing them of the visit.[1]

[1] Letter to Wesley Fishel from Howard W. Hoyt, March 7, 1958, Letter to H. W. Hoyt from Carl Rumf, March 6, 1958, Michigan State University, Fishel Papers, Vietnam Project, Aid to Vietnam, Police Administration, Municipal Police Section, box 684, folder 4; hereinafter

This anecdote illustrates a common thread in the relationship between the Americans and the Vietnamese. The further one got from Saigon, tensions between the two became more and more discernable. For local officials, including those fiercely loyal to Diem for their positions, maintaining the Americans at arm's length proved vital. Chief Ly's predecessor had been "too friendly . . . to the Americans," which caused his dismissal. Ly's actions showed that he was aware of the danger of similar cozy relations with the Americans and wanted to maintain his own position.[2] During the numerous years of American involvement in Vietnam beginning in 1954, a similar tension existed between the Americans and the Vietnamese at almost every level of contact. Perhaps the best known and most written about involved Diem himself at times refusing aid, demanding more, agreeing to reforms and then refusing to implement, spending aid monies on projects his American backers counseled against, and refusing to broaden his government. Diem understood that American aid would continue. For their part, the Americans convinced themselves that Diem would eventually come around. As historian David Anderson has explained, "self-assured Americans failed to perceive that their proud but insecure allies might prefer self-government to good government."[3] As the American aid mission expanded and encroached upon new aspects of Vietnamese life after 1957, this tension became more pronounced. Paralleling the growing U.S. state-building mission during 1958–1960, the U.S. Congress also began to scrutinize the aid program amid charges of waste and corruption; the revolution in the countryside grew into a substantial, organized force opposing Diem's rule, while the regime struggled for legitimacy below the seventeenth parallel. Indeed, it was not at all clear by 1960 whether the United States had moved forward or backward in achieving its objectives in Vietnam.

MSUG Papers, followed by specific collection information. MSUG personnel reported a similar incident, to then chief advisor Wesley Fishel, on an inspection tour of Rach Gia. The MSUG team concluded that the problem, at least in this instance, stemmed from the fact that the province chief of Rach Gia was "a military man" and that cold receptions such as these came from "military province chiefs." Letter to Wesley Fishel from M. A. Sanderson, February 19, 1957, *MSUG Papers*, box 660, folder 76.

[2] Ibid., letter of March 7, 1958.

[3] David Anderson, *Trapped by Success: The Eisenhower Administration and Vietnam, 1953–1961* (New York: Columbia University Press, 1991), 155.

THE AMERICAN MISSION AND BUILDING VIETNAM

The American aid program for Vietnam had necessarily focused on emergency relief measures during the period 1954–1957. In 1954, only the most rudimentary infrastructure existed to receive a substantial volume of aid. The French colonial system differed so markedly from that which the Americans began to create that the two contradicted and contravened each other. The French had sought to limit development, finding its absence more conducive to the maintenance of colonial rule. Furthermore, years of warfare badly eroded that system, culminating in a complete withdrawal of the French by 1956 and the concomitant withdrawal of private investment and a vital source of employment. The French, and the Americans as well, "dumped mountains of equipment" on southern Vietnam over the years. Everything from jeeps, engines, tires, small arms, ammunition, tanks, aircraft, and a multitude of spare parts estimated into the tens of millions simply lay abandoned, according to the U.S. Army's study of the early years of American involvement.[4] The American effort in Vietnam began with the removal of these materials and a vast rebuilding campaign.

French withdrawal created a power vacuum as well. Because the colonial system restricted the opportunities of Vietnamese, and because those that did manage to obtain high position were now seen as coolies, few emerged that could seriously be called nationalist. Outside of Ho Chi Minh, virtually no one commanded national attention. Local leaders in the southern part of Vietnam were themselves divided and busy collecting the spoils of France's defeat. The selection of Ngo Dinh Diem was one of the consequences of these limitations. Diem certainly had the best nationalist credentials, having quit a post within the colonial administration. Diem was also aided by his Catholic faith, which served him better in the United States than in Vietnam.[5] In any case, as far as the United States was concerned, he had few rivals for power as Vietnam

---

[4] Ronald Spector, *Advice and Support: The Early Years, The U.S. Army in Vietnam* (Washington, DC: Center of Military History, 1983), 257–58.

[5] *The Pentagon Papers: The Defense Department History of United States Decisionmaking on Vietnam*, Senator Gravel ed. (Boston: Beacon Press, 1971), I:296–98; hereinafter *PP*. Seth Jacobs, "'Our System Demands the Supreme Being': The U.S. Religious Revival and the 'Diem Experiment,' 1954-1955," *Diplomatic History* 25 (Fall 2001): 589–624. Joseph Morgan, *The Vietnam Lobby: The American Friends of Vietnam, 1955-1975* (Chapel Hill: University of North Carolina Press, 1997).

emerged from colonialism. And as no political system then existed to buttress Diem's ascension to power, one had to be created.

In 1954, communication and transportation infrastructure also badly needed development before a new government could be placed in power and become the recipient of U.S. development aid. Consequently, the United States cobbled together an elaborate, if also haphazard, aid program to remedy these and other shortcomings through the development of various training programs, a police network, an import substitution program, and other measures to bolster the position of Ngo Dinh Diem. By 1957, the American country team measured its work to date against the calamities of 1954–1955 and, not surprisingly, concluded that the "newly created nation would survive successfully the series of crises which threatened its existence at the outset," according to the MSUG.[6] The overall aid project could now move from crash programs on to long-term development projects.

Beginning in 1958, the aid mission, in conjunction with the Saigon regime, pursued a number of these long-term projects. Particularly important to the MSUG, its advisors could begin the serious business of developing the state now that "armed conflict has been replaced by peaceful tensions and internal struggles," according to a telling statement by MSUG consultant Ralph Turner.[7] Now that the general outlines of MSUG's program for building a police and administrative infrastructure had been laid, advisors anticipated several years more in which to complete their task. Many of their numbers, and other American advisors as well, accepted that the period of emergency had passed, and, if anything, economic development and the creation of a modern national infrastructure would occupy the lion's share of their energies into the later years of the decade.[8] Thus the Police Administration program and the National Institute of Administration (NIA) expanded training, facilities, and personnel over the course of the next couple of years.[9] The MSUG expanded the Vietnamese Bureau of Investigation (VBI),

---

[6] *Final Report* of MSUG, 6.

[7] "Law Enforcement in South Viet Nam," January 10, 1958, p. 12, *MSUG Papers*, box 682, folder 11.

[8] See *Final Report* of MSUG for repeated statements that 1957 and early 1958 was a turning point in the aid program.

[9] At the same time, however, MSU personnel actually decreased in number over the period, as planned. See *Final Report* of MSUG, introduction.

helped introduce a new and modern fingerprinting system, and launched an ambitious identity card program that, by 1962, had cataloged the identity of over 3 million Vietnamese. The NIA continued to train in Vietnam, abroad in the United States, and elsewhere. Reliance on American staff to teach courses began to diminish. The American advisors now focused on improving the quality and content of the courses and on research. The NIA expanded until, in 1960, the school boasted a sixteen-member Vietnamese staff.[10]

MSUG personnel expressed probably the most satisfaction, both then and later, with the effort to train personnel and build the police system. By the late 1950s, the Vietnamese National Police and Security Service boasted a full-fledged training center, providing both general and specialized programs. The regime's policing capacity had, in the process, become national, with municipal police precincts in all provinces. The program established a broad communications system and fingerprinting and identity tracking systems, and the MSUG believed that "the concept of training within the service seemed well ingrained and likely to be continued, within the limitations of local capabilities."[11] Local capabilities aside, southern Vietnam had not been so thoroughly policed since the days of colonial rule. Indeed, current force levels dwarfed those of the French system. The VBI consisted of over six thousand officers, and the various other police forces totaled more than forty-five thousand. By mid-1963, the combined strength of just the Civil Guard and the Self Defense Corps topped 150,000.[12]

As the police system grew, the MSUG conducted numerous field trips from 1957 onward to survey and inspect municipal police in every major city (and every province), including Saigon, to standardize the growing network of police in southern Vietnam.[13] In early 1958, the

[10] *Final Report* of MSUG, 25.

[11] *Final Report* of MSUG, 45–46; USOM News Release, October, 1958, *MSUG Papers*, box 684, folder 43; Letter to Arthur F. Brandstatter from Ralph H. Smuckler, October 15, 1958, *MSUG Papers*, box 681, folder 10; "Fourth General Report on Vietnam Project," December 18, 1958, *MSUG Papers*, box 658, folder 73.

[12] Robert Scigliano, *South Vietnam: Nation under Stress* (Boston: Houghton Mifflin, 1963), 165.

[13] For much more detailed information on field reports and more general monthly reports spanning the years from 1958 through 1960, see *MSUG Papers*, Vietnam Project, Police Administration, PSD/ICA/W Monthly Reports (Bound), 1957–1960, box 679, folder 33, Municipal Police Reports, box 684, folders 2–9, and box 683, folders 63, 66, and 69 for specific field reports on a variety of locations around southern Vietnam.

director of police for Saigon, Tran Van Tri, sent a routine report to MSUG municipal police advisor George Kimball. The report contained detailed statistics on a wide variety of criminal violations and related arrests for the month of February. From littering and traffic violations to gambling and prostitution, the report served as a kind of justification for time and energy poured into the training program. In Saigon alone, for example, police made over six thousand arrests for the month, recorded many thousands more violations (over fifteen thousand traffic violations), and issued thousands of fines. The report's author ensured Kimball that the situation in Saigon was "quite calm," and there was no reason to suspect that "foreigners living in the city resist our Republic Government."[14]

The city of Saigon was likely the most policed of all the cities in southern Vietnam. Diem's 1960 appointments for chief of police in the districts of Saigon, for example, were all military officers, and the president retained firm control. However, the outlying provinces proved far more difficult to police. More importantly, advisors found routine inspections and maintenance of good relations with outlying units difficult. Results often were "rather spotty," leaving "plenty of room for frustration," as MSUG chief advisor Smuckler reported late in 1958.[15] Travel through the countryside remained difficult, if not at times dangerous. Local police officials reported shortages in a number of areas, and methods and effectiveness were anything but uniform from one office to the next.[16] During routine inspections, and when the inspectors met with no resistance from local officials, supplies that had been sent to outlying units were often missing. Many units lacked basic equipment such as phones, radios, and uniforms, while others had an abundance of equipment. Stockpiles of ammunition, guns, radios, and other items procured through aid channels also sat in warehouses.[17] Advisors complained

---

[14] Report from Director of Police, Saigon to MSUG Police Advisor, Kimball, February 1958, *MSUG Papers*, Vietnam Project, Saigon Police Department, box 684, folder 16.

[15] Letter to Arthur Brandstatter from Ralph Smuckler, October 15, 1958, *MSUG Papers*, box 681, folder 10.

[16] USOM, "Review and Observation of Civil Police Administration and Improvement of Municipal Police and Surete," May 20, 1960, 17.

[17] Ibid., 15–20. Letter from Ralph Smuckler to Arthur Brandstatter, October 15, 1958, 2, *MSUG Papers*, box 681, folder 10; "VBI Field Survey, Long-An Province," November 5, 1958, *MSUG Papers*, box 684, folder 26; "Field Trip to Central Vietnam Highlands, etc.," November 10, 1959, *MSUG Papers*, box 684, folder 6.

from time to time of the inadequacies in the distribution of aid and realized that certain police units were clearly favored by Diem. Following
Diem's decision to retain the Civil Guard as a paramilitary force in 1958,
the idea of a wholly civil police presence that might win over the people
rapidly faded.[18] The Saigon regime's police forces became increasingly
militarized, and as this happened, MSUG's influence diminished.[19] Others within the aid mission, such as Military Assistance Advisory Group
(MAAG) chief Samuel Williams, had for years promoted an increased
military/security emphasis.[20] The U.S. military, along with Diem, continued to place primary emphasis on the establishment of tighter security.
Almost prophetically, his own emphasis on security and the campaigns
to control the people led to a greater need for security, as opposition to
his policies and popular resentment among the people grew.

In addition to police and public administration training, the U.S.
Operations Mission (USOM) oversaw substantial development aid to
southern Vietnam for projects in a number of other fields. The USOM
contracted with a variety of companies to facilitate internal economic
growth and build the necessary basic infrastructure. Thomas B. Bourne
Associates surveyed the Tan Son Nhut Airport project; Daniel, Mann,
Johnson, and Mendenhall provided engineering services for a canal
system; Television Associates of Indiana provided guidance on a regional
telecommunications network; Russell Wright Associates aided in hand-
icraft development; McIntosh Laboratories worked on the Radio Vietnam Project; and Capitol Engineering Corporation and Johnson, Drake,
and Piper engaged in several large-scale highway and bridge projects.[21]
The USOM awarded lucrative contracts to numerous private firms to
conduct business in Vietnam. As USOM director Arthur Gardiner told a

---

[18] Scigliano, *South Vietnam*, 165–66. In 1958, 36 percent of the province chiefs were military
officers. By 1960, over 87 percent were military officers. The numbers, according to
Scigliano, were 13 of 36 and 36 of 41, respectively.

[19] See source for note 1 as an example of the decreasing ability of the MSUG to influence
events once Diem had asserted his control.

[20] General Williams believed that "the population of South Vietnam, like any other, is more
responsive to fear and force than to an improved standard of living. The conclusion is
clear: The paramount consideration is to gain and maintain a superiority of force in all
parts of the country. This is done by developing the military and police potential as the
most urgent objective of our national program in Vietnam" (February 1960). Quoted in
Marilyn B. Young, *The Vietnam Wars, 1945–1990* (New York: Harper Perennial, 1991),
60.

[21] USOM, *Vietnam Moves Ahead, Annual Report for Fiscal Year 1960*, 71.

Senate investigative committee in 1959, "You would be astonished ... at the amount of business that has gone on in Vietnam under that [aid] program without any interference by the diplomats or the bureaucrats."[22] His agency released VN$259 million (or $7.4 million) for counterpart financing of road and bridge construction to the American firms Capitol Engineering and Johnson, Drake, and Piper for 1959.[23]

These and other companies surveyed, planned, and carried out an array of building projects below the seventeenth parallel. In the arena of public works involving canals, roads, bridges, and telecommunications, infrastructure was either nonexistent, destroyed, or in disrepair. The canal system consisted of over nine hundred miles of primary, over six hundred miles of secondary, and approximately one thousand miles of tertiary waterways. The USOM furnished heavy dredging equipment, training, and funding, and in 1960, Vietnamese and American teams removed 5.3 million cubic yards of infill from the canal system and opened new areas to transport. The USOM also delivered a twelve-hundred-horsepower ocean-going tugboat to assist vessels along the forty miles of the Saigon River en route to the only deep water port. Meanwhile, Capitol Engineering and Johnson, Drake, and Piper worked to build a system of roadways stretching across southern Vietnam. National Route 21, completed in 1960 at a cost of $14 million, linked Ninh Hoa along the coast to Ban Me Thuot further inland and became the largest aid project since the resettlement of Catholic refugees during 1954–1955. Barely a road at all as late as 1957, the artery now boasted two well-surfaced lanes built according to "modern" standards and providing access during the whole year. Transportation costs were thereby dramatically reduced, and the road "greatly increased the exchange of commodities." The Saigon-Bien Hoa Highway consisted of nearly twenty miles of roadway, two major bridges (the two longest ever built in Vietnam), six intermediate bridges, drainage systems, and erosion and traffic controls. Surfaced in asphaltic concrete and over fifty-two feet in width, complete with stable shoulders for heavy (military) traffic and built through swamp conditions at or below sea level, this road showcased the technological and individual hubris of the American mission.

[22] U.S. Congress, Committee on Foreign Relations, *The Situation in Vietnam*, 86th Cong., 1st sess., July 30–31, 1959, 106.

[23] Letter from USOM Controller to Director General for National Budget, October 13, 1959, 5, *MSUG Papers*, Vietnam Project, Counterpart Files, box 689, folder 33.

Only a thinly veiled military project, the road cost more than was spent on labor, community development, social welfare, housing, health, and education combined.[24] Other road-building projects included National Route 19 from Pleiku to Qui Nhon, 100 miles in length and with forty-five new bridges, and National Route 14 from Ban Me Thout to Pleiku, at just over 110 miles long and with several new bridges. The American mission also provided maintenance equipment, including tractors, power shovels, other road-building machines, and spare parts, at a cost of $18 million. USOM provided training to thousands of Vietnamese for these projects, and contractors furnished technical training manuals for the trainees.[25]

Contractors also began work on proposals for the development of a regional telecommunications system covering Vietnam, Thailand, and Laos. Television Associates of Indiana analyzed the feasibility of creating a microwave system of telecommunication, a high-frequency radio system, and a telephone system to connect outlying provinces to Saigon. Plans called for a series of radio terminals stretching from Quang Tri in the northern zone to Saigon and Can Tho in the southern zone, in conjunction with dozens of stations littered along the lengthy coast of Vietnam. The related electrification of Vietnam was also under way with the importation of power generators and construction of power distribution plants throughout Vietnam. In 1955, Vietnam produced 92,298 kilowatts of electric power. Planners estimated the country's needs by 1975 at 1,339 million kilowatt hours.[26] Vietnam required

---

[24] Diem was on record almost constantly advocating road building for security purposes, and MAAG chief Williams is often very supportive. See Telegram from the Ambassador in Vietnam (Durbrow) to the Department of State, February 8, 1958, 12–13, Memorandum of Conversation, Saigon, November 21, 1959, 250–254, Despatch from the Ambassador in Vietnam to the Department of State, 350–351, all in *Foreign Relations of the United States*, vol. I (Washington, DC: GPO, 1958–1960); hereinafter *FRUS*. Contracts were awarded on a "cost-plus" basis, and no penalties were built in for either going over budget or taking too much time for completion of the projects. The highway program, for example, began with an estimate of $15 million based on inaccurate data and ended up costing over $66 million. For a detailed critique of the program, see U.S. Congress, Committee on Foreign Relations, *United States Aid Program in Vietnam*, 86th Cong., 2nd sess., 1960, 25–26. For specific data on road building, see USOM, *Vietnam Moves Ahead*, 7–10; USOM, *Vietnam Meets Its Challenge: USOM Annual Report for Fiscal Year 1961*, 22–37. Scigliano, *South Vietnam*, 115.

[25] USOM, *Vietnam Moves Ahead*, 11–12.

[26] Ibid., 15–18. Vietnam's annual per capita usage during the early 1950s had been 17 kilowatt hours. The average usage of Japan for the same period was 731, Singapore, 305, and Hong Kong, 243.

modernization in these and in other areas if it was to make the leap from a traditional to a modern state.

In an effort to industrialize the country and to integrate it into a market economy, the U.S. aid mission and the Saigon leadership established, in late 1957, the Industrial Development Center (IDC).[27] Prior to partition, the absence of industry was not a shortcoming at all, but rather part of the symbiotic relationship between northern and southern Vietnam. The north relied on southern agricultural production and the south on northern industry for its manufacture needs. The south possessed small-scale industrial concerns such as cigarette making, rice milling, small ship building, some sugar refining, and cottage industry textile manufacturing. Following partition, however, the American aid mission needed to expand and further develop industry if it was to prevent the eventual unification of the country under Ho Chi Minh and his Communist Party. The USOM saw possibilities in developing coal, limestone, iron, gold, and copper mines and in constructing hydroelectric dams in central Vietnam. Although resources turned out to be less abundant than initially hoped, advisors believed the economy had to be made more diverse if it was to survive a volatile world market. Relying on rice production and limited coal production left southern Vietnam vulnerable. The IDC sponsored greater diversification through financial as well as technical assistance to foster the growth of a variety of industries. Funded by $6 million and VN$100 million, the project provided incentive through loans to would-be entrepreneurs and provided advice through the American consulting firm Day and Zimmerman Inc. The Commodity Import Program (CIP) also aided in this by financing imported capital goods for industrial projects such as heavy equipment and machinery. The project oversaw the launching of a variety of businesses, from textiles, ceramics, and soap to tobacco, pencils, and dinnerware.[28]

Though initially ambitious, the IDC began with a number of entrenched and stubborn handicaps. The idea behind the scheme was to foster the growth of business and industry, to create an internal source of wealth, and to wean the client from American aid. A center for financing

[27] M. N. Trued, "South Viet-Nam's Industrial Development Center," *Pacific Affairs* 33, (1960): 250–67.
[28] USOM, *Vietnam Moves Ahead*, 38–40.

and promoting industry was virtually the only way Saigon could reduce its enormous and growing balance of trade deficit. Increasing industrial production would, in the eyes of American planners, encourage foreign and private investment and private ownership. American experts, not surprisingly, considered the development of a free market entrepreneurial system vital to the evolution of the kind of economy they envisioned. Diem and his brother Nhu, however, envisioned a different kind of business sector with a different relationship to the government. They placed heavy emphasis on government ownership of business enterprise. As Nhu explained to the American ambassador, he wanted to pursue a "third way" between communism and heavy state planning and capitalism and the attendant emphasis on private ownership and market forces. Nhu believed other third world nations struggling to leave behind colonialism also found this third way an appealing option. Asian countries wanted to avoid copying both the Soviet Union and the Western capitalist nations, associating the latter historically with colonialism. A "mixed" economy of some government-owned enterprise and private ownership solved the dilemma of a lack of expertise, managerial skill, and risk capital since the government provided initial financing for capital ventures. Ultimately, as Nhu and Diem both pointed out, private concerns would take over these business enterprises.[29]

From the outset, Saigon and the U.S. advisory mission clashed over these differences. Ironically, the compromise hammered out to begin the IDC undermined the program. The compromise determined that American aid would remain available to government firms, while at the same time, counterpart financing was available to would-be importers. As mentioned, the latter reaped enormous profits before any real exchange of commodity, thus discouraging manufacturing. Since the exchange rate alone guaranteed profit, and Diem tightly controlled access to funding, private foreign investment remained very limited. The capital flow

---

[29] Memorandum of Conversation, Saigon, January 30, 1958, *FRUS*, 1958–1960, I:6–8. Trued, "South Viet-Nam's . . . ," 259–60. Bernard Fall, *The Two Viet-Nams: A Political and Military Analysis*, rev. ed. (New York: Praeger, 1964), 298–99. John Montgomery, *The Politics of Foreign Aid: American Experience in Southeast Asia* (New York: Praeger, 1962), 94–95. Douglas Dacy, *Foreign Aid, War, and Economic Development: South Vietnam, 1955–1975* (New York: Cambridge University Press, 1986), 5–6, 8–9.

out of Vietnam, in fact, continued almost unabated into the 1960s. An observer of the program commented in 1960 that "at the end of 1959 [the IDC] remained relatively unknown and unpublicized" and had no real plan. Of the more than one hundred loan applications received by the spring of 1959, only four of the applicants received any assistance. Consequently, the IDC became, in effect, "a holding company for government enterprises," and the flow of American aid provided safe and certain profit to a business class eager to take the path of least resistance.[30] In short, the IDC "withered on the vine," and investment in southern Vietnam's industrial development remained limited, while those individuals seeking quick profit looked to the American aid program and the CIP.[31]

Industry remained a minor part of the overall economy. As some industrial enterprises, such as coal, sugar, textiles, and glass, expanded and were nurtured along by the regime, the industrial sector never approached the level necessary to reverse the constant trade imbalance. Imports fluctuated from $232 million in 1958 to $225 million in 1959 and back to $240.3 million in 1960 and continued to outstrip exports. Exports for the same years were $55.2 million, $75 million, and $84.5 million. From 1960 until 1972, in fact, the largest growth sector for the economy was government, with a growth rate of 10.6 percent. In contrast, the agriculture sector grew by a scant 0.6 percent.[32] By 1960, southern Vietnam even imported some agricultural goods to feed itself. Vietnam's rice and rubber mainstays continued to contribute overwhelmingly to the export economy, accounting for 80–90 percent of all exports through the 1950s and into the 1960s. Even those products, however, fell short of requirements based on population growth. For example, while officials touted expanded rice production as evidence of growth, they often failed to point out that rice production did not keep pace with growth in the Vietnamese population. Historian Bernard Fall estimated that food availability in Vietnam had actually fallen off by 48 percent by the early 1960s. Rubber exports continued

---

[30] Trued, "South Viet-Nam's . . . ," 258–61.
[31] Taylor, "South Viet-Nam," 250. Kolko, *Anatomy of a War*, 225.
[32] United States Economic Assistance to South Viet Nam, 1954–1975 (henceforth *USEASV*), Agency for International Development, volume I, 94–95, 98–99. Taylor, "South Viet-Nam," 252. Dacy, *Foreign Aid*, 106, 61.

to rise but could not alone make Vietnam independent of American aid. Other crops, such as sweet potatoes, sugar cane, peanuts, and corn, also steadily expanded, although they never contributed significantly to the trade imbalance.[33] The aid program nurtured greater dependency, rather than modernization and eventual independence, for the new state.

Vietnam had long been primarily an agricultural nation. Four-fifths of southern Vietnam's labor force worked in agriculture, and of a population of 13 million, 11 million lived in the rural environment. No more than an estimated 20 percent of American aid ever reached the countryside in a way that was recognizable to the people.[34] The Saigon regime would never be a legitimate ruling body unless and until the people in the countryside had been brought into the fold. Perhaps more importantly, southern Vietnam could not be effectively modernized and developed into a separate, sovereign state if the vast majority of the people remained isolated in their villages and hamlets. The aid mission envisioned the "transformation" of the Vietnamese agricultural economy by discarding "out-moded traditional production methods" and creating a "self-reliant nation of high proficiency," according to USOM. This could be done by implementing the most modern farming techniques and technology from the west. Soils needed to be analyzed to determine the crops they best supported. Fertilizers and pesticides would reduce the amount of crop lost to parasites. New varieties of fruits and vegetables, such as okra, eggplant, peppers, dry onions, potatoes, and garlic, would be introduced to further diversify Vietnam's agriculture economy. Technicians also planned to introduce improved strains of sugarcane to replace and revitalize that aspect of Vietnamese agriculture. Individual farmers needed to become more efficient and the yield per hectare dramatically increased.[35] This aspect of the agrarian reform program aimed at increasing levels of production in Vietnam to be able to increase exports of a variety of commodities and ultimately to make Vietnam self-sufficient. Improved infrastructure, such

---

[33] USOM, *Vietnam Meets Its Challenge*, 4–8. Fall, *Two Viet-Nams*, 292–297. Scigliano, *South Vietnam*, 107. Dacy, *Foreign Aid*, 99.

[34] James B. Hendry, "American Aid in Vietnam: The View from a Village," *Pacific Affairs* 33 (December 1960): 389–390. Scigliano, *South Vietnam*, 121.

[35] USOM, *Vietnam Moves Ahead*, 19. One hectare is a little more than 2 acres.

as roads and bridges, would enable farmers to get their increased yield to a greater market. The whole process would make the peasant both more self-interested and interested in the maintenance of the new system of production as his livelihood now depended upon it. Furthermore, failure to reach out to the countryside threatened not only to fatally delay the ultimate goal of expanding agricultural production, it also threatened the continued existence of the regime in Saigon.

For this reason, Diem continued to channel American aid to the countryside through the construction of roads and bridges, but also through an increased overt military presence, harassing and jailing thousands of people, and a propaganda campaign aimed at the growing opposition. A number of officials recognized that Diem paid insufficient attention to either the issue of industrialization or that of expanding and developing agriculture. As the situation in the countryside deteriorated during the late 1950s, economic development became less and less urgent. That deterioration brought about significant fissures within the American country team and between it and Vietnamese officials in Saigon. By 1959, divisions over the proper use of American aid reached a critical juncture as a few key events drew much greater public attention and scrutiny than had been the case since 1954.

INVENTING VIETNAM AND THE POLITICS OF AID

Ambitious and far-reaching, the American aid program proved increasingly divisive through the decade of the 1950s. From 1957, the Diem regime had to deal with the threat of a shrinking aid budget from the United States. A wary American Congress began to look on various American foreign aid programs with a purser's eye. Along with the Senate's ever-present Indochina expert Mike Mansfield, Senators Wayne Morse of Oregon, William Fulbright of Arkansas, John F. Kennedy of Massachusetts, and others in the Congress urged the Eisenhower administration to at least redirect American aid to Vietnam from military toward economic aid projects.[36] Mansfield, who gradually became an outspoken critic of the American role in Southeast Asia, went even further in suggesting quitting all aid by the late 1950s, believing it resulted

---

[36] Anderson, *Trapped by Success*, 180.

in a dependent relationship and that the Diem government had moved beyond the point of emergency aid and relief.[37]

Not surprisingly, these debates caused alarm among Diem and his advisors. The regime in Saigon only survived courtesy of American largesse, and Diem recognized the real danger should that aid be substantially cut. Consequently, he repeatedly begged, cajoled, and threatened various U.S. officials for more aid, which he then channeled increasingly into military and security projects.[38] Late in 1958, Diem sent his secretary of state for foreign affairs, Dr. Vu Van Mau, to the United States to make the case for increased aid aimed at both security and economic development. Angered that other Asian nations received more aid and a larger American security presence than Vietnam and that Vietnam had seen a $5 million reduction[39] in its aid allotment, the secretary instructed his American audience that Vietnam remained the most threatened by communist subversion. Vietnam lacked the American military presence of other nations in the region. Additionally, Vietnam lacked the means

---

[37] Montgomery, *Politics of Foreign Aid*, 221–24. See also U.S. Congress, *Viet Nam, Cambodia, and Laos, Report by Senator Mike Mansfield for the Senate Committee on Foreign Relations*, 84th Cong., 1st sess., 1955. Regarding Senator Mansfield, his views on the situation in Vietnam are available via the *Congressional Record* under appropriate years. Additionally, Mansfield was not generally the Senate's Indochina expert for nothing. He made significant contributions to the growing debate over Vietnam in his somewhat famous "Reports on Indochina," the first of which he launched in 1953 and continued well into the 1960s. See, e.g., U.S. Congress, *Indochina: Report on a Study Mission to the Associated States of Indochina, Vietnam, Cambodia, Laos*, 83rd Cong., 1st sess., 1953; U.S. Congress, *Report on Indochina*, 83rd Cong., 2nd sess., 1954; U.S. Congress, *Vietnam, Cambodia and Laos*, 84th Cong., 1st sess., 1955; U.S. Congress, *United States Aid Program in Vietnam, Report to the Committee on Foreign Relations*, 86th Cong., 2nd sess., 1960; *Two Reports on Vietnam and Southeast Asia to the President of the United States, 1962 & 1965* (Washington, DC: GPO, 1973), among others. See also Gregory A. Olson, *Mansfield and Vietnam: A Study in Rhetorical Adaptation* (East Lansing: Michigan State University Press, 1995), esp. chap. 5 and p. 334, for a more thorough bibliography of Mansfield's various contributions on Asia.

[38] Telegram from the Ambassador in Vietnam (Durbrow) to the Department of State, February 8, 1958, Memorandum of Conversation, the President's Palace, Saigon, October 29, 1958, *FRUS, 1958–1960*, I:10, 91, respectively.

[39] U.S. aid to Vietnam was actually cut initially, then partially restored so that, ultimately, its aid was cut by only 7 percent, rather than the standard 10 percent cut dealt to others. See Memorandum of Conversation, Department of State, Washington, November 17–18, 1958, *FRUS, 1958–1960*, I:100–2. U.S. foreign aid as a percentage of the gross national product (GNP) consistently declined from the late 1940s to the present. From 1957 to 1958, aid fell from 1.10 to .89 percent of the GNP overall. See Doug Bandow, "Economic and Military Aid," in *Intervention into the 1990s: U.S. Foreign Policy in the Third World*, 2nd ed., ed. Peter J. Schraeder (Boulder, CO: Lynne Rienner), 1992, 78.

to ensure security in the countryside that the maintenance, and even the increase, of American aid would permit. At one point, Mau suggested a $30 million increase over the current level of approximately $250 million annually.[40] Dramatic increases in aid were almost certainly out of the question due to global cold war commitments. The Eisenhower administration was not, however, prepared to consider large reductions in aid either, given the precarious situation then prevailing in Vietnam that Diem and influential American officials continued to emphasize to good effect. As Eisenhower himself put it in April 1959 at the end of much discussion, the Diem government would continue to receive whatever "military strength [was] necessary to its continued existence in freedom."[41] The term *freedom* might well be relative, but America's relationship with Diem would stay its rocky course.

That relationship became increasingly controversial toward the close of the decade. As more policy makers, journalists, military figures, and advisors came to question the efficacy and use of aid monies, the added attention exposed numerous problems. Some leveled charges of outright corruption; others charged enormous waste and inefficiency. Part of the problem stemmed from the noted inability on the part of various officials to point to substantive results. Many could and did point out specific numbers of railroad track mileage, roadways rebuilt, canals dredged, police and military personnel trained, and so on. But on the question of South Vietnam becoming self-sufficient, the reports were less than glowing and shot through with inconsistencies and ambiguities. These problems were brought to light in 1959 as the result of a series of articles published by Scripps-Howard newspapers and authored by Albert Colegrove.

The Colegrove articles also came on the heels of the publication of a popular and very critical quasifictional account of America's role in foreign countries, *The Ugly American*.[42] The book became a runaway

40 Memorandum of a Conversation, Seattle, November 11, 1958, *FRUS*, 1958–1960, I:96–100; statement is on 97. Of the $250 million already being channeled to Vietnam, $170 million was spent on military projects.

41 Anderson, *Trapped by Success*, 179–80. Eisenhower quote in William Appleman Williams, Thomas McCormick, Lloyd Gardner and Walter LaFeber, *America in Vietnam: A Documentary History* (New York: W.W. Norton, 1989), 143.

42 William J. Lederer and Eugene Burdick, *The Ugly American* (New York: W. W. Norton, 1958). By the time of the Colegrove articles, the book had sold one hundred fifty thousand copies and had been serialized to 5.7 million readers in *The Saturday Evening Post*. John

best seller and, in 1959, was handed out to each member of the U.S. Senate by a handful of other senators, including John F. Kennedy.[43] The novel's characters, apparently borrowed from Graham Greene's earlier novel *The Quiet American*,[44] were based on real-life participants whose identity was only thinly disguised. Colonel Edwin B. Hillendale bore a striking resemblance to Colonel Edward G. Lansdale. Hillendale, like his real-life model, specialized in counterinsurgency tactics or what would later be termed "winning the hearts and minds" of the people. He, too, had just come from the Philippines, where his skills (on the harmonica especially) had been crucial in besting a communist insurgency led by the Huk rebels and bringing about the election of Ramon Magsaysay. Hillendale was then sent to the kingdom of Sarkhan, "a small country out toward Burma and Thailand" for a repeat performance. Lansdale, like Hillendale, believed that since communists hid among the people, all one had to do was "win the people over to your side," leaving the enemy "no place to hide. With no place to hide, you can find them. Then, as military men, fix them."[45] Lansdale became the indispensable man in Vietnam, always everywhere and nowhere at the same time, attached to no formal group but right beside and in the ear of Ngo Dinh Diem.

The American mission in the book also had its compliment of figures whose grand ideas might just rescue Sarkhan, or Vietnam, from its own backwardness. The book's John Colvin, a former Office of Strategic Services (OSS) officer turned businessman, looked to sell dried milk and assorted products to Sarkhanese, along with importing special cows to eat a particularly stubborn grass that covered large areas of land and made farming it near impossible. Colvin puts it this way:

If the people of Sarkhan could be taught to use milk and its by-products, there was no reason why cattle would not prosper on land that was otherwise useless. Also, there were good markets in Asia for the by-products. The butter

---

Montgomery's *The Politics of Foreign Aid* contains an aggressive refutation of the articles. See his Appendix III, 304.

[43] Robert D. Schulzinger, *A Time for War: The United States and Vietnam, 1941–1975* (New York: Oxford University Press, 1997), 98.

[44] Graham Greene, *The Quiet American* (New York: Viking Press, 1955).

[45] Sarkhan quote found in Lederer and Burdick, *Ugly American*, 14. Lansdale quotes found in Stanley Karnow, *Vietnam: A History* (New York: Penguin Books, 1997), 236.

could be reduced to *ghee* and sold to India, the leather could be tanned and made into finished goods by the artisans of Sarkhan, the entrails could be used in the native medicines preferred by non-Christians.[46]

Indeed, Sarkhan could play a large and important role in the economy of that part of the world. Never mind the fact that the Sarkhanese had no use for milk. They could be "taught." The author's exaggerated characters John Colvin, Colonel Hillendale, the blissfully ignorant and personally sensitive Ambassador Louis Sears,[47] the well-intentioned construction engineer Homer Atkins, who suggested "a couple of bulldozers" to "rip out the roads" from the interior to the coast to allow peasants to contribute to a larger market, all demonstrated to a broad American audience the callous and cavalier nature by which U.S. foreign aid programs were attempting to remake societies.[48]

Albert Colegrove's investigation found evidence that substantially supported this view of American aid to Vietnam. Colegrove spent nineteen days in Vietnam, during which time he turned up numerous examples of waste, mismanagement, favoritism, fraud, and widespread disinterest in the way American funding spread through the southern half of the country. Published under the title "Our Hidden Scandal in Vietnam," the articles were carried in over fifteen newspapers and read by a nationwide audience of over 2.6 million. In them, Colegrove charged the aid mission with losing twenty-seven hundred vehicles, failing to account for $34 million given to the Saigon regime, paying for more than a dozen radio towers that did not exist, subsidizing lavish living standards for Americans in-country who never left the confines of Saigon, and allowing $8 million to be lost in a 1955 fire, among others.[49] *The Ugly American* had whetted the public appetite

---

[46] Lederer and Burdick, *Ugly American*, 22.

[47] The parallels between the novel and the real events in Vietnam are quite obvious. Take, e.g., congressional testimony given by then ambassador Elbridge Durbrow. After boasting of his "open house" parties thrown routinely in Saigon, Durbrow was asked by a senator, "Do the Vietnamese respond generally to the open house?" The ambassador responded, "No, sir; they don't come very often." The American ambassador to Sarkhan had the same problem as no Sarkhanese had been to one of his open house parties in two years. For Durbrow's testimony, see U.S. Congress, Committee on Foreign Relations, *The Situation in Vietnam*, 86th Cong., 1st sess., July 30–31, 1959, 22.

[48] Homer Atkins quote from Lederer and Burdick, *Ugly American*, 209.

[49] Montgomery, *Politics of Foreign Aid*, Appendix III.

and increased the visibility of U.S. government programs abroad. Not surprisingly, when the articles ran, they caused a sensation in the media, and Congress quickly convened hearings to investigate the aid mission to Vietnam.[50]

Immediately, Colegrove and the Scripps-Howard newspapers were widely condemned. Before Congress, USOM director Arthur Z. Gardiner testified that the claims were completely erroneous. Assistant Secretary of State for Far Eastern Affairs J. Graham Parsons testified similarly, as did Ambassador Durbrow, MAAG Chief Lt. General Samuel T. Williams, regional director for Near East and South Asia Leland Barrows, and deputy director of the International Cooperation Administration Leonard J. Saccio. Each in his turn denied any legitimacy to the claims made by Colegrove. The MAAG chief argued that there simply was no record of the twenty-seven hundred vehicles mentioned; Durbrow argued there was no cost-of-living allowance that provided "luxury" to some among the American mission; and Gardiner assured the investigators there were no such missing fourteen radio towers worth twenty-eight thousand dollars, as Colegrove suggested. Colegrove himself took the witness chair and maintained his ground, even suggesting he could provide additional witnesses before the committee, if needed.[51] The hastily convened hearings ended in a kind of stalemate. Not surprisingly, no conclusive evidence emerged that the program was quite as corrupt as the articles had portrayed. Such evidence, under the circumstances, could have come only through outright admission of guilt from the aid mission or from an admission of falsifying his story on the part of Colegrove.[52]

Diem's American advocates rallied and quickly scuttled the Colegrove exposé. The American Friends of Vietnam publicly denounced the

---

[50] Memorandum from the Assistant Secretary of State for Far Eastern Affairs (Parsons) to the Secretary of State, August 6, 1959, *FRUS*, 1958–1960, I:225–27.

[51] U.S. Congress, *Situation in Vietnam*, esp. 1–96.

[52] The dilemma was explicitly recognized by a member of the House during that body's own investigation into the matter. Representative Meyer stated, "Our committee actually should have its own independent staff...in the field" and "we rely too much entirely on the words and reports of the State Department and naturally, as Mr. Colegrove says in his report, they are going to paint it for us the way they want it painted." See U.S. Congress, *Current Situation in the Far East, Hearings before a Subcommittee of the House Committee on Foreign Affairs*, 86th Cong., 1st sess., August 14, 1959. Also quoted in Montgomery, *Politics of Foreign Aid*, 226.

reporting as "grist for the Communist propaganda mill." The chairman of that organization, General John "Iron Mike" O'Daniel, went on to call Colegrove's effort "a disgraceful example," even "yellow journalism" larded with "misinformation" and "plain unvarnished sidewalk gossip."[53] Meanwhile, Wesley Fishel tracked down and reported to the American embassy Colegrove's brief itinerary while in Vietnam to discredit his story. Fishel also dashed off a letter to Senator Mansfield, who had recently engaged in "increasingly frequent attacks" on the aid program himself, to inform the latter that Colegrove was merely a "malicious sensationalist" who would soon be discredited as the facts came out.[54] The Michigan State University professor also played the public relations angle, organizing a conference on Social Development and Welfare in Free Vietnam and cajoling President Diem to allow Vice President Nguyen Ngoc Tho to attend to increase the regime's visibility within the United States and to showcase "the progress which can be expected when a Southeast Asian country is well led and when its ideological guidons keep it stable, peaceful, and progressive." Fishel cited the Colegrove articles and the attention they attracted as threats to continued approval of aid monies from the U.S. Congress.[55]

Almost simultaneously in Vietnam, however, the situation seemed to give the lie to the claims of these various officials of the American mission. From May to July, for example, the periodical *Times of Vietnam*, noted for its pro-American perspective, reported on the arrest of three well-placed Vietnamese officials for an array of crimes. In May, Tran Quoc Thai, a militia second lieutenant, was arrested for embezzling VN$925,648; in June, Ngo Van Huan, an official of the Commissariat for Refugees, was arrested and convicted for the embezzlement

[53] Letter from General John W. O'Daniel to Walker Stone, August 21, 1959; American Friends of Vietnam News Release, August 24, 1959; General John O'Daniel, "Statement on Recent Charges against the American Aid Program to Free Vietnam," August 24, 1959, all in *MSUG Papers*, Fishel Papers, Organizations, American Friends of Vietnam, Committee Meetings, box 1203, folder 46.

[54] Letter from Wesley Fishel to Howard Elting, American Embassy, July 29, 1959, box 1184, folder 17; Letter from Wesley Fishel to Ngo Dinh Diem, May 30, 1959, box 1184, folder 33; and Letter from Wesley Fishel to Senator Mike Mansfield, July 25, 1959, box 1184, folder 31, all in *MSUG Papers*, Fishel Papers.

[55] Fishel noted acidly the "increasingly frequent attacks on various aspects of the foreign aid program even by such good friends of ours as Senator Mansfield and Senator Humphrey." Letter from Wesley Fishel to Ngo Dinh Diem, May 30, 1959, *MSUG Papers*, Fishel Biographical Files, Correspondence, Diem, Ngo Diem, 1951–1962, box 1184, folder 33.

of VN$1,266,015; in July, Captain Dang Nhu Tuyet was found guilty and sentenced for embezzlement, false arrests, and receiving bribes. So concerned with growing corruption was the Saigon government that it made embezzlement of government funds punishable by death.[56] As officials of the Saigon effort to create a government currently bankrolled by the United States, these arrests came at a particularly bad time.[57]

In October, the Scripps-Howard newspapers published a story that alleged fraud within the MSUG as well. What came to be termed the Rundlett Affair involved MSU advisor Lyman Rundlett letting contracts to Motorola, his former employer. The USOM reported that the company to which Rundlett awarded the contract actually bid lower than competitors "on only two of the 31 items contained in the Invitation to Bid." Furthermore, the American Justice Department had reportedly been investigating the allegation that Rundlett made the decision as part of a deal with Motorola in which he would receive financial kickbacks for allowing the company to supply police radio equipment to meet the Diem regime's needs.[58] Charges were never brought against Rundlett, and he soon departed Vietnam and resumed employment with Motorola.

Following up on the investigation, a delegation from both houses of the U.S. Congress journeyed to Vietnam late in 1959 to conduct on-site hearings, interviews, and inspections. At the head of that delegation were Senators Albert Gore, Gale McGee, Carl Curtis, and Bourke Hickenlooper and Representatives John Pilcher, Harris McDowell, Dante

---

[56] Foreign Service Despatch from American Embassy Saigon to the Department of State, Washington, May 2, 1960, National Archives, Record Group 59, 851K.00/1–760, 5; hereinafter RG and appropriate filing number.

[57] "Militia Second Lieutenant Sentenced to 5 Year's Permanent Confinement on Charge of Embezzlement," *Times of Vietnam*, May 27, 1959; "Comigal for Refugees Official Accused of Embezzling over 1 Million Piasters: Sentenced to 20 Years of Hard Labor," *Times of Vietnam*, June 19, 1959; "Captain Dang Nhu Tuyet Convicted of Embezzlement, Illegal Arrests Gets Five-Year's Hard Labour Sentence," *Times of Vietnam*, July 1, 1959, all from *MSUG Papers*, Fishel Papers, Vietnam Project, MSU Advisory Group, box 1206, folder 31.

[58] USOM, "Review and Observation of Civil Police Administration and Improvement of Municipal Police and Surete," May 20, 1960, 12. Jim Lucas, Scripps-Howard staff writer, press release, November 16, 1959, *MSUG Papers*, Vietnam Project, Coup d'etat Correspondence (1960), box 661, folder 46. John Ernst, *Forging a Fateful Alliance: Michigan State University and the Vietnam War* (East Lansing: Michigan State University Press, 1998), 75.

Fascell, Marguerite Church, and Walter Judd.[59] While in Vietnam, this subcommittee investigated many of the claims made by the Colegrove articles, although officially distancing the proceedings from them.[60] This investigation, also very brief, produced little in the way of satisfactory, concrete evidence of either a corrupt aid program or one that was exemplary and effective. There was no shortage of waste and excess to stir up the already tense sessions. For example, the investigators spent a considerable amount of time discussing two deep freezers kept in the well-furnished Saigon home of Arthur Gardiner; the fact that Americans were provided not only vehicles, but chauffeurs as well; the refusal of Saigon officials to allow the Americans to review the counterpart fund; the fact that the United States paid for a luxurious penthouse (VN$25,000 per month) apartment lived in by a wealthy American businessman; and so on. MSUG member Robert Scigliano later wrote that "the American community in Vietnam . . . lives far better than it would in the United States . . . which tends to cut it off from Vietnamese society."[61] Despite such waste and excess, the delegation could not agree on what it all meant. Did the U.S. mission just need more congressional oversight? Certainly some, such as Senator Mansfield, thought so.[62] Or did the mission need to be overhauled, redirected, or simply scrapped altogether? Opinions ran across several alternatives.

Almost immediately, Senators Gore and McGee sharply disagreed over what they saw. McGee observed "the most exciting and imaginative [aid program] of any . . . around the world." Gore was "shocked and disturbed" at the "slack-jawed laxness with which our tax money is being handled." The Saigon hearings also cast in relief the tense relations between all parties involved: the U.S. Congress seemed not to believe the official story given by aid mission members; the ambassador and the MAAG chief squared off over who actually was in charge; the Vietnamese were miffed at the arrogance of the delegation in assuming

[59] Quarterly Economic Summary, October–December 1959, RG 59, 851K.00/1–760, 4–5.
[60] Explicit effort is made in numerous places within the published account of the hearings to present the hearings as being conducted as the normal business of the Congress's oversight capacity, for obvious reasons. U.S. Congress, *Situation in Vietnam*.
[61] Scigliano, *South Vietnam*, 195.
[62] See Mike Mansfield's conclusions in U.S. Congress, *United States Aid Program in Vietnam*, 1–2. Olson, *Mansfield and Vietnam*, 79–83.

authority on Vietnamese soil; tensions between the MAAG, the ambassador, the Saigon government, and the MSUG also were strained by the added scrutiny.[63]

Senator Mansfield ultimately steered Congress's conclusions away from the fundamental question of the efficacy of the U.S. aid programs currently carried out in Vietnam. Rather, he gave assurances that despite what was said publicly by Senators Gore and McGhee, the issue "would be framed in such a way that [the subcommittee's] recommendations would be generalized for the whole aid program rather than specifically directed toward Vietnam."[64] Consequently, the final report is littered with detailed criticisms, from the way contracts were awarded to the chain of command within the American mission. All recommendations, however, point to greater command and control, increased congressional oversight, and a general tightening of the budgetary belt. Mansfield wrote to the chairman of the Committee on Foreign Relations J. W. Fulbright to explain that while "Vietnam has made a great deal of progress," the time had come for a "reshaping" of the aid program to make it more "efficient" and "effective."[65] Mansfield recognized that deeper questions and greater scrutiny of the program threatened Congress's ability to continue to provide support for the Diem regime, and also to control that support.[66]

Even as contrary evidence piled up, Mansfield continued to believe that the Vietnam the United States wanted to create below the seventeenth parallel could only be built around Ngo Dinh Diem. As the senator submitted his report, he was well aware that the regime in Saigon had earned the fear and hatred of many Vietnamese and that, as far as some were concerned, the U.S. aid program made Diem's authoritarian rule possible. Recognizing the relationship between the United States

---

[63] See U.S. Congress, *Situation in Vietnam*, and U.S. Congress, *Current Situation in the Far East*. See also *FRUS*, 1958–1960, I:273–74; Senator Gore leaked a good deal of information regarding the hearings in Saigon to Scripps-Howard writers Jim G. Lucas and Marshall McNeil. Their articles, which make much more interesting reading than do the hearings themselves, can be found collected in *MSUG Papers*, box 661, folder 46. Also see Montgomery, *Politics of Foreign Aid*, 224–35.

[64] Memorandum of a Conversation between Senator Mike Mansfield and the Under Secretary of State (Dillon), Department of State, Washington, December 18, 1959, *FRUS*, 1958–1960, I:273–74.

[65] U.S. Congress, *United States Aid Program in Vietnam*, III.

[66] Olson, *Mansfield and Vietnam*, 81–82.

and Ngo Dinh Diem, many Vietnamese came to refer to Diem, and even local officials, as *My-Diem*, meaning "America's Diem." In the eyes of many Vietnamese, "the war of Resistance against French-Bao Dai rule never ended; France was merely replaced by the U.S., and Bao Dai's mantle was transferred to Ngo Dinh Diem."[67]

MY-DIEM AND THE RISE OF THE INSURGENCY

I get around at one hell of a lot of social functions, and official dinners out here, and I've never met a native Communist yet.[68]

The Saigon regime had, by this time, a well-established presence beyond that city. Aside from the development of transportation and communication infrastructure, Diem had simply eliminated many elected village council posts in favor of direct appointments he could then control. As he larded these village and municipal councils with his own people (many outsiders), he eliminated an important degree of local autonomy and further centralized his administration. Saigon further alienated the people by carrying out, through these appointees, denunciation campaigns aimed ostensibly at communists, but reaching well beyond that goal. By mid-1956, and less than one year into the "denounce the communists" campaign, officials reported that over ninety-four thousand cadres "rallied to the government," over fifty-six hundred surrendered, and officially, fifteen thousand to twenty thousand were placed in camps. Between 1954 and 1960, almost fifty thousand people were jailed. The official numbers only reflect a portion of the real damage done. As oppressive tactics became normalized, channels of political and social expression ceased to exist for ordinary Vietnamese. Local officials jailed hundreds of people without evidence as a means of extorting money and/or eliminating possible rivals for power. In Long An Province, for example, the Cong An security agents became notorious for the terror they brought and for demanding payments from the people.[69]

---

[67] George M. Kahin, *Intervention: How America Became Involved in Vietnam* (New York: Anchor Books, 1987), 101.

[68] U.S. Ambassador Louis Sears in Lederer and Burdick, *Ugly American*, 75.

[69] Kahin, *Intervention*, 96–98. Scigliano, *South Vietnam*, 167–69. Jeffrey Race, *War Comes to Long An: Revolutionary Conflict in a Vietnamese Province* (Los Angeles: University of California Press, 1972), 65–68.

Diem rounded out the building of a police state with the introduction of Law 10/59 in May 1959. This law, reaching well beyond earlier
efforts, prescribed the death sentence without right of appeal for any
act that could be construed as "sabotage" or as "infringing upon the
security of the state."[70] Diem's security forces rounded up suspected
subversives – Viet Minh cadres – and those suspected of supporting
them or related to them, tried them before military tribunals, and sentenced them, all in three days. Although it disrupted the revolutionary
effort in the countryside, this decree also caused a great deal of backlash
among villagers, who came to fear and resent the regime's representatives far more than ever before.[71] By 1959–1960, American observers
expressed growing concern that the whole experiment might be undermined by such policies. Even such indomitable supporters as Wesley
Fishel warned Diem of the growing image within some circles in the
United States of an emerging dictatorship in Vietnam and the damage
that would have on continued support.[72] In a lengthy and thought-
ful memorandum, Ambassador Durbrow also warned, "We should be
prepared to acknowledge to ourselves that even over the longer term
democracy in the Western sense of the term may never come to exist in
Viet-Nam." Instead, the United States would have to learn to live with
autocratic leadership and not attempt "to make over Viet-Nam in our
own image."[73] It was within the breathing space created by this contradiction that the Diem regime flourished and redoubled efforts to tighten
security over the whole of southern Vietnam.

It should be noted that Diem based his increasing concerns over security issues on mounting evidence of a growing opposition. As early as
1957, an attempt was made on the president's life at the opening of the
Ban Me Thout Economic Fair in the light of day.[74] Bombings, night

[70] Kahin, *Intervention*, 98. Law 10/59 is partially reprinted in Marvin E. Gettleman, Jane
Franklin, Marilyn B. Young, and H. Bruce Franklin, *Vietnam and America: The Most
Comprehensive Documented History of the Vietnam War* (New York: Grove Press, 1995),
156–60.

[71] David W. P. Elliott, *The Vietnamese War: Revolution and Social Change in the Mekong
Delta, 1930–1975* (New York: M. E. Sharpe, 2003), I:195–203.

[72] Letter from Wesley Fishel to Ngo Dinh Diem, April 1960, *MSUG Papers*, Fishel Biographical Files, Correspondence, Ngo Dinh Diem, 1951–1962, box 1184, folder 33.

[73] Despatch from the Ambassador in Vietnam (Durbrow) to the Department of State,
December 7, 1959, *FRUS*, 1958–1960, I:255–71; quote is on 269.

[74] "Monthly Report on the Civil Guard Program," March 1957, *MSUG Papers*, Vietnam
Project, Police Administration, box 679, folder 29.

ambushes on military outposts, and sabotage as well as intimidation, harassment, and assassination of various officials loyal to the Diem government had been on the rise for several years. For example, in 1958, approximately seven hundred officials were assassinated; by 1960, the number was twenty-five hundred.[75] The regime's ramped up security and aggressive ferreting out of suspects outside of Saigon contributed to the opposition. The program of forced resettlement into *agrovilles* in 1959, for example, generated a great deal of resentment from the people.[76] The first of many similar schemes introduced over the years, the *agroville* program attempted to relocate large numbers of Vietnamese into concentrated zones along major transportation routes. Once concentrated, the peasants no longer provided the insurgency with a base of operations and sustenance. The effort smacked of the old colonial system of corvée labor, as the people were forcibly removed from their farmlands and ancestral tombs to build their new quarters, occasionally out of materials from their dismantled former homes, and to work to construct the camp, all without recompense.[77] Local officials took advantage of the confinement to extort money and goods, while meting out physical abuse and torture. Not surprisingly, within the barbed wire surrounding these camps, opposition only grew. Amid obvious

---

[75] Despatch from the Ambassador in Vietnam (Durbrow) to the Department of State, March 2, 1960, *FRUS, 1958–1960*, I:296–99. Bernard Fall, *Viet Nam Witness, 1953–1966* (New York: Praeger, 1966), 160. George Herring, *America's Longest War: The United States and Vietnam, 1950–1975*, 4th ed. (New York: McGraw-Hill, 2002), 82.

[76] Loosely conceived, the resettlement effort was only a small part of a much broader agrarian reform program that included the expansion and modernization of the agricultural sector of the economy and land transfer to reverse the highly inequitable distribution pattern then prevalent. For reasons outlined in the text, Diem focused most of the government's energies on the resettlement campaign. The expansion of agriculture did not live up to American expectations, and the land transfer or land reform program resulted in relatively little land being distributed to the peasant, a prerequisite of land reform and of economic development aimed at economic self-sufficiency. Rent ceilings and limitations on the size of individual holdings were routinely violated to the benefit of Diem's cronies and other well-heeled landlords. Ultimately, less than 10 percent of tenant households received any land under the program. See James B. Hendry, "Land Tenure in South Viet Nam," *Economic Development and Cultural Change* 9 (October 1960): 27–44; Hendry, *The Small World of Khanh Hau* (Chicago: Aldine, 1964); J. Price Gittinger, *Studies on Land Tenure in Vietnam*, Terminal Report, Division of Agriculture and National Resources (Washington, DC: United States Operations Mission to Viet Nam, 1959); David Wurfel, "Agrarian Reform in the Republic of Vietnam," *Far Eastern Survey* 26 (June 1957): 81–92; Scigliano, *South Vietnam*, 121–24.

[77] Joseph J. Zasloff, "Rural Resettlement in South Viet Nam: The Agroville Program," *Pacific Affairs* 34, no. 4 (1962): 327–40.

failure and growing protest over the camps, the regime finally abandoned the effort, but not before it had demonstrated to large numbers
of Vietnamese the necessity of resistance.[78]

In April 1960, a group of eighteen well-placed officials demonstrated
that even in the cities, the government generated hostility. The group,
including a former minister of education, a former minister of defense, a
former minister of agriculture and labor, and a former minister of public
health and social action, issued their manifesto calling for a recognition
and inclusion of opposition parties and asking the president to "liberalize the regime, promote democracy" and "guarantee minimum civil
rights" to end the government's alienation of the people and stave off
collapse. This "Caravelle Manifesto" was widely publicized, particularly in the United States, and caused considerable alarm among Diem's
supporters both in Vietnam and the United States. Wesley Fishel, who
had warned his friend earlier of the betrayal of the intellectuals, now
advised "discrediting its authors by presenting to the world their records
of past collaboration with the French and with Bao Dai." Fishel urged
Diem to forward brief biographies on each of the signers and promised
he would "see what can be done" in the United States to counter their
sinister designs.[79] The regime immediately attacked the group as enemies of the state and moved to malign their individual reputations.[80]

[78] For some detail on the controversial nature of the *agrovilles*, see Open Letter to President
Ngo Dinh Diem about Agrovilles, October 6, 1960; Secretariat of State for Information,
press release, July 8, 1960; "Vietnamese Exiles Join Plot on Diem," press release, June 20,
1960(?), all in *MSUG Papers*, Vietnam Project, Government Information, Criticism of
Diem, box 661, folder 46. Elliott, *Vietnamese War*, I:198–205. Also see Despatch from
the Ambassador in Vietnam (Durbrow) to the Department of State, Current Security
Problem Facing GVN, February, 16, 1960, Despatch from the Ambassador in Vietnam
(Durbrow) to the Department of State, March 7, 1960, *FRUS*, 1958–1960, I:283, 302,
respectively. For a more thorough critique written by Ambassador Durbrow, see Despatch
from the Ambassador in Vietnam (Durbrow) to the Department of State, Subject: GVN
Agroville Program, June 6, 1960, *FRUS*, 1958–1960, I:485–89.

[79] The Caravelle Manifesto is reprinted in Fall, *Two Viet-Nams*, Appendix III. Fishel's
comments and advice are in Letter to Ngo Dinh Diem, May 2, 1960, *MSUG Papers*,
Vietnam Project, box 1184, folder 33. Fishel's earlier warnings contained a bit of advice
as well. He suggested the government employ its intellectuals in writing textbooks to keep
their collective hands busy so they would be less inclined to cause trouble. Fishel wrote,
"The object, unspoken of course, would be to make them feel 'useful' and 'wanted.'" See
Letter from Wesley Fishel to Ngo Dinh Diem, December 30, 1958, in ibid.

[80] The group of eighteen, foreseeing the effort to discredit them, issued a rebuttal of the
charges against them later that month. See Public Notice, April 30, 1960, *MSUG Papers*,
Vietnam Project, Government Information, Criticism of Diem, box 661, folder 46.

Diem refused to allow the publication of the manifesto and followed up by harassing and arresting some of those involved. As David Anderson has pointed out, however, "the complete ineffectiveness of the protest laid bare the truth of its charges." The government was not about to reform or to allow such criticism. The episode exacerbated tensions between different elements of the country team, with the ambassador, MAAG chief, and Diem increasingly at odds over how to proceed, as the people grew restless and protests and demonstrations mounted.[81]

The regime became increasingly paranoid. The Can Lao, or Personalist, Party enveloped the president and his family to prevent encroachment from outsiders but also to prevent the intrusion of unwanted criticism and advice. Officially known as the Revolutionary Labor Personalism Party, this organization was the party of the ruling elite and served as an anticommunist, pro-Diem propaganda machine tightly controlled by Diem's brother Ngo Dinh Nhu.[82] With its emphasis on conservatism, hierarchy, and position, personalism justified rigid and authoritarian rule. It should also be pointed out that the doctrine mattered little because very few Vietnamese actually adhered to or even understood it.[83] It became another weapon panoply used by the regime to silence opposition and safeguard the Ngo hold on power.

By most accounts, security, and not democratic reforms, compelled the Diem regime. From his perspective, he had ample evidence of mounting opposition to his rule. The countryside teemed with opposition. Despite a variety of tactics aimed at destroying it, the insurgency, which Diem and others came to refer to derisively as the "Viet Cong," continued to grow and continued to rely on the population that both made up its members and sustained it. That insurgency really grew out of a decades-old revolutionary movement spanning all of Vietnam that had defeated the French and now opposed the Americans and Diem. By late 1960, this revolution attracted thousands of insurgents from all over southern Vietnam and formed itself into the National Front for the

---

[81] Anderson, *Trapped by Success*, 184–86.
[82] Robert Scigliano, "Political Parties in South Vietnam under the Republic," *Pacific Affairs* 33 (December 1960): 327–47; specific data on 329–30. Much more detailed descriptions of personalism are Despatch from the Ambassador in Vietnam (Durbrow) to the Department of State, December 12, 1958, *FRUS*, 1958–1960, I:109–13, and Fall, *Two Viet-Nams*, 246–52.
[83] Scigliano, "Political Parties," 330.

Liberation of Vietnam (NLF). It received formal recognition for aggressively opposing Diem's rule from Hanoi by the close of the year.[84] Additionally, a broad spectrum of workers, students, civil servants, and the military continued to make their opposition to the government known in a variety of ways.

Only weeks earlier, opposition reached crisis proportion as a coalition of military officers attempted a coup and very nearly succeeded. Led by an elite parachute regiment and a marine battalion, in the early hours of November 11, the rebels stormed the presidential palace and took over army headquarters and the airport. As this fragile and divided coalition conferred about the composition of the new "provisional government," Diem used phony concessions to stall for time. Once loyal troops arrived the next day to surround the palace and its captors, the coup crumbled, and its leaders fled to exile in Cambodia. The *Times of Viet Nam* shortly reported that things had "returned to normal." On November 14, Diem announced, "the Government continues to serve the nation in accordance with republican and personalist principals."[85] The coup came and went quickly, and seemingly without disturbing the balance of forces in Saigon. For the time being, Diem remained in power.

[84] The story of the birth of the NLF is much more complex as Hanoi officials remained bitterly divided over whether or not to sanction some southern actions. The efforts of Le Duan, the Lao Dong Party's Nam Bo regional secretary, proved critical in bringing about the transition from primarily political struggle to a combination of political and armed struggle. Citing armed resistance in a number of locales in the south in response to Diem's repression, the party formally sanctioned armed struggle, and a group of sixty revolutionaries formed the National Front for the Liberation of South Viet Nam (NLF) on December 19, 1960. Hanoi, after the decision to support armed struggle, continued to conceal its hand so as not to provoke increased American intervention. See Robert Brigham, *Guerrilla Diplomacy: The NLF's Foreign Relations and the Vietnam War* (Ithaca, NY: Cornell University Press, 1999), chap. 1. William Duiker, *Sacred War: Nationalism and Revolution in a Divided Vietnam* (New York: McGraw-Hill, 1995), 128–34. For a detailed and illuminating analysis of the revolution in the village of My Tho from 1930 to 1975, see Elliott, *Vietnamese War*.

[85] Telegram from the Ambassador in Vietnam (Durbrow) to the Department of State, November 12, 1960, *FRUS*, 1958–1960, I:641–43. "Rebellion Collapses; Situation Normal," *Times of Viet Nam*, November 14, 1960. "Revolt Revealed Cracks in Viet Nam Regime," *New York Herald Tribune*, Paris, November 17, 1960. Letter from Lloyd Musolf to Ruben Austin, Additional News Release on Recent Attempted Coup, November 23, 1960, *MSUG Papers*, Vietnam Project, Coup de tat Correspondence, box 661, folder 39. Details of the coup attempt are numerous. For an able account, see Kahin, *Intervention*, 123–26.

The coup did, however, expose an ominous trend in that it revealed, and even nurtured, a politicized military and pitted that military against incompetent and, in many quarters, illegitimate political leadership. For the American mission, the event further divided Durbrow, who increasingly demanded reform, and now-retired MAAG chief Williams, who believed the ambassador had perhaps had a hand in encouraging the plot or at least did not give wholehearted support for Diem in his hour of need.[86] Diem clung to power in Saigon for the next several years, during which time the situation only worsened. The NLF gained more power, engaging increasingly in armed clashes with Diem's forces. Insurgent guerrillas became ubiquitous in numerous villages and came to control large areas of rural Vietnam, as peasant dissatisfaction with *My-Diem* grew. The Ngo family maintained its intransigence and continued to aggressively squash dissent and opposition. The American mission shifted as well, as circumstances drifted toward open armed conflict and away from any real focus on economic development. Indeed, the events of 1958–1960 in Vietnam set in motion tensions and divisions over American policy that became deeply entrenched and significantly informed U.S. policy toward Vietnam for years to come.[87]

CONCLUSION

From the late 1950s into the early 1960s, the Eisenhower administration continued to increase its aid to the regime in Saigon, in part to encourage its development, but largely to stave off collapse. As part of that effort, a wide array of experts, academics, elected officials, private groups, charity organizations, and the Central Intelligence Agency continued to build the new state. Starting with a traditional society, advisors hoped to accomplish more than just the containment of communism. If the United States could replicate its own national development experience, including modernization, industrialization, development of

---

[86] Anderson, *Trapped by Success*, 192–93. In a telegram of November 12, 1960, at 7:00 A.M., Durbrow seemed eager to embrace the new military government, in which he thought Diem had agreed to participate. Perhaps Durbrow viewed any transition in power as tolerable under the circumstances. See *FRUS, 1958–1960*, I:644–45.

[87] See Robert Buzzanco, *Masters of War: Military Dissent & Politics in the Vietnam Era* (New York: Cambridge University Press, 1996), esp. chaps. 2 and 3.

infrastructure, harnessing of national resources, and the building of political, social, and economic institutions, the success of this bold experiment could be proof to the world of the efficacy of state building and the power of Western democracies in the Cold War. An attempt at simple containment through an overt military presence, or occupation, would demonstrate force, not superiority. The American mission in Vietnam acted on the latter.

From the outset, the two goals of economic development and military/security preparedness competed for the dominant role in creating the new Vietnam. That competition gave rise to an odd pattern of infrastructural development: an overdeveloped security infrastructure and underdeveloped economic, social, and political institutions. Certainly the authoritarian rule of the Ngo family quite purposefully retarded institutional development. At the same time, however, the emphasis U.S. officials placed on security and military preparedness as essential elements of the overall program also set important limitations on the project's ultimate results. In the process, policy makers, both U.S. and Vietnamese, invented a Vietnam below the seventeenth parallel that required constant aid and support to maintain. The overall program of economic development had still not reached its objectives. By 1960–1961, the state invented below the seventeenth parallel, to the extent that it existed at all, was not yet what planners imagined. The Diem regime required more and more aid of a military nature. The revolution in the countryside became better organized and expanded its resistance to the regime. All the while, the aid program designed to build a modern state infrastructure around Vietnamese leadership had grown exponentially, although not uniformly. The administration of John F. Kennedy assumed office early in 1961 and responded to the situation in Vietnam with much greater military aid and U.S. military personnel. The new administration also shifted from what had been an advisory role to one of direct assistance in an attempt to counter some of these trends.

5

"A PERMANENT MENDICANT": SOUTHERN VIETNAM, 1960–1963

During the first week of January 1960, the U.S. embassy in Saigon reported to the State Department with disappointment that the regime had just broken a major strike using military force. The strike, begun only days before, was actually part of the ongoing struggle in the rubber-growing industry to obtain an agreement between the regime and workers. The use of force to break the strike thus undermined the negotiations. Diem perceived actions such as strikes as direct threats to his family's hold on power. Official sources soon reported that some 90 percent of workers had returned to their jobs, while workers' representatives reported that barely 10 percent had come back to work. Diem's American advisors understood the potential danger in using troops to break a strike, referring to the episode as "most unfortunate."[1] This action certainly did not improve the regime's image among the Vietnamese or among the Americans. Far more important in the context of constructing the state, however, was the fact that the rubber sector was the major foreign exchange–earning sector in an economy desperate for any earnings independent of American aid. The regime soon followed up with "wide scale arrests" and intimidation of labor leaders. Additionally, the continued presence of troops and tanks in the area during and after the strike only fed the growing opposition to the regime.[2]

---

[1] *Saigon Weekly Economic Review*, no. 1 (December 28, 1959–January 6, 1960): 5, National Archives, Record Group 59, box 851K.oo/1-760; hereinafter RG and appropriate filing number.
[2] *Saigon Weekly Economic Review*, no. 2, January 7–14, January 16, 1960, RG 59, box 851K.oo/1-760. See also *Quarterly Economic Summary*, October–December 1959, March 23, 1960, RG 59, box 851K.oo1/1-760.

Viewed in isolation, the outcome of the strike is of only minor importance to the American role in Vietnam into the early 1960s. However, the event should be viewed as part of a growing laundry list of missteps, violations, abuses, and tragedies committed by the Diem regime and enabled by continued and growing U.S. funding and training. The Saigon regime's obstinacy in dealing with workers translated to the rest of the Vietnamese people and actually impeded the overall effort. This and similar instances of the Ngo family's strong hand and general intolerance for opening up the regime presented formidable obstacles to U.S. ambitions. The anecdote also illustrates the considerable tensions and contestations amid the state-building efforts that permeated the relationship between the Vietnamese and the Americans.

At the same time, the American aid program, initiated with the hope and promise of constructing a state around Saigon, sustained an unpopular regime that otherwise would have collapsed. The regime's sustenance came to require far greater levels of currency, commodity, and military support, which both distorted the economy in important ways and undermined the long-term aims of U.S. policy. And although the events then unfolding in Vietnam did not yet capture the national leadership's undivided attention, mounting problems with internal security, political legitimacy, and the growing movement among ordinary Vietnamese to oppose the rule of *My-Diem* all combined to bring about a significant change in policy toward the effort in southern Vietnam from 1961 forward. From 1961 to 1963, the American role in southern Vietnam shifted from advice and aid to direct assistance and preparation for war aimed at military victory. In state-building terms, these policy shifts also required the reinvention of Vietnam.

SOUTHERN VIETNAM IN THE DECADE OF DEVELOPMENT

The young and dynamic Kennedy administration embraced a threatening Cold War environment as one of its touchstones when the president issued his famous promise to "pay any price, bear any burden, meet any hardship, support any friend, oppose any foe, to assure the survival and success of liberty."[3] As a senator, Kennedy believed America

[3] Public Papers of the President (*PPP*), JFK, 1961, 1.

shouldered a unique responsibility in the postcolonial age, that it "must supply capital ... technicians ..., [and] guidance to assist a nation taking those first feeble steps toward the complexities of a republican form of government."[4] He had campaigned for the presidency under the banner the "New Frontier," on a pledge to reverse the foreign policy setbacks handed to the United States under the previous administration. The advisors surrounding the new president, which journalist David Halbertam termed the "best and the brightest," believed that with the proper application of American know-how, technology, and experience, the problems that so threatened the kind of world they hoped to create could be solved.

The ideas of economic development and modernization for the third world had already become formative in the crafting of American foreign policy by 1960. John Kennedy had himself warmed to the ideas of academics and intellectuals for solving the problems of poverty and instability in the world several years earlier. In particular, he became an advocate of the use of American economic power and technological prowess in the ambitious objectives of "nation building." As Massachusetts senator in 1957, Kennedy had consulted a group at the Massachusetts Institute of Technology's (MIT) Center for International Studies on the economic development of Southeast Asia, already considering the subject a potential campaign issue.[5] That same year, in an article published in *Foreign Affairs*, Kennedy wrote, "Old liberal bromides have no appeal to nations which seek a quick transition to industrialization and who admire the disciplined attack which Communism seems to make upon the problem of economic modernization and redistribution." For these reasons, the senator argued for a new approach, one of increased development and military aid to the former colonial world.[6]

At MIT, Kennedy found able and committed academic intellectuals like Max Millikan and Walt Rostow already hard at work on the problems left over from the collapse of colonialism. Rostow's *The Stages*

[4] John F. Kennedy, *Speech at Rockhurst College, Kansas City, Missouri, June 2, 1956*, 84th Cong., 2nd sess., *Congressional Record* 102 (1956): 9614–9615.

[5] Walt W. Rostow interview, Oral History Program, John F. Kennedy Library (hereinafter JFKL), 2–4.

[6] John F. Kennedy, "A Democrat Looks at Foreign Policy," *Foreign Affairs* 36, no. 1 (1957), 44–59; quote is on 53.

of Economic Growth (1960) laid out a formula explaining the linear development of nations and, more importantly, a solution to communism, which the author viewed as nothing more than "the disease of the transition."[7] Rostow's work and his contribution within the Kennedy administration were directly connected to the opening of what officials termed the "decade of development" in the realm of foreign affairs. Following promises to aid "those people in the huts and villages of half the globe," the president launched a number of efforts aimed at greater development of the areas in the third world, or the global south.[8] With the administration's backing, Congress passed an expanded Foreign Assistance Act for 1961 as part of a one-third increase in U.S. aid to developing countries. While aid for Europe trailed off between 1950 and 1960, aid for Asia, the Middle East, Africa, and Latin America increased dramatically, demonstrating in another way the shift the Cold War had taken. U.S. aid for Asia now doubled aid provided for Europe, far more than reversing the pattern of ten years before.[9] The administration also established the White House Office of Food for Peace, embracing that program, inaugurated the Peace Corps, and supported the United Nation's Economic Commission for Latin America, along with launching the Alliance for Progress for Latin America; it facilitated development through the Inter-American Development Bank and the International Development Association, and it created, by executive order, the organization to preside over this increased emphasis on development aid, the Agency for International Development.[10]

The new reality called for bold initiative and innovation to win over the vast "uncommitted" peoples and states of the third world.[11]

---

[7] Walt Rostow, *The Stages of Economic Growth: A Non-communist Manifesto* (New York: Cambridge University Press, 1960), 162–64.

[8] *PPP, JFK*, 1961, 1. On the "decade of development," see Chester Bowles, "Foreign Aid: The Great Decision of the Sixties," *Department of State Bulletin* XLIV, no. 1142 (1961): 703–09; hereinafter *DSB*. Adlai Stevenson, "The Search for Balanced Economic and Social Development," *DSB* XLV, no. 1157 (1961): 363–69.

[9] The aid figure for Europe in 1950 was $25.5 billion, and for Asia, $3.4 billion. Doug Bandow, "Economic and Military Aid," in *Intervention into the 1990s: U.S. Foreign Policy in the Third World*, 2nd ed., ed. Peter J. Schraeder (Boulder, CO: Lynne Rienner, 1992), 75–97.

[10] See, e.g., Michael Latham, *Modernization as Ideology: American Social Science and "Nation Building" in the Kennedy Era* (Chapel Hill: University of North Carolina Press, 2000), esp. 30–59.

[11] Kennedy, "Democrat," 53.

Eighteen new nations gained independence in 1960 alone as the old pre–World War II colonial system continued crumbling. The Kennedy team embraced these crises, priding itself on its "crisis management" approach to foreign policy. As it happened, the formula spelled out by Rostow and others and adopted by the administration for bringing development and order to the third world came to rely on a combination of American economic aid and military force. Developing nations seemed to defy facile development formulae. Economic aid did not necessarily result in improved living standards or increased per capita income. Furthermore, increased per capita income did not necessarily translate into development or uplift for the people. And few of the developmentalist solutions gave much attention and emphasis to widespread revolutionary nationalist resistance. In the face of myriad difficulties and obstacles to controlling the destinies of the third world, the administration quickly began to alloy its liberal developmental approach with the more familiar military force. In its first year, the Kennedy administration chose to make its Cold War stand in Southeast Asia. Vietnam not only became a Cold War hot spot, but also the venue for implementing the development formula articulated over the preceding few years. The combination of these two factors resulted in an important shift in the U.S. state-building strategy in southern Vietnam.

COUNTERINSURGENCY, STRATEGIC HAMLETS, AND THE MILITARIZATION OF U.S. POLICY

Just a few days into his administration, President John Kennedy received from Edward Lansdale a sobering report based on the latter's recent two-week observation trip to Vietnam. The report painted a rather grim picture of the situation in Vietnam and of the Diem regime. At best, the report warned, Diem could only postpone ultimate defeat. The report concluded the country should be treated as a cold war hot spot in need of "emergency treatment" by the "best people" who were dedicated and who not only understood Asia, but also "really like[d] Asia and Asians." The situation cried out for able American leadership (on this, Lansdale had himself in mind), a sustained effort to develop a "responsible opposition," and a renewal of the commitment to Diem as the only reliable candidate. Relying on the American national historical experience to explain the dilemma faced in Vietnam, Lansdale reported "plenty of Aaron Burr's" and, unfortunately, "practically no George Washington's, Tom Jefferson's or Tom Paine's in Saigon today."[12]

The report and subsequent discussion of it energized Kennedy. According to the notes of the meeting, it gave him "for the first time . . . a sense of the danger and urgency of the problem in Viet-Nam." The meeting also focused on a new plan of action developed by the American mission in Vietnam over the preceding months and eventually known as the counterinsurgency plan.[13] Among other measures, the counterinsurgency plan called for augmenting the level of Diem's military forces (the Army of the Republic of Vietnam [ARVN]) from 150,000 to 170,000, ramping up the training and more than doubling the size of his thirty-thousand-man Civil Guard forces, and expanding military aid to Diem another $42 million over and above the $225 million annually committed to his regime.[14]

A couple of days following this meeting, the president approved the counterinsurgency plan, adding marginally, "Why so little?"[15] The president wanted to get moving in Vietnam, to change the nature of America's role there and to bring about a victory. Kennedy prodded those around him with questions about the utility of the added forces, about whether or not guerrillas could be infiltrated into Viet Minh areas. He talked of getting saboteurs, guerrillas, and spies to work in northern Vietnam as well. The action-oriented Kennedy administration soon embarked on an ambitious counterinsurgency program. The president

---

[12] *United States-Vietnam Relations, 1945–1967: A Study Prepared by the Department of Defense,* V.B.4, "U.S. Involvement in the War, Internal Documents, the Kennedy Administration: January 1961–November 1963," 1–12.

[13] Paper prepared by the Country Staff Committee, "Basic Counterinsurgency Plan for Viet-Nam," January 4, 1961, in *Foreign Relations of the United States,* vol. I (Washington, DC: GPO, 1961–1963), 3–6; hereinafter *FRUS.*

[14] "Meeting Saturday Morning, January 28, in the President's Office, on Viet-Nam," January 30, 1961, Vietnam Country File, National Security File, box 193, JFKL. "Summary Record of a Meeting, the White House, Washington," January 28, 1961, *FRUS,* 1961–1963, I:13–15. "Basic Counterinsurgency Plan for Viet-Nam," ibid., 1–12. Marilyn B. Young, *The Vietnam Wars, 1945–1990* (New York: Harper Perennial, 1991), 75. Diem's military force was the Army of the Republic of Vietnam, or ARVN, and usually pronounced "arvin."

[15] Memorandum for the Secretary of State, Secretary of Defense from President Kennedy, January 30, 1961, VN C.F., NSF, box 193, JFKL. William C. Gibbons, *The U.S. Government and the Vietnam War: Executive and Legislative Roles and Relationships, v. II, 1961–1964:15.*

involved himself directly from the start, reading the writings of revolutionaries Che Guevara and Mao Tse-tung and encouraging those around him to do the same. He authorized the army's Special Forces to wear a green beret to signify their new counterinsurgency emphasis and called for expanding the service in general. The president was interested in new gadgetry and technology as well and, after reading several training manuals, found them inadequate and obsolete. Closely following his new "green berets," he later attended an all-day counterinsurgency demonstration at Fort Bragg, complete with some of the new technology and weapons associated with counterinsurgency. As historian Douglas Blaufarb has written of the demonstration, "the high point of the day was an exhibition of a tiny rocket which, strapped to the back of a soldier, enabled him to fly over obstacles and across streams in the style of a comic-book hero." Aside from the dubious utility of personal rockets in the jungles of Vietnam, the goal of counterinsurgency was to change course, to break from the tradition of the equipment-laden soldier tied to cumbersome units moving sluggishly about in response to orders from faraway places.[16] Through new technology and improved strategic and tactical organization, the U.S. military could achieve success where predecessors had failed. These "counterguerrillas" were to be lighter, faster, and more mobile than traditionally trained and supplied combat soldiers.

American officials expressed an eagerness to "get on with the war," and demanding reforms which were unpalatable to Diem only held up the implementation of the counterinsurgency plan's military features that, as its advocates believed, could bring about the defeat of the insurgents.[17] As early February stretched into late April, support for

---

[16] Douglas Blaufarb, *The Counterinsurgency Era: U.S. Doctrine and Performance, 1950 to Present* (New York: Free Press, 1977), 55–56. For the intellectual or theoretical evolution of counterinsurgency ideas, see 57–71. See also Lionel McGarr, "Tactics and Techniques of Counter-Insurgent Operations," VN, C.F., NSF, box 204, JFKL.

[17] *The Pentagon Papers: The Defense Department History of United States Decision Making on Vietnam*, Senator Gravel ed., vol. II (Boston: Beacon Press, 1971), 27–30; hereinafter *PP*. By late April, in fact, Durbrow himself advocated implementing the twenty-thousand-man increase in Diem's military, writing "enough has been accomplished in arriving at agreed CIP to warrant proceeding with MAP procurement for 20,000 force increase." Although, he added the Diem regime should not be told of this decision. See Memorandum from Saigon to Secretary of State, April 15, 1961 (9:44AM), VN, C.F., NSF, box 193, JFKL.

Ambassador Durbrow and the carrot and stick approach to obtaining agreement waned in favor of moving forward with counterinsurgency and shelving any demand for substantive changes in the American client. Durbrow himself relented under pressure and recommended ramping up the military aid, even though he believed Diem clearly intended to "use all possible pressure [to] obtain increased defense support aid [in order] to obviate [the] necessity [of] unpopular internal...reforms."[18] By late February, the decision to replace the ambassador in Saigon with Frederick "Fritz" Nolting had in fact been made. The administration wanted someone on the ground in Saigon who was "on Diem's wavelength" and gave Diem less cause for questioning the American commitment to him.[19]

The president's recently created Vietnam Task Force soon produced *A Program of Action to Prevent Communist Domination of South Vietnam*, which emphasized military features of the problems in southern Vietnam and suggested military solutions.[20] Though the *Program* included recommendations for sending U.S. troops to Vietnam as instructors and advisors, the administration hedged its bets and instead opted to increase aid to Diem and to scuttle the demands for reforms. The key now was to make Diem confident of American support, to allay any concerns that the goal of reforming his regime superceded aiding him in maintaining his security.[21] National Security Action Memorandum (NSAM) 52, approved on May 11, reinforced this position by placing particular emphasis on winning the confidence of Diem as a

---

[18] Telegram from Saigon to Secretary of State, April 15, 1961 (7:51AM), VN, C.F., NSF, box 193, JFKL. White House advisor Walt Rostow wrote the same day, "Durbrow should relax with Diem from here on out and leave the arm-twisting to men with fresh capital." See Memorandum for the President, April 15, 1961, VN, C.F., NSF, box 193, JFKL.

[19] Elbridge Durbrow had been in Vietnam for fours years and was due to be replaced. President Kennedy submitted Nolting's nomination February 17, and he was confirmed on March 15, 1961. "Wavelength" quote is *PP*, II:3.

[20] This report itself has an interesting story and several incarnations. For a brief history of its evolution, see "Note for Researchers," April 12, 1976, VN, C.F., NSF, box 193, folder: 4/25/61–4/31/61, JFKL. The report cited here is *A Program of Action to Prevent Communist Domination of South Vietnam*, 1, May 1961, FRUS, 1961–1963, I:93–115. For another, significantly different version, see above folder, JFKL, under same title but dated 26 April, 1961. For an analysis, see Gibbons, *U.S. Government*, II:37–39; *PP*, II:31–55.

[21] *PP*, II:52–54.

means to influence him in the future. The demands for reforms, however, were quieted. The president also deferred the question of sending U.S. troops to Vietnam, preferring instead a "full examination" of the possible forces needed in the future. NSAM 52 also directed that a study be undertaken to discover the implications of increasing Diem's forces, again, from the 170,000 ceiling to 200,000.[22] Only days later, increased military aid included radar and surveillance equipment, U.S. funding for arming and training the whole of the Civil Guard, providing advice and support for the forty-thousand-strong Self Defense Corps, training of a Junk Force to prevent infiltration through water courses, and training Diem's own "Special Forces."[23]

Vice President Johnson landed in Vietnam the day Kennedy signed NSAM 52 to carry out in person the policy directive. Johnson publicly reaffirmed the U.S. commitment to Diem in glowing terms, offered U.S. forces, if needed (an offer Diem declined), suggested a bilateral pact to abrogate the Geneva Accords that had now been officially violated and jettisoned, and capped off the visit, referring to the Saigon client as the "Winston Churchill of Southeast Asia." He successfully shifted the emphasis away from the regime's lack of popular support and legitimacy and onto the threat posed to Diem's rule by the insurgency.

This shift in emphasis was apparently no accident. The president himself later echoed the theme following a mission to Vietnam by General Maxwell D. Taylor. The "gut issue," Kennedy claimed, "is not whether Diem is or is not a good ruler." The important thing was that the United States not "continue to accept the systematic infiltration of men from outside and the operation from outside of a guerilla war against him."[24] Not unlike the previous administration, these officials believed they possessed the ability to influence Diem once the aid was

---

[22] National Security Action Memorandum No. 52, May 11, 1961, *FRUS*, 1961–1963, I:132–34.

[23] The ramped up military aid was part of what became known as the Presidential Program for Vietnam. It also explicitly mentioned a study of the feasibility of sending U.S. troops to Vietnam. For text, see Telegram from Department of State to Amembassy Saigon, May 20, 1961, VN, C.F., NSF, box 193, JFKL. See also Lawrence Basset and Stephen Pelz, "The Failed Search for Victory," in *Kennedy's Quest for Victory: American Foreign Policy, 1961–1963*, ed. Thomas G. Paterson (New York: Oxford University Press, 1989), 231.

[24] George M. Kahin, *Intervention: How America Became Involved in Vietnam* (New York: Anchor Books, 1987), 137.

3. Vice President Lyndon Johnson's farewell breakfast with Diem, 1961.

no longer conditioned upon reforms and they had won his confidence. And just as he had with the previous administration, Diem continued to refuse all but the most superficial changes. Both sides tacitly agreed, however, that the growing insurgency necessitated a greater military preparedness. Consequently, security concerns and military prepared- ness now became the backbone of the U.S. effort. By the end of 1962, the administration had increased not only the numbers, training, and equipment of those forces protecting Diem and the Saigon regime, it had increased the American role there as well by introducing more than ten thousand American military advisors, helicopters, over two hundred intelligence officers at the province level, M-113 personnel vehicles, defoliants, napalm, an expanding Junk fleet for patrols, and other features of "modern military technology."[25]

In concert with the policy of increased military aid and assuaging Diem's nationalist sensibilities, administration officials simultaneously pursued an ambitious program aimed ostensibly at developing a political, economic, and social infrastructure in the countryside and bringing it into direct contact with the regime in Saigon. The population, so long as it remained isolated in thousands of villages strung out across the southern half of Vietnam, stood in the way of the development of a separate and sovereign state below the seventeenth parallel. Modernization and economic development required that the people become a part of the infrastructure of the new state, that their latent energies be exploited and put to work for development. Officials also continued to believe that those same Vietnamese peasants whose energies would be required if the project was to succeed also represented the very backwardness and underdevelopment on which the "enemy" thrived. The strategic hamlets introduced in early 1962 became the vehicle for this transformation. Peasants would be relocated and/or have their villages refashioned to better expedite the development of the new state. The administration sought to modernize Vietnam by extirpating all vestiges of the traditional. It was to be an assault upon tradition, particularlism, superstition, ignorance, clannishness, isolated and ignorant world views, and general rural backwardness. In short, the Kennedy administration assailed the people themselves. Therein lay the inescapable contradiction: the peasants of Vietnam were both the target of modernization and economic development initiatives and the key to the success of those initiatives.

The presence of a revolutionary movement actively organizing in the villages around southern Vietnam in opposition to the regime meant that the people became the centerpiece in a tug-of-war over influence, control, and territory. In his important study of the revolution in the village

---

[25] Memorandum for Mr. McGeorge Bundy, Developments in Viet-Nam between General Taylor's Visits – October 1961–October 1962, October 8, 1962, VN, C.F., NSF, box 197, JFKL, 5.

of My Tho in the Mekong Delta, for example, historian David Elliott points out that the decades-old revolutionary forces had been successfully organizing new recruits, networks, and a command structure. The advent of counterinsurgency and strategic hamlets placed severe pressure on that infrastructure. The revolution viewed U.S. military escalation with great caution and carefully calculated its response; the famous battle at Ap Bac in January 1963 is an example of this careful, if costly, assessment of enemy capabilities. The movement sought to, and did in dozens of instances, destroy the hamlets being put in place by the Americans and the regime.[26] For the next several years the forces of the revolution coupled military with political initiatives to thwart the ambitions of the regime and its American backers. A presence within and some degree of control over the countryside was vitally important to both parties.

Diem and his American advisors believed it of utmost importance to reach beyond Saigon and extend the regime's influence into the countryside to develop a governmental infrastructure. Conceived in large measure to deal with a deteriorating situation, the strategic hamlet program was nevertheless lauded as a development tool that would bring the blessings of modernization to the people of rural Vietnam. According to the author of the *Pentagon Papers*, the hamlet concept was "an attempt to translate the newly articulated theory of counterinsurgency into operational reality." As the centerpiece of the Kennedy administration's counterinsurgency doctrine, designers believed the program should include political, social, economic, and psychological as well as military features.[27] It was to transform the latent energies of the rural peasants into a bulwark of support for the Diem regime. The idea for the project emerged from earlier Vietnamese practices, British counter-guerrilla expert Robert G. K. Thompson's experience in Malaya, and

---

[26] David W. P. Elliott, *The Vietnamese War: Revolution and Social Change in the Mekong Delta, 1930–1975* (New York: M. E. Sharpe, 2002), I:397–406.

[27] Douglas Blaufarb, *The Counterinsurgency Era: U.S. Doctrine and Performance* (New York: Free Press, 1977), chap. 4. Quote is in *PP*, II:128. Secretary of Defense Robert McNamara referred specifically to the strategic hamlets as the "backbone of Presidents Diem's program" to defeat the insurgency. Of course, that also made it the backbone of the U.S. effort as the latter created and bankrolled the former; see *PP*, II:149. See also Latham, *Modernization as Ideology*, chap. 5.

American State Department intelligence officer Roger Hilsman's ideas. They conceived of strategic hamlets as only one of a multiphased counterinsurgency process whereby the peasant's loyalties would be won through a variety of measures.[28] In its initial phases, the overall process would involve setting up a government presence, as opposed to an overt military presence and show of force, to establish basic security. Villages would be organized for protection, requiring military forces on a limited basis, and gradually, they would be cleared of all insurgents or revolutionaries. A police force would remain in the area as part of a "clear and hold" strategy. Outlying villages or communities would thus have been brought into greater contact with an expanded and modernized Vietnam, with the Saigon regime at its center. Thus, from the start, the strategic hamlet program was the embodiment of the administration's combination of military and developmental solutions for Vietnam.

Launched in March 1962 in the province of Binh Duong and dubbed Operation Sunrise, the hamlet program attempted the mass relocation of peasants from this area into fortified hamlets. Lying a short distance north of Saigon, this area was chosen by Diem over the objections of some advisors, who suggested instead an area in which there was little insurgent activity. The insurgency enjoyed considerable support in Binh Duong and was thoroughly ensconced in the northern part of the province. Consequently, the operation began with Diem's forces sweeping through and forcibly removing insurgents, who simply "melted into the jungles." Having removed the insurgents, temporarily at least, the resettlement of the people into new hamlets began. Of more than two hundred families, only seventy could be persuaded to move. The remaining 135 had to be removed at gunpoint. Shortly, the dwellings, tools, and whatever belongings had to be left behind were burned to deprive the

---

[28] Philip E. Catton, *Diem's Final Failure: Prelude to America's War in Vietnam* (Lawrence: University of Kansas Press, 2002). R. G. K. Thompson, at the request of Diem, provided a detailed proposal on how to pacify the Vietnamese people. His paper served as the basic blueprint for strategic hamlets. See his Memorandum, November 11, 1961, USVN Relations, 1945–1967, V.B.4, book I, 345–58. Roger Hilsman adopted much of the Thompson proposal for his own report to the president in *A Strategic Concept for South Vietnam*, February 2, 1962, *FRUS*, 1960–1963, II:73–90; see also Roger Hilsman interview, Oral History Program, JFKL, 18 and 20, and Roger Hilsman, *To Move a Nation: The Politics of Foreign Policy in the Administration of John F. Kennedy* (New York: Doubleday, 1967), 427–35.

insurgency of their use and to ensure that no one returned to this area to resume their former lives. The U.S. Operations Mission (USOM) provided three hundred thousand dollars for those resettled, an average of about twenty-one dollars per family. Very little of the money, however meager, reached the people as the regime held up its delivery to ensure the settlers would not simply leave their new homes. Those young men had likely also melted into the jungle prior to the beginning of the operation. Six weeks into the operation, only 7 percent of the people had been resettled, either by force or voluntarily. By June, the guerrillas demonstrated their continued presence by attacking a military convoy, killing twenty-six of Diem's soldiers, two American officers, and a number of civilian public works advisors.[29]

Strategic hamlets could potentially "reconstruct the socio-politico-economic structure of the countryside," according to an analysis from the American embassy. The "multitude of advantages" following such a reconstruction included "centralization of market places,... establishment of modern commercial channels," increasing "the availability of labor (and incidentally military age youth),... more rapid monetization of the countryside," and, ultimately, "economic viability." The report concluded, "The new communities with appropriate institutional structures... are really tantamount to the modernization of Viet-Nam and the identification of a truly national entity." Unfortunately, one had to "cast aside consideration of the affirmative political values" and "the present essentially defensive nature of the strategic hamlet" to discern these positive attributes. This report suggested that by mid-1962, the strategic hamlet system functioned primarily as a weapon of counterinsurgency and that forced labor only promoted fear and distrust among the people.[30]

---

[29] *PP*, II:149; on the planning for Operation Sunrise, see Memorandum from the Naval Aide to the President's Military Representative (Bagley) to the President's Military Representative (Taylor), March 10, 1962, *FRUS, 1960–1963*, II:212–14; John C. Donnell and Gerald C. Hickey, "The Vietnamese 'Strategic Hamlet': A Preliminary Report," September 1962, U.S. Air Force Project Rand, Research Memorandum; Latham, *Modernization as Ideology*, 180–81. The number of resettled after six weeks was 2,769 out of 38,000. Bernard B. Fall, *The Two Viet-Nams: A Political and Military Analysis*, rev. ed. (New York: Praeger, 1964), 374–79.

[30] Telegram from U.S. Embassy, Saigon to Department of State, Viet-Nam – Approach to Economic Development; Certain Policy Suggestions, July 26, 1962, RG 59, 851K.00/7-1262. The chief complaint in this report was that the peasants were forced to build the hamlets and were not paid for their labor.

The opposing themes of economic development and uplift on one hand and an emphasis on security and population control on the other are less contradictory than they appear. Many American and Vietnamese officials muted their concerns over the treatment of the people in the countryside in favor of simply establishing a presence in and controlling certain areas of rural Vietnam. In the Central Highlands, for example, the combat-induced flight of the Montagnards from their lands was viewed as an opportunity. As the security situation deteriorated, both the Americans and the Vietnamese took advantage of the mobility of the mountain tribes to train them as combatants and ultimately employed them to defend the Vietnamese, who had historically viewed them as savages and dominated them. They thus became a tool exploited by the Americans and Diem in his campaign to control southern Vietnam.[31] Nor did the plight of lowland Vietnamese compel changes in the strategic hamlet system. Many thousands of peasants became refugees, had their homes destroyed, their livelihoods ended, and their communities divided as the project unfolded. Although progress toward reforming and reshaping the Vietnamese peasants was "uneven," according to an October 1962 report, Diem's chief advisor, Nhu, continued to hail strategic hamlets as the "democratic revolution in the countryside." The report's author was less upbeat, warning that an "underdeveloped [nation] with 2,000 years of authoritarian traditions does not quickly or easily become a modern democracy."[32] American USOM advisors, military advisors, and various Vietnamese officials interpreted counterinsurgency and pursued its ends in varied ways and with varied results. While some emphasized winning the hearts and minds of the people, others believed top priority should be given to combating the insurgency. Some advisors certainly understood the problems being created by the reckless nature of pacification.

Despite serious shortcomings, the program proceeded rapidly through 1962. Operations of varying scope, method, and success were

---

[31] Fall, *Two Viet-Nams*, chap. 14; John Prados, *The Hidden History of the Vietnam War* (Chicago: Ivan R. Dee, 1991), chap. 8; Memorandum of Conversation, Department of State, Washington, September 19, 1962, *FRUS*, II:652–53. In this memorandum, a Saigon official assured American officials that it was of utmost importance to kill the crops in Montagnard areas, saying, "If the VC can't get food they can't live there." Of course, neither could the tribes.

[32] Memorandum for Mr. McGeorge Bundy, October 8, 1962, VN, C.F., NSF, box 197, JFKL.

begun in Phu Yen, Binh Dinh, and Quang Nai Provinces immediately. Numerous other hamlets were begun elsewhere. The regime's Ministry of the Interior reported 157 completed hamlets within two months in Phu Yen Province. By October, the regime boasted 3,225 hamlets completed out of 11,316 planned, housing approximately 4.3 million people.[33] Their zeal to produce large numbers of hamlets led Saigon officials to very broadly define what could be called a secure hamlet. That same month, a report on central Vietnam found "the strategic hamlet program is mostly pure façade." Some strategic hamlets were inaugurated, for example, once a moat had been dug. Others were established on the basis of having gathered together the requisite villagers. Supplies such as radio equipment, weapons, barbed wire, concrete, and other building materials often arrived late or never. In a pattern that became familiar through the decade of the 1960s, officials nevertheless proclaimed success in establishing a large-scale strategic hamlet system that pacified the people and won them over to the regime in Saigon.[34]

Meanwhile, the ARVN, in conjunction with American advisors, carried out the overtly military aspect of the counterinsurgency program. Beginning with the creation of the Military Assistance Command and the appointment of former tank commander Paul Harkins to head it in early 1962, that effort included decidedly conventional measures. Missions now involved substantial firepower, set-piece units aggressively searching after other insurgent units, and increasing aid by American personnel, helicopters, weapons, and advice. Though poorly coordinated, if at all, the two sides of the counterinsurgency effort reached well beyond Saigon to sweep across much of southern Vietnam during 1962. The two approaches also began the large-scale destruction of the rural environment and the movement of people that became so commonplace in later years and cynically referred to as "voting with the

---

[33] *PP*, II:150–51. The next month, General Taylor argued that instead of the official 3,353 hamlets proclaimed completed by Diem, 600 was likely a more accurate number. See Memorandum from the Chairman of the Joints Chiefs of Staff (Taylor) to the Secretary of Defense (McNamara), November 17, 1962, *FRUS*, II:736.

[34] See sources for note 47. Memorandum from the Assistant Director for Rural Affairs, United States Operations Mission in Vietnam (Phillips), to the Director of the Mission (Brent), May 1, 1961, *FRUS*, 1960–1963, III:256–58. Memorandum from Robert H. Johnson of the Policy Planning Staff to the Counselor of the Department of State (Rostow), October, 16, 1962, *FRUS*, II:704. Hilsman, *To Move a Nation*, 450–53. Donnell and Hickey, "The Vietnamese 'Strategic Hamlets': A Preliminary Report," 10–19.

feet." In 1962, however, conventional firepower and the concentration of peasants into fortified encampments seemed to answer the insurgent problem.[35]

THE POLITICAL ECONOMY OF STATE BUILDING

As the American military presence grew alongside Diem's security apparatus during this period, economic development initiatives, so important to the state-building effort, receded into the background of what was fast becoming a war against Vietnamese insurgents. And although American officials from the Eisenhower through the Kennedy administrations pressed Diem for reforms, those reforms increasingly emphasized the danger of a growing insurgency and related internal security problems. The dramatic increases in military aid and the buildup of Diem's security, military, and police forces clearly demonstrated the centrality of this concern. Of the $203 million in economic aid the USOM committed to Vietnam for 1963, for example, over $184 million went to the military budget and counterinsurgency, while just $9.4 million went for economic and social development.[36]

As 1961 stretched into 1962, officials in Vietnam voiced more frequent complaints that the economy, such that it was, had now become "stagnant" and that by most measurements, it had not only failed to achieve pre–World War II levels of per capita income, but had actually lost ground since 1954, despite considerable foreign investment in rebuilding projects. Efforts such as agrarian reform and industrialization went largely unimplemented or only partially so. The regime seemed to focus its energies on security and on protecting its narrow base of support in and around the Saigon-Cholon area to the detriment of the

---

[35] Memorandum for Mr. McGeorge Bundy, Developments in Viet-Nam between General Taylor's Visits – October 1961–October 1962, October 8, 1962, VN, C.F., NSF, box 197, JFKL. Report by the Joint Chiefs of Staff's Special Assistant for Counterinsurgency and Special Activities (Krulak), undated, *FRUS*, III:455–65.

[36] United States Operations Mission, Operational Report, 1963–1964, Agency for International Development, Vietnam, 82. This figure excludes technical support, monies for food distribution, and, of course, military assistance, which accounted for $275 million for 1963. Data for each year in Douglas C. Dacy, *Foreign Aid, War, and Economic Development: South Vietnam, 1955–1975* (New York: Cambridge University Press, 1986), 200.

larger agrarian sector. That sector, at nearly 5.7 million workers, represented the vast majority of a workforce numbering about 6.3 million. Agricultural production still accounted for the overwhelming majority of exports, and exports remained dwarfed by imports, thus resulting in negative economic growth. Exports fell again in the first half of 1962 by almost half, and the regime recorded no export of its staple, rice. Additionally, industrial concerns remained relatively small and concentrated in such sectors as textiles and handicrafts. Though generally accorded protection in the form of tariffs and American aid, the industrial sector remained limited by the serious political/economic constraints then prevailing in Saigon and extending to the hinterland.[37]

By 1962, American experts and planners found themselves in a corner of their own making. While tentatively holding out hope for a brighter future for the project, they also pointed to the role of the U.S. aid program itself as threatening to undermine the whole effort. In January, the Economic Affairs desk of the U.S. embassy issued a memorandum detailing the problems associated with the counterinsurgency plan. Dozens of commodity imports, from raw materials to finished goods, from industrial equipment to consumables, entered Vietnam with substantial U.S. Agency for International Development (AID) financing. The U.S. program financed a record 59 percent of all import licenses in just the first quarter of 1962 and 85 percent of all goods into Vietnam for the year. Officials viewed this arrangement, or one very similar, as necessary since the 1950s. Altering the scheme by the early 1960s proved virtually impossible, according to the report, because "Viet-Nam's foreign exchange earnings have fallen drastically; Viet-Nam finds itself in a crucial struggle for national survival; and Viet-Nam is imposing new financial reforms [devaluation] . . . which are expected to increase the price of some imports." Because the regime used funds derived directly from U.S. financed imports to pay for its expanding military budget, "the economy cannot afford supply problems" even if the current supply mechanism

---

[37] The numbers on employment and the workforce vary from report to report. Those used here are from Dacy, *Foreign Aid*, 48. For export/import data, see Telegram from U.S. Embassy, Saigon to Department of State, July 26, 1962, RG 59, box 851K.oo/7-1262, 12. Quarterly Economic Summary, April–June, 1962, RG 59, box 851K.oo/7-1262, 5–6. *Saigon Bi-Weekly Economic Review*, no. 17, August 13–August 16, 1962, RG 59, box 851K.oo/7-1262.

kept the regime aid dependent in perpetuity.[38] Similar political obstacles prevailed beyond Saigon as well.

To illustrate one example, the city of Da Nang provides insight into the political obstacles to the development of a viable economic infrastructure in southern Vietnam. One of the key ingredients of any economic development plan involved bringing outlying areas into direct connection with Saigon. The building of roads, bridges, and rail lines into the hinterland really was only one part of the whole. Other urban areas beyond Saigon needed a liberal commercial environment as well. Diem, however, continued to frustrate these efforts by tightly controlling and further centralizing trade policy so that no one outside the Ngo family could have significant influence or wield economic power. Consequently, American economic advisors decried a "poor" Da Nang economy, in which "construction, sales, investment and banking activity are lethargic" and "purchasing power is low and there is a good deal of unemployment and underemployment."

Da Nang did not lack economic activity or opportunity. Rather, one businessman with ties to Diem's brother Ngo Dinh Can monopolized all economic activity in the area. Nguyen van Buu began by dominating cassia export, then muscled out the competition in the export of forest and agricultural products, took over coastal shipping (including trade from Saigon) and much of the construction business, and possessed considerable real estate holdings. Buu, in effect, enjoyed monopoly privileges that local businessmen believed grew out of his relationship with the ruling family. They also blamed the poor state of the local economy on Buu as much as on the security situation. He either crushed or completely controlled small business and heavily influenced local officials. One American official reviewing this report commented marginally, "and

---

[38] Memorandum on Price and Supply Effects of the Limited Procurement Policy on AID-Financed to Viet-Nam, January 18, 1962, RG59, 851K.00/1-1862110.4-AID. *Quarterly Economic Summary*, January–March, 1962, May 9, 1962, RG59, 851K.00/5962, 6. At the same time, U.S. officials scrambled to secure greater levels of third country aid to Vietnam to stave off economic collapse and increase the regime's revenues. Some of those officials, however, remained wary of the United States taking the lead in that effort for fear of "embarrassing [the Diem regime] as [a] supplicant" and the "implication we are more concerned than Diem about the survival [of] his government." See Telegram from Kuala Lumpur to Secretary of State, February 6, 1962, RG59, 851K.00 Second Fine/7-562.

the colonials were exploiters?" Privately, local businessmen told American advisors that Buu did not reinvest his profits into the local economy. Consequently, their collective attitudes toward the economic development of central Vietnam ranged from "pessimistic" to "downright skeptical." Ultimately, no profitable business activity took place without first accommodating Buu.[39] Such an atmosphere obviously inhibited the growth of industry and the spreading of economic opportunity.

This situation was most unfortunate, as one American consultant found, because it kept Vietnam stuck "in the same stage of underdevelopment." Aside from this kind of cronyism, the Vietnamese people eagerly awaited development according to that consultant. A "young population, with a sizable portion between the age of 15 and 30 providing a relatively high reservoir of manpower, and despite the tropical climate and the simple diet [of fish] the Vietnamese is energetic, alert and adaptable. His adaptability makes him extremely susceptible to the 'demonstration effect'"; that is, the people should be able to quickly imitate whatever the American trainers demonstrate. From this perspective, the real impediment to economic development was the tight control exercised by Diem from Saigon. The people themselves, thanks to French colonialism, had undergone a "'preconditioning' essential to economic development" and were thus prepared.[40] Leaving aside the shortcomings of this analysis, economic development no doubt suffered as a direct consequence of political realities.

Over time, these deficiencies became intractable. As the budgetary needs of the regime mounted in response to growing security problems, this set of economic policies served those needs without collapsing the entire project. The expansion of the counterinsurgency plan would generate greater revenues to expand the budget. It also necessarily increased the number of import licensees. The shrinking of local production that followed reduced business opportunities and also reduced incomes. Meanwhile, prices for imported goods rose, while the regime persisted in maintaining price ceilings. As an American economic advisor concluded, "this price policy generally favors the urban consumer at the

---

[39] Telegram from Embassy in Saigon to Department of State, November 26, 1962, RG 59, box 851K.00/10-862, 6–7.

[40] Telegram from U.S. Embassy, Viet Nam – Approach to Economic Development; Certain Policy Suggestions, July 26, 1962, RG 59, box 851K.00/7-1262, 2–4.

expense of the rural producer, whose production costs in the case of fertilizers alone has increased by 20 to 25 percent."[41] However, while inflation hovered around 24 percent, the money supply expanded by 134 percent, proving the utility of the commodity import program. The particular structure of the aid program prevented hyperinflation, while it also kept the client regime in a state of dependency.[42]

Diem's overcentralization, refusal to liberalize the economic and political system, fierce loyalty to the Ngo family, and almost phobic preoccupation with security likewise presented obstacles to reform right up until his death in late 1963. What a number of the embassy reports demonstrated, some implicitly and others explicitly, was the role played by the United States in not only permitting, but even encouraging the regime in Saigon to maintain a political economy that defied fundamental economic principles. Any effort to create sustained economic growth while still maintaining the status quo proved futile. The aid program itself, ostensibly aimed at building a modern political, economic infrastructure, perpetuated the problem by financing the majority of imports and import taxes and allowing an unrealistic rate of currency exchange, which created windfall profits for Vietnamese importers but sharply restricted exports.[43] The rate of exchange, thirty-five piasters to one U.S. dollar, allowed importers to purchase goods at well below market prices and sell them months later at significantly higher prices. Vietnamese farmers, while also victims of high prices for some imported goods, faced the prospect of exporting their produce at considerable disadvantage in terms of the exchange rate. This system was a bonanza for Diem and the small band of importers granted license by his regime.

Though some suggested a more realistic rate of exchange would be around seventy to eighty piasters to one dollar, and the black market rate was around one hundred to one, the regime had for years refused to consider devaluation. Diem feared the political consequences of spiking inflation. For their part, U.S. advisors grudgingly recognized the very real limitations placed on their own leverage through these economic

[41] Ibid., 9.
[42] U.S. Agency for International Development, *United States Economic Assistance to South Vietnam, 1945–1975*, volume I (Washington, DC: U.S. AID, 1975), 98; (hereinafter *USEASV*).
[43] Chi Do Pham, "Inflationary Finance in Wartime South Vietnam: 1960–1972," PhD diss., University of Pennsylvania, 1976, 14.

arrangements. Each year, aid officials forecast the level of import aid to southern Vietnam for the coming year based on the anticipated level of demand. The formula for doing so was based upon the artificial exchange rate. Thus any serious devaluation would have not only curtailed the level of real aid the regime received, but would also have sent inflation skyward. Under the current arrangement, profits accrued to importers, and this delicate balance prevented, at least for the time being, more severe economic and political costs. Owing to mounting pressures from various sources, the regime indirectly devalued the piaster in 1962 to sixty to one U.S. dollar, although it maintained the *official* rate of thirty-five to one to avoid any economic backlash. The regime continued to collect import taxes (largely from the U.S. program) based on that official rate. American officials also pointed out that the devaluation in effect raised taxes to meet "the expanded military budget for 1962."[44]

The aid program created a precarious and artificial system. The amount of American aid and infrastructural investment that flowed into Vietnam, without intervention of some kind, would have caused serious inflation. Runaway inflation would have jeopardized Diem's already difficult position as the economy spiraled out of control and goods became affordable to fewer and fewer Vietnamese. To control inflation, the United States agreed on one hand to a fixed rate of exchange for the piaster and, on the other, began to import the lion's share of goods needed (and some not needed) and even to pay for those goods as part of its aid program, hence the commodity import program. The dilemma created by this arrangement was that the aid program actually perpetuated underdevelopment by preventing the growth of home industry and of an export economy. Although officials could not overcome lackluster consumer spending in the early 1960s, they nevertheless had to continue to encourage greater levels of imports to increase the regime's revenue to pay for the growing costs of the project.[45]

---

[44] *Quarterly Economic Summary*, April–June, 1962, 6. Vietnamese officials chose to satisfy the demand for devaluation through a complex scheme of taxation and further aid from the United States to avoid the political costs of devaluation. See *USEASV*, I:101–4. *Quarterly Economic Summary*, October–December, 1961, RG59, 851K.00/2-1262. Pham, "Inflationary Finance," 12.

[45] Not surprisingly, southern Vietnam could not adequately expand a consumer base under conditions then prevalent. Price increases, a large majority of the population living in the rural environment, and a "general uneasiness" also inhibited consumption. See "Economic Assessment," Viet-Nam, March, 1962, RG59, 851K.00/3-2962, 2–3.

Putting aside their own role in creating these circumstances, American officials routinely complained that their Vietnamese allies did not share their enthusiasm for development. They criticized a Vietnamese "Tentative Five-Year Plan" put forward in 1961 as "a political weapon" used to "imbue the people with a sense of expectation of better things to come." They saw as evidence of the leadership's lack of interest in real development the fact that of all the officials assigned to the Planning Directorate, only three "had any qualification or knowledge concerning economic development planning."[46] An independent Vietnam below the seventeenth parallel could not develop under the circumstances. Furthermore, to fundamentally shift the aid program away from enormous subsidization of imports would bring back the specter of inflation. This was not a new problem.[47]

For some time, economic advisors warned this formula prevented any real economic growth. Milton Taylor, an economist for the Michigan State University Vietnam Advisory Group (MSUG), found that the American aid program had emphasized military concerns too heavily. As the program became further militarized, the level and scope of the counterinsurgency plan and of American aid also increased. Both perpetuated Vietnamese dependence. As Taylor concluded, "the greater proportion of merchandise imports has been used for the maintenance of living standards rather than for the development of the economy." Another analysis found that of a population of over 12 million, only about fifteen thousand individuals declared taxes. Of that number, approximately 12,500 were civil servants and military personnel. In 1962, the regime generated only about $10 million in taxes, a figure American advisors found "shockingly low." From 1961 through 1972, the tax base never amounted to even 10 percent of the gross national product, while American aid climbed from just under $400 million to well over $3 billion annually for the same period. This lack of tax base was one of the reasons

---

[46] Development Planning; GVN "Tentative" Five-Year Plan – 1961–1965, July 28, 1961, RG 59, 851k.oo/7-2861, 3–4.

[47] One can immediately glean the implications of these economic problems from even a cursory reading of the economic reports from the U.S. embassy during this period. See, e.g., *Quarterly Economic Summary*, January–March 1961, June 8, 1961, RG 59, 851K.oo/6-861; *Quarterly Economic Summary*, April–June, 1961, July 28, 1961, RG 59, 851k.oo/7-2861; *Quarterly Economic Summary*, October–December, 1961, February 12, 1962, RG 59, 851k.oo/2-1262; "South Viet Nam – An Assessment of Its Economy – September, 1961, September 19, 1961," RG 59, 851k.oo/9-1961.

for the effort to reach into the countryside and to "monetize" the rural economy. Until that effort succeeded, the American aid program functioned in lieu of an internal revenue capability. Designed under emergency or crisis circumstances to aid in the construction of modern state infrastructure, the system instead created what Taylor termed "a permanent mendicant" in southern Vietnam.[48] The American aid program made the Saigon client and all of southern Vietnam aid-dependent and import-oriented, and altering these arrangements would have brought a quick end to the whole experiment.

Taylor was not alone in his appraisal of the project. His criticisms and those of other MSUG advisors also attracted considerable attention. Published beginning in the early 1960s, the articles sharply contrasted with the optimistic appraisals of the situation in Vietnam coming out of Washington. They highlighted corruption, lethargy, wrongheaded advice, and a vast aid program that was ill-conceived and ill-administered, among other failings.[49]

For example, Michigan State University political scientist Robert Scigliano published "Political Parties in South Vietnam under the Republic" in 1960, in which he cast Diem's one-man rule in stark terms. The author pointed out the range of noncommunist, nationalist opposition groups legitimately vying for power in southern Vietnam.

---

[48] Milton C. Taylor, "South Viet-Nam: Lavish Aid, Limited Progress," *Pacific Affairs* 34, no. 23 (1961): 246, 256; Telegram to Saigon, Subject: GVN Budget, February 15, 1963, VN, C.F. NSF, box 197, JFKL, 2; Dacy, *Foreign Aid*, 200, 222–23; John D. Montgomery, *The Politics of Foreign Aid: American Experience in Southeast Asia* (New York: Praeger, 1962), 114. For a general statement regarding the lack of revenue capability of the Saigon regime, see *USEASV*, 104–6. For specific numbers on a yearly basis for revenues and expenditures, see Pham, "Inflationary Finance," 99.

[49] See, in addition to Taylor's essay, Frank C. Child, "Vietnam – The Eleventh Hour," *New Republic* 145 (December 1961): 14–16; Adrian Jaffe and Milton Taylor, "A Crumbling Bastion: Flattery and Lies Won't Save Vietnam," *New Republic* 144 (June 1961): 17–20; Joseph Zasloff, "Rural Resettlement in South Viet Nam: The Agroville Program," *Pacific Affairs* 35, no. 4 (Winter 1962–63): 327–40; Robert Scigliano, "Political Parties in South Vietnam under the Republic," *Pacific Affairs* 33 (December 1960): 327–47; Scigliano, *South Vietnam: Nation under Stress* (Boston: Houghton Mifflin, 1963); Scigliano and Guy Fox, *Technical Assistance in Vietnam: The Michigan State University Experience* (New York: Praeger, 1965); James B. Hendry, "American Aid in Vietnam: The View from a Village," *Pacific Affairs* 33 (December 1960): 389–90; Hendry, "Land Tenure in South Viet Nam," *Economic Development and Cultural Change* 9 (October 1960): 27–44; M. N. Trued, "South Viet-Nam's Industrial Development Center," *Pacific Affairs* 33, (1960): 250–67; among others.

He also explained how the regime had either marginalized, exiled, jailed, harassed, or simply outlawed those groups and/or their leaders. Scigliano suggested the regime allow a freer press, a real role for the National Assembly, tolerance for public expression, and generally, a greater level of public freedom.[50] Michigan State advisor Frank Child offered a much more acerbic critique. On the basis of his own travels around the countryside of Vietnam, Child believed that Diem had created a "police state with all the normal accouterments of a police state" and that the regime's insularity prevented long-term political and economic viability. Child's criticism of the regime did not center on its undemocratic nature, but on the fact that "it is a failure. It has neither of the two saving graces of an 'acceptable' dictatorship: it is neither benevolent nor efficient."[51] Michigan State advisors Adrian Jaffe and Milton Taylor concurred in their own essay, "A Crumbling Bastion: Flattery and Lies Won't Save Vietnam," published in 1961. Both believed Washington had deluded itself by continuing to proclaim success in Vietnam. In their view, "Vietnam is not stable, not viable, not democratic, and not a bastion" of the "Free World," as officially claimed. The United States had presided over little political or economic development despite six years and $1.5 billion investment. The U.S. effort had yielded instead an autocratic regime scarcely distinguishable from the communists.[52] The force of this combined assault on the project from so many of its most committed planners and advisors was undeniable.

Sometime in early 1962, Diem decided not to renew the MSUG contract, and he cited the offending articles as his rationale. Observers at the time accepted that Diem allowed the MSUG contract to lapse because of these former advisors and their indictments of the project. There can be little doubt that Diem chafed under the added criticism from supposed insiders, those granted a modicum of trust and access.[53] He had retaliated against criticism from the press corps as well, even expelling

---

[50] Scigliano, "Political Parties," 346.
[51] Child, "Vietnam – The Eleventh Hour," 15.
[52] Jaffe and Taylor, "A Crumbling Bastion," 17, 19.
[53] Letter from Wesley R. Fishel of the Michigan State University Group in Vietnam to President John A. Hannah of Michigan State University, February 17, 1962, FRUS, II:148–52; Memorandum from the Chief Adviser, Michigan State University Group in Vietnam (Fox), to James B. Hendry of Michigan State University, February 19, 1962, FRUS, II:152–55.

journalists from Newsweek, CBS, and NBC.[54] The termination of the university's contract, however, also dovetailed with the shift in emphasis away from development and reform and onto counterinsurgency and military preparedness during 1962. Perhaps the MSUG really did "work itself out of a job," as had been its mission. Having established or aided in the establishment of police, governmental, economic, and other infrastructure, the team from Michigan State really had outlived its utility by 1962.

Much greater aid now focused on military projects such as strategic hamlets, the buildup of the ARVN, and the growing American military presence. The United States directly involved itself in the regime's survival. Diem was, if nothing else, an astute political operator, and he understood the changes occurring during 1961–1962. Though the published critiques of the regime were no doubt a factor, Diem also dismissed the MSUG because, with increased direct military aid assured in 1962, he could afford such a move.[55] In late 1961, he had declared a state of national emergency and used the occasion to split the regime's budget in two, civil and military, and removed the latter from the National Assembly entirely, making it solely the responsibility of the executive branch – himself. Thus the expanding military budget was no longer subject to the scrutiny of the legislature, obscuring its details for both the National Assembly and U.S. advisors.[56]

At the time of the dismissal of the MSUG, officials had begun "a very urgent revamping" of the economic program for Vietnam for fiscal years 1962 and 1963. As part of that reassessment, programs found not to "support...the war directly" were to be terminated, or at least curtailed. The director of the Vietnam Task Force wrote, "While we want to continue successful, long-range development projects, we are going to defer new starts for the time being, and we are reviewing other long-range development projects to modify them or terminate them."

---

[54] Robert D. Schulzinger, *A Time for War: The United States and Vietnam, 1941–1975* (New York: Oxford University Press, 1997), 116.

[55] "Out of a job" quote in MSUG *Final Report*, 4. On the articles written by former MSUG personnel as a major factor in the group's dismissal, see, inter alia, Scigliano, *South Vietnam*, 205–06; Herring, *America's Longest War*, 109; John Ernst, *Forging a Fateful Alliance: Michigan State University and the Vietnam War* (East Lansing: Michigan State University Press, 1998), 121.

[56] *Quarterly Economic Summary*, October–December, 1961, RG59, 851K.00/2-1262, 5.

The emphasis on security became top priority. The memorandum continued, "We especially want to work out civilian (and military) projects that will have the swiftest impact in winning the peasants to the government, i.e., civilian and military civic action progress."[57] Some officials nevertheless continued to champion the ideas of economic development.

Upon his departure from Saigon in the spring of 1962, Arthur Gardiner, formerly head of USOM and embassy counselor for economic affairs, delivered a speech before the Saigon Rotary Club, in which he warned his audience that the Vietnamese themselves must take "responsibility" for their country's "development." Echoing warnings issued earlier by American state builders of the chaotic nature of the process, Gardiner urged that "men of vision and good will ... struggle against rootlessness engendered by vast social change" to bring about the "development of economic and other organizations to implement democratic ideas." In naming the tools of democracy, he invoked "credit," "new techniques," "modern methods," "buying power," "growth," and "Western technology." Though lauding "new and challenging vistas" and quoting Disreali on the importance of education, Gardiner really admonished those gathered before him, calling on them to "develop your many untapped resources" and to "realize that legitimate profits are the mainspring of growth." Though generally congratulatory and upbeat, the speech really pointed out that so far, the entire program in southern Vietnam had met with little long-term success.[58]

Beginning that same year, 1962, the American mission gave way to increased military involvement, expanding Diem's fighting forces, and a marked attention to counterinsurgency and strategic hamlets to consolidate the rule of the Ngo family and to bring outlying regions into the fold. Aside from the economic system already described, the systems of roads, bridges, canals, ports, national police, and paramilitary groups, however inadequate for the new level of military activity, became crucial for the buildup that followed. A growing war and preparations

---

[57] See Memorandum from Robert H. Johnson of the Policy Planning Council to the Director of the Council (Rostow), February 15, 1962, FRUS, II:132–36, quote is 135; Memorandum from the Director of the Vietnam Task Force (Cotrell) to the Assistant Secretary of State for Far Eastern Affairs (Harriman), February 17, 1962, FRUS, II:144–47, quote is 147.

[58] Speech on Viet-Nam Economic Development by USOM Director Arthur Z. Gardiner, May 18, 1962, RG 59, 851k.00/5-1862.

for it necessitated further increases in American imports, expansion of the counterinsurgency plan to offset the real costs, and further currency manipulations to slowly expand the money supply to pay for the changes. Economic development would have to wait. In a comprehensive summary report, the AID pointed out this shift from economic development and toward greater emphasis on counterinsurgency and increased warfare, adding that "this shift in direction was not universally heralded within A.I.D.," as many of the new responsibilities lay well beyond its members' scope of training.[59] Military construction and building projects got under way over much of southern Vietnam during 1962 and into 1963 to accommodate a growing ARVN, a growing number of American military advisors, and a rapidly expanding strategic hamlet program and war against the opposition rooted in the countryside.

Despite the infrastructural developments of the previous six or seven years, southern Vietnam lacked the capacity to receive the level of direct military aid the United States began providing in 1962–1963. The network of roads needed expanding. Ports needed extensive dredging, while others needed building. Military bases needed constructing. As construction activity stepped up, the USOM announced that the "port facilities, road networks, and inland waterways of Vietnam may soon be described as distinctly good." Construction projects included building 250 miles of new roads, expanding and updating 935 miles of existing roads, expansion of railroad track mileage, acquisition of new rolling stock, building airports, including a jet airstrip at the Tan Son Nhut facility, importing a fleet of dredges to clear new waterways for transportation, and expanding radio communications capacity. Although only a very few could land heavy jet aircraft, southern Vietnam soon possessed more airfields per square mile than any other nation in Southeast Asia.[60]

Infrastructure development related directly to counterinsurgency, and officials now spoke of the "war" in Vietnam, rather than economic or development aid and assistance to Vietnam. The expansion and

---

[59] *USEASV*, I:39–44. The AID report also maintained that "economic and other technical assistance projects were not discontinued, merely overshadowed in the new emphasis on counterinsurgency." See *USEASV*, I:101.

[60] USOM, *Annual Report for Fiscal Year 1962*, 27–31.

improvement of the communications and transportation network was seen in this light.[61] As the president himself made clear in 1963, "what helps to win the war, we support; what interferes with the war effort, we oppose."[62] Although responding specifically to a question regarding continued support for a corrupt and ineffective Saigon regime, Kennedy laid bare the administration's own view of its mission in Vietnam.

By the end of 1963, that mission had grown into a formidable presence of both personnel and material. The U.S. military presence stood at more than 16,000, up from approximately 680 in 1960. And although still officially slated as advisors, American military personnel participated in missions, flying helicopters and carrying out ground operations, from the start. Additionally, that force brought with it helicopters, personnel carriers, defoliants, small arms, and napalm. Diem's own forces stood at more than one quarter million for the ARVN and more than 150 paramilitary forces. From 1961 to 1963, the administration had raised the stakes for the United States in Vietnam and had, at the same time, significantly undermined its own program in Vietnam. When the ideas and language of modernization and economic development were invoked, they often appeared perfunctory and not as fundamental policy. In short, the administration had come to see winning a war in southern Vietnam as its major objective. Consequently, the twin aims of economic development and state building that had launched the project beginning in 1954 now fell into abeyance, despite the fact that neither had been accomplished.

In papering over these facts, the administration painted itself into a corner in Vietnam. Senator Mansfield pointed explicitly to the problem in another of his reports to the president in 1963: "We have intensified our support of the Vietnamese armed forces in ways which those responsible believe will produce greater effectiveness in military operations. This intensification, however, inevitably has carried us to the start of the road which leads to the point at which the conflict in Viet Nam could become of greater concern and greater responsibility to the United States than it is to the Government and people of south

---

[61] USOM, *Operational Report, 1963–1964*, 21–33.

[62] Lloyd Gardner, *Pay Any Price: Lyndon Johnson and the Wars for Vietnam* (Chicago: Ivan R. Dee, 1995), 65.

Viet Nam."[63] This point had been reached by 1963, as Diem provoked another series of crises involving suppression of the Buddhists.

The Americans looked about for new forms of leverage to compel Diem to change. Not surprisingly, few could be found. Once again, officials attempted to use their ability to withhold some portion of the aid package to get what they wanted.[64] The union that now existed between economic aid and the war effort posed a serious problem, for it essentially reduced leverage that a threat of aid suspension might otherwise possess. As a report from General Taylor and Secretary McNamara late in 1963 pointed out explicitly, "any long-term reduction of aid cannot but have an eventual adverse effect on the military campaign since both the military and the economic programs have been consciously designed and justified in terms of their contribution to the war effort."[65]

Simply put, as a result of the shift from advice and aid to assistance and a larger direct military role, the United States now aided and financed its own effort to build the political, social, economic, and military infrastructure below the seventeenth parallel. Withdrawing that aid, while certain also to anger Diem, only further reduced options and restricted the conduct of the war against the countryside. Among the variables that could not be controlled, Diem certainly ranked high on the list. His brutal tactics in suppressing growing dissent, and of the Buddhists in particular, threatened to bring down the house of cards from within. More generally, however, there remained much uncertainty in southern Vietnam through the early 1960s. Many American advisors were slowly beginning to grapple with the inherent contradictions contained in the aid program, and their somber assessments reflect this shift. Even the most optimistic forecasts included the qualification that all planning anticipated no real change (either reduction or expansion) of the conflict. Of course, no one really knew what lay ahead. As the U.S. embassy's economic affairs counselor ominously concluded in a 1962 assessment, "the outlook is obscured by imponderables."[66]

[63] Mike Mansfield, "Viet Nam and Southeast Asia, 1963," VN, C.F., NSF, box 197, JFKL.

[64] This threat was recommended in a report submitted following an observation trip to Vietnam by General Taylor and Secretary McNamara. See Memorandum for the President, Report of McNamara-Taylor Mission to South Vietnam, October 2, 1963, *PP*, II:751–66.

[65] Memorandum from the Chairman of the Joint Chiefs of Staff (Taylor) and the Secretary of Defense (McNamara) to the President, October, 2, 1963, ibid., 345.

[66] "Economic Assessment," Viet-Nam, March 1962, RG59, 851K.00/3-2962, 5.

CONCLUSION: POLITICAL COLLAPSE AND THE FALL OF DIEM

Despite steadily increasing military aid (now more than $1 million per day) and a more aggressive effort to maintain the regime in Saigon, Diem continued to frustrate his American backers. An ardent nationalist himself, he now balked at the number of Americans in both urban and rural locales. He complained more frequently that the growing advisory presence perpetuated the notion that the whole project was really run by the Americans. His brother Nhu had also become more vocal and more of an influence. In May, he suggested that the Americans remove half of their military forces from Vietnam.[67] At the same time, the brothers used that American aid and assurance to extend the regime's control to the whole of southern Vietnam. Against the advice of his financers, Diem also went after various opposition groups and imposed harsh penalty for their impudence. The most visible of these confrontations involved the crackdown on Buddhists that began in May 1963 and brought relations between the regime in Saigon and the U.S. government to a crisis point.

Celebrating the birthday of Buddha in Hué on May 8, several thousand gathered to hear a speech broadcast over loudspeaker. The Catholic authorities, however, abruptly cancelled the speech, citing lack of approval by censors, and ordered armored cars to the area, along with police and Civil Guard units. Authorities demanded the crowd break up and leave and then began firing on the unarmed people. In the melee that ensued, a woman and eight children were killed, and fourteen others were injured, some of them shot, others crushed by armored cars.[68] Efforts by the authorities to blame the insurgency on the communists had little impact. People laid blame for the episode at the feet of the regime, and of Ngo Dinh Diem in particular. The Buddhists quickly organized in protest of the regime and its refusal to punish those responsible. Over ten thousand marched the next day in Hué. Demonstrations sprung up all over southern Vietnam in the weeks that followed.

---

[67] Telegram from Saigon to Secretary of State (section one of three), April 5, 1963, VN, C.F., NSF, box 197a, JFKL, 2–3. Warren Unna, "Viet-Nam Wants 50% of GIs Out," *Washington Post*, May 12, 1963. Diem and Nhu both believed that American force levels stood at twelve to thirteen thousand. The actual numbers were kept from them to avoid further problems.

[68] Telegram from the Consulate at Hue to the Department of State, May 9, 1963, *FRUS*, III:277–78.

While Diem largely ignored the coming storm and demands from the Buddhists, the movement itself gathered force and quickly galvanized disparate anti-Diemist elements. Diem compounded the crisis by attempting to smash the opposition, breaking up demonstrations with tear gas and tanks in June. The Buddhists used the eager Western press to great advantage and coordinated demonstrations, meetings, and public statements to have the most impact. On June 11, activists alerted the press to an episode that spread their message well beyond Saigon. On that day, Thich Quang Duc, a Buddhist monk, calmly sat in the middle of a busy intersection and, his companions having doused him in gasoline, lit a match and burned to death before several hundred shocked bystanders and Western cameras.[69] Over the next several months, this practice of immolation by Buddhists continued and provoked shock and anger around the world.

By late June and into July, the Buddhists had evolved into a substantial political opposition. American officials also believed the crisis was "more political than religious," despite the Ngos' continued insistence that the whole movement was communist inspired and therefore without legitimacy. The movement's leaders also began to suggest political solutions such as removal of Diem and the Ngo family. This demand, substantially different than the initial "five demands" listed at the outset of the crisis, now became commonplace.[70] Diem and his family remained obdurate, attacking numerous Buddhist pagodas in cities around southern Vietnam in August. In one raid, Diem's forces arrested over fourteen hundred, killing several and injuring more than two dozen monks in the process. At the same time, Diem and Nhu declared martial law in an attempt to tighten the grip and preempt any popular response. Outraged and thunderstruck American officials looked on, uncertain how

---

[69] Telegram from Saigon to Secretary of State, June 11 (12:08am), 1963, VN, C.F., NSF, box 197a, JFKL; Telegram from Saigon to Secretary of State, June 11 (2:21am), 1963, VN, C.F., NSF, box 197a, JFKL; Telegram from Saigon to Secretary of State, June 11 (11:30am), 1963, VN, C.F., NSF, box 197a, JFKL. *PP*, v. II, 225–27.

[70] The "five demands" are from a manifesto issued on May 10 by Buddhist leaders. Those demands were the following: (1) freedom to fly their flag; (2) legal equality with Catholics; (3) an end of arrests; (4) freedom of practice; and (5) an indemnity for the May 8 tragedy and punishment for its perpetrators. See *PP*, II:226. On political danger of politicized Buddhist opposition, see Telegram from State Department to Embassy in Saigon, June 11, 1963, VN, C.F., NSF, box 197a, JFKL; Telegram from CIA, Saigon, July 8, 1963, VN, C.F., NSF, box 198, JFKL.

to respond. Just as he had during the 1954–1955 crises involving the sects, Diem employed violence to put down native groups whose power could rival his own.

The problem now was that Diem had, for over eight years, been the central figure around which the United States carried out its policy. It was now more difficult than ever to remove him, and all potential replacements had been eliminated. When that decision came late in the year, many dreaded its consequences, with good reason. After an aborted coup plot in August, a cabal of military officers planned and organized a coup and made its move in early November. Assured of American support, the group quickly removed Diem and Nhu, loaded them into the back of a van, drove them a short distance through Saigon, and shot them both while tied and bound in the back of the vehicle. Immediately, the prison doors were thrown open, and broken and tortured men and women by the thousands were released. Stories of the secret prisons and torture remained secret no longer. People filled the streets and celebrated the end of the regime, tearing down all signs, pictures, statues, and other vestiges of Ngo family rule. In the countryside, peasants either destroyed the strategic hamlets or simply abandoned them.[71] Diem's long and crisis-ridden rule was at an end, but the state-building campaign remained troubled and in a state of flux.

Three weeks later, President Kennedy was assassinated in Dallas, Texas. Many of the administration's goals and ambitions for inventing Vietnam remained unrealized. Others had proved failures. The strategic hamlet program died with Diem without having achieved its aims, at least as far as could be reliably measured. The regime required much greater aid by 1963 just to pay its costs and the growing costs associated with putting down internal rebellion. The sudden and violent end of Diem's rule ushered in political, economic, and social crises in southern Vietnam. For many months afterward, instability reigned as the United States scrambled to put in place new leadership that could pursue the changed objectives. A full-fledged war now raged in southern Vietnam; the new state would now have to be built by force of arms, rather than economic aid and advice. Tragically, American officials never seemed to realize that the state and its accompanying infrastructure upon which a U.S. success depended had yet to emerge.

---

[71] Hilsman, *To Move a Nation*, 521.

The brief period from 1960 to 1963 witnessed substantial changes in U.S. policy in Vietnam. The state-building objectives, though reduced in emphasis, essentially remained in place, while the preferred solution to a range of problems relied increasingly upon military technology and firepower. During the brief period, U.S. troop levels expanded from less than one thousand to more than sixteen thousand; the military forces supporting the regime in Saigon expanded to a combined total of more than two hundred thousand. In part reflecting this shift, U.S. direct military assistance grew from less than $80 million to more than $275 million, while economic aid grew from $180 million to $195 million for the period.[72] The MSUG was effectively fired; the Civil Guard continued to expand after gaining the direct support of the USOM and was coupled with a range of paramilitary forces supporting the regime; the revolution expanded the number of insurgents as well as its own fighting capability, as each side fought an increasingly violent and large-scale battle for control of the people and territory of southern Vietnam.

The important shift in the U.S. role in the state-building effort during this period turned out to be a useful indicator of future trends. The U.S. share of subsidization and financial support for the Vietnamese economy had grown from approximately 25 to 30 percent to well over 60 percent. The share of U.S. direct supplied commodities grew from 18 to more than 45 percent for the same period. The aid program now included military aid, direct and indirect commodity aid, currency support mechanisms, piaster purchases, and Public Law 480 (PL-480 or Food for Peace) agricultural support.[73]

---

[72] Dacy, *Foreign Aid*, 200.
[73] USOM, *Annual Report for 1962*, 33.

APPENDIX I. *Simplified Balance of Payments, 1964–1968 (US$, in millions)*

	1964	1965	1966	1967	1968
A. Balance of trade					
1. Exports	49	40	25	22	16
2. Commercial imports	−233	−288	−572	−635	−548
Balance of trade	−184	−248	−547	−613	−532
B. U.S. support					
1. U.S. aid	139	203	335	347	239
[CIP]	[105]	[155]	[259]	[194]	[101]
[PL 480 Title I]	[34]	[48]	[76]	[153]	[138]
2. U.S. piaster purchases	15	126	333	327	301
[Official]	[8]	[94]	[233]	[212]	[246]
[Personal]	[7]	[32]	[100]	[115]	[55]
Total U.S. support	154	329	668	674	540
C. Net invisibles and other	−11	−41	17	−46	−3
D. Change in GVN reserves from operations	−41	40	138	15	15

Source: U.S. Agency for International Development, *United States Economic Assistance to South Vietnam, 1945–1975*, vol. I (Washington, DC: U.S. Agency for International Development, 1975), 133.

APPENDIX II. *U.S. Economic and Military Assistance to South Vietnam by Fiscal Year, 1955–1975 (US$, in millions)*

Fiscal Year	AID	PL-480	Piaster Subsidy	Total Economic Aid	Military Assistance	Total Assistance
1955	320.2	2.2		322.4		322.4
1956	195.7	14.3		210	176.5	386.5
1957	259.4	22.8		282.2	119.8	402
1958	179.4	9.6		189	79.3	268.3
1959	200.9	6.5		207.4	52.4	259.8
1960	170.6	11.3		181.9	72.7	254.6
1961	140.5	11.5		152	71	223
1962	124.1	31.9		156	237.2	393.2
1963	143.3	52.6		195.9	275.9	471.8
1964	165.7	59.1	5.8	230.6	190.9	421.5
1965	225	49.9	15.4	290.3	318.6	608.9
1966	593.5	143	57.4	793.9	686.2	1480.1
1967	494.4	73.7	98.5	666.6	662.5	1329.1
1968	398.2	138.5	114.4	651.1	1243.4	1894.5
1969	314.2	99.4	146.9	560.5	1534	2094.5
1970	365.9	110.8	178.7	655.4	1577.3	2232.7
1971	387.7	188	202.3	778	1945.6	2723.6
1972	386.8	67.8	133.1	587.7	2602.6	3190.3
1973	313.3	188.3	29.5	531.1	3349.4	3880.5
1974	384.3	269.9	3.2	657.4	941.9	1599.3
1975	191.3	49.6		240.9	625.1	866
Total	5954.4	1600.7	985.2	8540.3	16762.3	25302.6

APPENDIX III. *South Vietnam Trade Deficit, 1956–1974*
(US$, in millions)

Year	Trade Deficit	Exports as Percentage of Imports	Deficit as Percentage of National Income
1956	172.5	21	18
1957	208.2	28	20
1958	176.9	24	16
1959	149.5	33	13
1960	155.5	35	13
1961	189.8	27	16
1962	219.4	20	18
1963	238.7	24	19
1964	278.2	15	20
1965	352.2	9	23
1966	579.6	5	36
1967	727.6	2	38
1968	695.8	2	36
1969	825.8	1	34
1970	703.6	2	28
1971	692.6	2	27
1972	730	2	29
1973	710.5	8	25
1974	802.1	10	23

Source: Douglas C. Dacy, *Foreign Aid, War, and Economic Development: South Vietnam, 1955–1975* (New York: Cambridge University Press, 1986), 83.

6

A PERIOD OF SHAKEDOWN:
SOUTHERN VIETNAM,
1963–1965

Shortly following his presidency, Lyndon Johnson wrote, "As for nation-building, . . . I thought the Vietnamese, Thai, and other peoples of Asia knew far better than we did what sort of nations they wanted to build. We should not be too critical if they did not become thriving, modern, twentieth century democracies in a week."[1] This statement sounds very much like those of others in the government whose faith in the project in Vietnam waxed and waned over the years. Lyndon Johnson was no different, given his penchant for involving government in reforming and transforming the lives of ordinary people within the United States. The statement is also, however, somewhat disingenuous. If Lyndon Johnson had truly believed what he later wrote, he would not have chosen to wage war in Vietnam in 1965. The fact is Johnson, like a number of others before him, had grown weary and disenchanted with the effort to build the new Vietnam. As he discovered during his tenure as president, bringing the heavy hand of the federal government to bear on remaking traditional and former colonial societies often met with less than total triumph. Finding little success in piecing together a developed state, American policy makers had much earlier begun to rely less and less on economic development and modernization initiatives and more on the tried-and-true use of military force.

As the new president learned during that first year of his stewardship of Vietnam policy, the situation defied easy solution. Consequently, during his administration, Lyndon Johnson followed two parallel paths in Vietnam: promises of modernization through such development

[1] Lyndon Baines Johnson, *The Vantage Point: Perspectives of the Presidency, 1963–1969* (New York: Holt, Rinehart & Winston, 1971), 44.

initiatives as the Mekong Delta project, coupled with greater overt military force and large-scale infrastructure projects to defeat "enemies." As will become clear, the former ideas and rhetoric, when introduced at all, had less to do with earlier state-building initiatives and more to do with the politics of waging war. During the period from late 1963 until the end of 1965, the Johnson administration struggled to define its goals and objectives in Vietnam under even more dire circumstances than had its predecessors. The range of options narrowed as the political base in Saigon crumbled. Eventually settling on full-scale war as the only alternative to withdrawal, the administration went on to invent its own Vietnam through the implementation of the largest infrastructure building effort yet undertaken in Vietnam.

"STABLE GOVERNMENT OR NO STABLE GOVERNMENT": RESCUING SOUTHERN VIETNAM FROM THE VIETNAMESE

As Lyndon Johnson assumed the presidency in late 1963, he also assumed responsibility for a fundamentally unstable client regime in Saigon. On November 24, 1963, two days following the assassination of John Kennedy, Johnson received a briefing on the situation in Vietnam. The presentations left little doubt that the project he had just inherited was precarious and could easily deteriorate over the next handful of weeks.

Before year's end, the new president received a veritable avalanche of news, most of it bad, from Vietnam. The Central Intelligence Agency (CIA) reported dramatic increases in "enemy activities," in which the Viet Cong (VC) numbered into the several hundreds. Other reports believed the VC capable of one-thousand-man operations following a string of successful attacks on several installations. The insurgents had also begun to attack aircraft with effect and now possessed the "capability for sustaining a high level of activity over a period of time spanning several weeks." Whatever effect the strategic hamlet program once had among the rural populace, it, too, lay in ruins, with the majority of hamlets in the delta either being overrun or abandoned. Attacks on hamlets actually decreased largely because there remained "few worth attacking," according to a U.S. Operations Mission (USOM) report. Another analysis from the field concluded that "the Viet Cong by and large retain de facto control of the countryside and have steadily increased

the overall intensity of the war." A better trained, equipped, and numer-
ically expanded enemy now attacked, and even altered the intensity of
combat operations at will.[2] The revolution and the insurgency built up
around it had developed into a broad-based, popular, highly organized
and effective resistance force during the previous few years.

Defense Secretary McNamara's own late-December report confirmed
a dire situation. The report concluded "that the situation has in fact
been deteriorating in the countryside since July to a far greater extent
than we realized," and "current trends, unless reversed in the next two
or three months, will lead to neutralization at best and more likely to
a communist-controlled state."[3] The American ambassador followed
this gloomy assessment with one of his own in January, writing, "We
are . . . just now beginning to see the full extent of the dry rot and las-
situde in the Government of Viet-Nam," and, deflecting criticism away
from the United States, "the extent to which we were given inaccurate
information."[4]

The post-Diem Saigon leadership, a military junta known as the Military Revolutionary Council (MRC) and led by Duong Van Minh, was
shoved aside in January and replaced by another military figure, Nguyen
Khanh. This latest change also seemed to have little impact. Reports
out of Vietnam in the following weeks expressed a palpable sense of
urgency to turn things around and of frustration that Khanh had so

---

[2] *CIA Information Report*, 2 December; Report from COMUSMACV to Washington,
4 December; Report from DIA/CIIC to CINCPAC, 11 December 1963, NSF, CF, VN,
box 1, Lyndon Baines Johnson Library (LBJL). Telegram from the Embassy in Vietnam
to the Department of State, December 7, 1963, in *Foreign Relations of the United States*,
vol. IV (Washington, DC: GPO, 1961–1963), 687–89; hereinafter *FRUS*. *The Pentagon
Papers: The Defense Department History of United States Decisionmaking on Vietnam*,
Senator Gravel ed., vol. III (Boston: Beacon Press, 1971), 28–29; hereinafter *PP*. See also
Telegram from the Joint Chiefs of Staff to the Commander in Chief, Pacific (Felt), Decem-
ber 2, 1963, *FRUS*, 1961–1963, IV:653. For detailed data on deterioration in the coun-
tryside, province by province, throughout the year, see *Quarterly Evaluation*, October–
December 1963, February 3, 1963, NSF, CF, VN, box 2, LBJL, 30–50, and Annex X,
Province Rehabilitation.

[3] Memorandum for the President from Secretary of Defense McNamara, 21 December
1963, NSF, CF, VN, box 1, LBJL. See also "Highlights of Discussions in Saigon 18–20
December 1963" and Office of Secretary of Defense to CINCPAC, 21 December 1963,
both in *PP*, III:31–32, 494–96. Johnson, *Vantage Point*, 62–63. A detailed, quarterly summary draws similar conclusions; see *Quarterly Evaluation*, October–December 1963, NSF,
CF, VN, box 2 (1 of 2), LBJL.

[4] Message from the Ambassador in Vietnam (Lodge) to the President, January 1, 1964,
FRUS, 1964, I:1.

far failed really to accomplish anything. The CIA found that since the Khanh coup, the situation had "steadily deteriorated," and the insurgents opposed to the regime "retain[ed] the initiative." From February through March, the insurgents gained ground and, with it, popularity among the peasants. Officials decried the absence of an "atmosphere of hopefulness" surrounding their own efforts, while the insurgents seemed to be creating such an atmosphere around theirs. The authorities in Saigon had no reach beyond that city, and instability reigned, as Vietnamese military officers assigned to command large areas of southern Vietnam now were rotated in and out too frequently. Thua Thien Province had seen five different chiefs since the previous summer; Da Nang had gone through the same number of police chiefs. Of forty-one province chiefs overall, thirty-five were replaced following the November coup. Almost all military commands changed as well, all while American military advisors worked feverishly to prevent the "virtual collapse of administration," and Khanh worked at "reorganizing his government and trying to improve its image." Secretary McNamara's fact finding trip in March confirmed the news, and he lamented that the "greatest weakness in the present situation" was the Khanh regime itself.[5] There still existed no government with the staying power, legitimacy, or political infrastructure necessary to realize the objectives sought over the previous decade by the United States.

Throughout spring and summer 1964, the Johnson administration devoted gradually increasing amounts of energy and time to reverse some of these troubling trends. Officials struggled to paste together a regime stable enough to carry the "war" to the insurgents. The objectives were not grandiose at this point. The president and his advisors pinned their hopes on greater military preparedness, increased engagement with the "enemy," and the willingness of Khanh to carry out a range of new programs. The president ordered Ambassador Lodge to

[5] Appraisal of the Conduct of the War in Vietnam, February 10, 1964, NSF, CF, VN, box 2 (1 of 2), LBJL; "Further Comments [material deleted] on the Situation in Vietnam," February 10, 1964, NSF, CF, VN, box 2 (1 of 2), LBJL; "Appraisal of the Situation in Vietnam," February 14, 1964, NSF, CF, VN, box 2 (2 of 2), LBJL; *South Vietnam Situation Report* (14–20 February 1964), NSF, CF, VN, box 2 (2 of 2), LBJL; "The Situation in South Vietnam (28 February–6 March 1964)," March 6, 1964, NSF, CF, VN, box 2 (2 of 2), LBJL. Memorandum for the President, 16 March 1964, *PP*, III:499–510 and 46–50.

vigorously stamp out all talk of neutralism "wherever it rears its ugly head... I think that nothing is more important than to stop neutralist talk wherever we can by whatever means we can."[6] Of course, they knew it increasingly reared its ugly head among the very Vietnamese for whose beneficence the Americans carried out all the assistance and aid.

In late August, Khanh became critically unstable and complained of high blood pressure and hemorrhoids, tendered his resignation, and dissolved the MRC. Leaving Saigon nearly consumed in violence and riots, he retreated north to Da Lat, where now Ambassador Taylor found him "practically a mental case" but managed to convince him to return.[7] Over the next several months, the political situation in Saigon deteriorated, and the president himself became nearly obsessed with the need for a stable government as the basis for any future action. At a December meeting with his top advisors, Johnson hammered away at the theme, insisting on the need for "stable government" at least eight times during the two-hour conversation.[8] Nevertheless, the decay in Saigon continued unabated. Following a failed coup in mid-September, the regime changed hands numerous times from November through January, until finally, the Americans aided in a final coup that brought Khanh's mercurial rule to an end in late February 1965.

By February, there had been more than a half dozen regime changes since the fall of Diem. Ambassador Taylor in particular grew increasingly frustrated and less certain that the project could be rescued at all. In the midst of this political collapse, he found it "impossible to foresee a stable and effective government under any name in anything like the near future."[9] Additionally, anti-American demonstrations had become almost commonplace, with episodes in Hué, Da Nang, Qui Nhon, and Nha Trang signaling a growing antipathy toward the increasing American presence and toward the regime's representatives. A CIA

---

[6] Message from the President to the Ambassador in Vietnam (Lodge), March 20, 1964, *FRUS*, 1964, I:184–85.

[7] Telegram from the Embassy in Vietnam to the Department of State, August 28, 1964, *FRUS*, 1964, I:717, and Telegram from the Embassy in Vietnam to the Department of State, August 31, 1964, *FRUS*, 1964, I:719. Stanley Karnow, *Vietnam: A History* (New York: Penguin Books, 1997), 395.

[8] John McNaughton Meeting Notes, December 1, 1964, LBJL.

[9] Robert Buzzanco, *Masters of War: Military Dissent & Politics in the Vietnam Era* (New York: Cambridge University Press, 1996), 177.

report found Saigon "almost leaderless" and the regime's apparatus in the countryside "near paralysis."[10] Meanwhile, the insurgents launched ever more audacious attacks. On October 31, the Bien Hoa air base came under an attack, which killed four and wounded thirty Americans, and on Christmas Eve, the insurgents hit the Brinks Hotel in the heart of Saigon, which served as a barracks for American military officers. This attack killed two and wounded thirty-eight.

Shortly before Khanh's final removal in late February, the opposition again attacked, this time an American air base at Pleiku in the Central Highlands of Vietnam, killing 9, injuring another 126, and damaging or destroying over twenty aircraft. This attack led directly to escalation and the Americanization of the whole effort that had been in planning stages for months. U.S. aircraft immediately began bombing territory north of the seventeenth parallel.[11] By early 1965, the United States embarked upon the course of Americanization in its pursuit of a military victory in Southeast Asia.

During these months, the political base, such that it was even in the best of times, atrophied. What remained could not be called a national government, but rather, a collection of competitive, ambitious, insecure, and war-weary men, whose internecine bickering occupied most of their energies. Administration officials were keenly aware of this problem, and the record is replete with their complaints, criticisms, and ruminations about alternatives.[12] When National Security Advisor McGeorge Bundy and McNamara bluntly informed the president in late January that the current policy could lead only "to disastrous defeat," Johnson responded, "stable government or no stable government, we'll do what

---

[10] Special National Intelligence Estimate, October 1, 1964, *FRUS*, 1964, I:806–11.

[11] *PP*, III:286–87.

[12] Alternatives were troubling, and the president struggled with the implications. In an early December meeting, he repeatedly admonished those present that the most important thing prior to moving against the north was a stable government in the south, or, as he put it, you could not "send [a] widow woman to slap Jack Dempsey." Though he and others recognized the lack of anything of substance in the south, they never directly dealt with the implications of this fact. See source in note 8. See also *FRUS*, 1964, I:965–69. The *PP* authors refer to 1964 as a year of "almost uninterrupted political upheaval in Saigon"; see *PP*, III:287, 292–94. Telegram from the Embassy in Vietnam to the Department of State, September 6, 1964, *FRUS*, 1964, I:733–36. Special National Intelligence Estimate, September 8, 1964, "Chances for a Stable Government in South Vietnam," *FRUS*, 1964, I:742–46. Instructions from the President to the Ambassador to Vietnam (Taylor), December 3, 1964, *FRUS*, 1964, I:974–78.

we ought to do. I'm prepared to do that. *We will move strongly.*"[13] In subsequent days and weeks, and following the Pleiku incident in particular, the president did just that. The administration had thus made the decision to pursue an expanded military agenda in southern Vietnam without a government in place. What had been the *raison d'être* for the entire project from 1954 was now jettisoned. Although the president and others at this point recognized there was no political apparatus on which to construct a new state, they proceeded anyway. The United States, and the administration of Lyndon Johnson in particular, soon set about reinventing Vietnam through a construction effort and subsequent military buildup of unprecedented scope.

Escalation, and ultimately Americanization, would be no mean task. The limited role of the United States up to this point had meant the development of only that infrastructure deemed necessary to connect Saigon to the provinces and to facilitate defense by the forces supporting the regime. That would prove inadequate if the United States was to bring the full weight of its military power to bear on the situation. Having been in the planning stages for months, military and civilian engineers and logistics specialists recognized this basic obstacle right away. Transportation infrastructure in southern Vietnam in particular remained essentially undeveloped. Only about one-third of an already meager railway system functioned. Much would need to be done, and it would need to be done quickly. A number of these decisions had already been taken in the intervening months since August 1964. By early 1965, a massive construction effort was already rapidly transforming southern Vietnam.

"THE CONSTRUCTION MIRACLE OF THE DECADE": THE MILITARY BUILDUP AND INVENTING VIETNAM

By the time the Johnson administration decided to escalate the war, the U.S. mission had already outstripped the capacity of southern Vietnam to receive it. Infrastructure was insecure, inadequate, or nonexistent. Significant portions of the road network became at times unusable due

[13] Memorandum for the President: Basic Policy in Vietnam, January 27, 1965, NSF, Memos to the President, McGeorge Bundy, box 2, LBJL. McGeorge Bundy meeting notes, January 27, 1965, McGeorge Bundy Papers, Notes on Vietnam, 1964–1965, LBJL. Emphasis in original.

to lack of security, decay, and war damage, or some combination of these. A memorandum prepared for McNamara in early spring lamented continued political decay and suggested the regime's control in the countryside had been reduced to small enclaves, preventing the regime and the Americans from reaching out into the provinces in a meaningful way. By all accounts, the administration faced a crossroads in its policy toward Vietnam by early 1965: either allow for complete collapse of the project and withdraw the United States from the situation, or undertake an American military takeover and an attempt to prevent what nearly everyone viewed as imminent.[14] The latter course, the one chosen, would mean a considerable investment beyond just large numbers of troops. It would also mean a commitment to establish a vast physical infrastructure – to remake southern Vietnam, again.

All of southern Vietnam had only three airfields capable of landing jet aircraft. Its national airline, 75 percent government owned, consisted of twelve aircraft, none of which was jet propelled.[15] Tan Son Nhut, the Saigon airfield serving as the principal hub, received some of the military aid but could not begin to keep pace with the flood of materiel. Of all the supplies destined for southern Vietnam, over 90 percent arrived by sea. Consequently, the increased volume of military hardware and Commodity Import Program (CIP) goods created significant port congestion. Saigon, in fact, was one of only two ports with deep draft berthing. Other port facilities, such as those at Da Nang, Nha Trang, and Hué, remained woefully inadequate. Over the next year, almost half of all military cargo and 90 percent of all Agency for International Development (AID) cargo passed through the port at Saigon. The congestion became infamous as ships and barges often waited a period of weeks

---

[14] George M. Kahin, *Intervention: How America Became Involved in Vietnam* (New York: Anchor Books, 1987), 310–11. At the same time, McNamara aid John McNaughton ranked the factors calling for greater American intervention in the following order: 70 percent, "to avoid a humiliating defeat," 20 percent, to keep the territory out of "Chinese hands," and only 10 percent, to "permit the people...to enjoy a better, freer way of life." Paper prepared by the Assistant Secretary of Defense for International Security Affairs (McNaughton), March 10, 1965, *FRUS*, 1965, II:427–32. See also *PP*, III:423–26, for a general assessment of the situation in southern Vietnam.

[15] AID Administrative History, LBJL, 424. U.S.AID, *U.S. Economic Assistance to South Vietnam, 1945–1975 (USEASV)*, II:408. Carroll H. Dunn, *Base Development in South Vietnam, 1965–1970* (Washington, DC: Department of the Army, 1972), 7–12.

or months for dock space to offload. As of early 1965, despite years of economic aid and infrastructure development, southern Vietnam still lacked anything like an integrated, modern, national infrastructure. In past years, though recognized periodically as an obstacle, this under-developed infrastructure was not nearly the problem it soon became. A congressional team explained the importance of the port situation following a series of investigative trips there in 1966: "Vietnamese port capacity is the chief factor bearing on the amount of assistance – both military and economic – that the United States is physically capable of providing to Vietnam."[16]

Significantly escalating the American presence in Vietnam thus required substantial physical development. The needed construction would quickly dwarf that which had come before. Dozens of engineers and construction teams had been at work building up that infrastructure since the late 1950s. They had built new, or had refurbished, canals, roads and bridges, residential areas, hospitals, port facilities, and air-fields. Beginning in 1962, much of this work was handed over to a consortium of private American construction corporations made up of Raymond International and Morrison-Knudsen (RMK). The work had been somewhat limited, however, by the limited nature of American involvement. Those placed in charge of various building projects assumed the work would be completed in only a few years. The pace of new projects seemed to confirm this as orders trailed off throughout the first half of 1964. In August, however, this trend was reversed as a series of new orders began to arrive at the offices of RMK.[17]

Originally contracted for around $15 million in construction work, RMK saw its responsibilities expand dramatically from late 1964 into

---

[16] U.S. Congress, *An Investigation of the U.S. Economic and Military Assistance Programs in Vietnam, October 12, 1966*, 89th Cong., 2nd sess., 1966, 64. See also Memorandum for Mr. Robert Komer, Subject: Report of Special Mission – Port of Saigon, Vietnam, June 14, 1966, NSF, Komer-Leonhart File, box 20, LBJL.

[17] A. H. Lahlum, *Diary of a Contract*, Saigon, July 1967, *RMK-BRJ Papers*, 22. Originally, the private consortium consisted of Raymond International and Morrison-Knudsen. In August 1965, Brown and Root and J. A. Jones Construction were both added to gain greater reach and access to greater resources commensurate with an expanded American military role and related construction needs in Vietnam. All documents referred to as *RMK-BRJ Papers* were obtained from the companies involved and came in no discernable order or arrangement. They are all in the author's possession.

early 1965.[18] By spring, construction allocations had soared to over $150 million, and RMK could hardly keep pace.[19] Because so much of the work had to be completed prior to escalation, the consortium knew of the imminent American expansion well before most others. At the same time, the scale of the work, the pace of the projects, and the funds allocated provided some early indication of things to come. Congress granted the administration $700 million in supplementary military spending for Vietnam in 1965, and $100 million was earmarked for construction. These projects quickly spread across much of southern Vietnam and involved ports, ammunition dumps, airfields, radio installations, refugee camps, barracks, fuel depots, hospitals, and warehouses. By May, the consortium had more than doubled its workforce from the 1964 level, hiring several hundred American construction workers and eleven thousand Vietnamese, mostly as nonskilled laborers.[20] Several months later, the orders still ran far ahead of the capacity of RMK alone. One exasperated MK official explained, "All we knew was that they wanted a lotta roads, a lotta airfields, a lotta bridges, and a lotta ports, and that they probably would want it all finished by yesterday."[21] In early August, RMK brought on board two other large American construction firms, Brown and Root and J. A. Jones Construction (BRJ), to form the RMK-BRJ. This consortium became the sole contractor for the federal government for construction projects in Vietnam. The U.S. Army, the navy's Seabees, and the air force's Base Engineering Emergency Forces (BEEF) construction units also played a role,

---

[18] Contract No. NBy-44105, "Raymond-Morrison-Knudsen Joint Venture Contractor for Airfields and Communications Facilities, Vietnam," U.S. Navy Bureau of Yards and Docks, January 19, 1962, *RMK-BRJ Papers*.

[19] "Military Construction in South Vietnam," *The Em-Kayan*, November 1963, 8–9, *RMK-BRJ Papers*. Captain Charles J. Merdinger, "Civil Engineers, Seabees, and Bases in Vietnam," *U.S. Naval Institute Proceedings*, no. 807 (May 1970): 261. The rate of work taking place was measured on a WIP basis. At the end of 1964, the WIP figure stood at $1.7 million. By the next spring, it had leapt to over $4 million. As plans for expansion continued, the amount of work expanded to an eventual peak of more than $65 million WIP.

[20] The Vietnamese workforce was increased from forty-nine hundred to eleven thousand, a leap of nearly 125 percent. As of April 1965, according to the *Diary of a Contract*, "every day some new and bigger phase of work was received and no diminishing of this trend was foreseen," *RMK-BRJ Papers*, 27–28. "Work Increases as War Expands," *Engineering News-Record*, May 13, 1965, 25–28. "Construction Expands in South Viet Nam," *The Em-Kayan*, June 1965, 7, *RMK-BRJ Papers*.

[21] John Mecklin, "Building by the Billion in Vietnam," *Fortune*, September 1966, 114.

but the RMK-BRJ accounted for the lion's share of all work, or about 90 percent of the total.[22] The RMK-BRJ negotiated a cost-plus-fixed-fee contract via the U.S. Navy and sped up work on an array of construction projects aimed to quickly prepare Vietnam below the seventeenth parallel for a major U.S. military presence.[23]

Quickly ramping up the direct American role accelerated the need for more projects. Once completed, a given project, such as barracks or warehouse space, was often quickly inundated, and more became necessary. In some instances, projects had to be expanded even before completion. In early March, the first contingent of combat troops, two Marine battalions, waded ashore at Da Nang officially to guard the air base there. More troop deployments soon followed. As it became clear that the Rolling Thunder bombing campaign had little effect on Vietnamese leaders in Hanoi and even less impact in the south, the White House authorized U.S. ground forces to engage in offensive operations.[24] Administration officials then recommended increasing U.S. troop strength by forty thousand following a hastily convened Honolulu conference in late April.[25] The period from July to December saw the greatest increase as the United States sent approximately 150,000 soldiers to Vietnam. By the end of the year, the troop total stood at 184,000, up from just 23,000 a year earlier.[26] A week prior to the March

[22] Letter from MK to Raymond Intl., Brown & Root and J. A. Jones, "Joint Venture Agreement," August 16, 1965; Letter from Lyman Wilbur (Morrison-Knudsen) to H. C. Boschen (Raymond International, Inc.), August 25, 1965, both in *RMK-BRJ Papers*. Carroll Dunn, *Base Development*, 27. Lieutenant David L. Browne, "Dust and Mud and the Viet Cong," *U.S. Naval Institute Proceedings*, no. 811 (September 1970): 53–57. Commander W. D. Middleton, "Seabees in Vietnam," *U.S. Naval Institute Proceedings*, no. 774 (August 1967): 55–64, 60.

[23] The contract was converted to a cost-plus-award-fee-type arrangement in late spring 1966. Supplemental Agreement No. 3 to Contract NBy 44105, May 25, 1966, *RMK-BRJ Papers*.

[24] NSAM-328, April 6, 1965, *FRUS*, 1965, II:537–39. *PP*, III:447–48.

[25] *PP*, III:436–40, 705–6. Buzzanco, *Masters of War*, 207. Larry Berman, *Planning a Tragedy: The Americanization of the War in Vietnam* (New York: W. W. Norton, 1982), 58–62.

[26] These troop increases were not, of course, without controversy and heated debate among the principals. The president, in particular, recognized that sending large numbers of American troops to Vietnam early in the year would certainly highlight changes in policy that he was keen to keep quiet, and would also serve as a lightning rod for critics in Congress whose support was being carefully cultivated during these weeks and months. See *PP*, III:330–32, 354. Randall Bennett Woods, *Fulbright: A Biography* (New York: Cambridge University Press, 1995), chap. 19. At least one of the utilitarian aspects of awarding private contractors the lion's share of responsibility for all construction in

deployment at Da Nang, Secretary McNamara had assured the military brass that there was an "unlimited appropriation" to meet the military requirements in Vietnam. A large part of that appropriation came, as it would in subsequent years, in supplemental military spending packages approved by Congress in May and again in August.[27] During these weeks, events moved with great speed, which accelerated the construction needs exponentially. Once landed, these troops needed a support network, including bases, supply lines, equipment, maintenance and repair facilities, messing and quartering facilities, water and sewage systems, power plants, and a communications network. The administration could only escalate the war in Vietnam as fast as an infrastructure to receive the influx could be built.[28]

Vietnam was that the considerable labor requirements would be met by Vietnamese and not by additional U.S. engineer forces. The RMK-BRJ employed a workforce, at the peak of construction, of over fifty thousand. Most of these were Vietnamese. Because of high turnover, the consortium employed overall an estimated 180,000 to 200,000 on its construction projects. To have relied on military construction units for the needs in building up southern Vietnam would have meant significantly larger deployments, and much earlier. See *Jones Construction Centennial: Looking Back, Moving Forward* (Charlotte: Laney-Smith, 1989), 154. See also Dunn, *Base Development*, 132. See also Senior Officers Oral History Program, Jean E. Engler, Lt. General, USA Retired, interviewed by Phillip G. Shepard, 1981, Jean E. Engler Papers, box 1 of 3, Military History Institute, Carlisle, PA.

[27] McNamara continued in this memorandum, "Under no circumstances is lack of money to stand in the way of aid to that nation." Each year, beginning in 1965, McNamara went before Congress to ask for military spending supplements for Vietnam. Through this device, much of the increased spending on Vietnam could be kept off the official budget and thus beyond public and congressional scrutiny. Leonard B. Taylor, *Financial Management of the Vietnam Conflict, 1962–1972* (Washington, DC: Department of the Army, 1974), 17–19. See also *PP*, III:474–75. U.S. Congress, Committee on Armed Services, "Supplemental Military Procurement and Construction Authorizations, Fiscal Year 1966," 89th Cong., 2nd sess., 1966.

[28] Interestingly, Hanoi officials and their Chinese allies had already anticipated these latest moves on the part of the United States. Hanoi asked for Chinese aid in building its own infrastructure in preparation for war. The Chinese assented, sending dozens of thousands of engineering troops into northern Vietnam during early to mid-1965. They began immediately building roads, bridges, and base areas. By the time the last of these Chinese units left northern Vietnam in summer 1970, they had completed hundreds of miles of new railway and repaired hundreds of miles of old lines, built dozens of bridges and tunnels, and established many new railway stations. Despite such aid, North Vietnam kept its Chinese benefactors at arm's length. The key difference in the relationship, according to historian Chen Jian, was that "Communist North Vietnam was a much more mature, independent, and self-confident international actor than the Viet Minh had been during the First Indochina War." Chen Jian, *Mao's China and the Cold War* (Chapel Hill: University of North Carolina Press, 2001), 221–23.

Historian John Prados has estimated that each U.S. soldier required fifty pounds of supplies a day when in the field. At this rate, the 184,000 troops in Vietnam by the end of 1965 required 138,000 tons of supplies per month. When the Vietnamese military forces being supplied and trained by the Americans are added, the overall figure jumps to more than 285,000 tons of supplies per month. This quantity far exceeded the entire port capacity of southern Vietnam.[29] These estimates only account for a relatively small percentage of the total supply volume required for the kind of escalated role now being planned and implemented. CIP goods for 1965, for example, had grown to $150 million, while total aid swelled to nearly $350 million.[30] Not counted in these numbers are additional military materiel requirements, which reached 650,000 tons per month in 1966. Throughout the year, AID commodities and war materiel continued to flood into Vietnamese ports and airfields, to fill up docks and consume all available warehouse space. Airfields, too, experienced sharp increases in the flow of goods. Traffic increased at Saigon's Tan Son Nhut airfield by 200 percent in just over a year, giving the airport a heavier traffic load than Los Angeles International. Air traffic at the Da Nang facility increased 5,000 percent from 1961, while Ban Me Thuot saw a 500 percent increase, and Hué, 300 percent.[31] Ship and barge traffic piled up while waiting offloading. By November 1965, 122 ships laden with goods sat idle, unable to find dock space.[32] An ad hoc construction program simply would not meet the tremendous needs. Something more systematic would be needed.

Military planners quickly pieced together a model for the development of a modern, integrated military infrastructure to encompass all of southern Vietnam. The plan called for heavy port construction at Da Nang, Qui Nhon, Cam Ranh Bay, and Saigon. These ports, once substantially developed, would form the keystones of the base development

---

[29] John Prados, "The Parameters of Victory," in *The Hidden History of the Vietnam War* (Chicago: Ivan R. Dee, 1995), 102–10.

[30] This figure excludes military aid and allocations for the military construction program. It includes the CIP, Food for Peace Program, Project Aid, and the cost of piaster purchases. See AID, *United States Economic Assistance to South Viet Nam, 1954–1975, Terminal Report*, December 31, 1975.

[31] "U.S. Ally in Vietnam: Civil Works," *Engineering News-Record*, May 5, 1966, 15–17.

[32] "Construction Escalates in Vietnam," *Engineering News-Record*, February 3, 1966, 11–14. Prados, *Hidden History*, 108.

plan and the centers of what eventually became semiautonomous logistical enclaves. These three port areas, complete with major air bases, would receive troops and supplies and then feed both into the interior and to smaller ports all along the coast. In mid-1965, and aside from these coastal facilities, the U.S. military had no way to deliver the expanding volume of supplies into the southern Vietnamese interior. There simply was no system as such extending into the countryside capable of delivering goods on anything like the scale rapidly becoming necessary. At the same time, they realized that however grandiose their initial planning, it would not begin to accommodate the forces and equipment requirements being assembled in the coming months. These basic plans were revised and expanded almost constantly over the next two years. The result would be an immense grid complex of airfields, bases, ports, canals, ammunition depots, military hospitals, dumps, warehouses, and light industry for military production, all woven together to form a kind of military "matrix." Needed supplies and materiel of all kinds could simply be plugged in to the system at any point and conveyed to any other point along the grid. Airfields, both large and small, would dot the landscape as well. The plan was to have no spot anywhere in southern Vietnam more than fifteen miles from an airfield, and airfields would have ready access to other larger airfields and/or the system of ports.[33]

By late 1965 and into early 1966, the transformation of southern Vietnam was well under way. The builders completed or neared completion on a number of projects at Cam Ranh, Da Nang, Qui Nhon, Pleiku, and Chu Lai and farther south at Vung Tau, Bien Hoa, Soc Trang, and Saigon. Projects were under way at dozens of construction sites simultaneously to assemble all of the pieces of the larger grid and get it up and functioning to relieve massive congestion and allow for the assembly of even greater forces and related materiel.[34] At Saigon, planners decided on a brand-new facility just upstream from the existing pier. The new, deep-draft facility would consist of multiple deep-draft berths and receive military cargo exclusively. Traffic teemed at numerous lesser ports all over southern Vietnam.[35] Hundreds of thousands of square

[33] Dunn, *Base Development*, 38–40, 63.
[34] *Diary of a Contract*, 91–122, *RMK-BRJ Papers*.
[35] "Vietnam – Paradox of Construction and Destruction," *Power Parade* 20, no. 2 (1967): 6. For a listing of the "nine principal ports" in southern Vietnam and estimated capacity

feet of new warehouses overflowed with goods, and more space was hurriedly being built. Numerous airfields, some that had only recently come into existence at all, now accommodated hundreds of flights daily, and others were in various stages of construction. An extensive road-building program was also under way, involving hundreds of miles of new and refurbished roadways linking towns along the coast to each other and to the interior. Whole new industries sprang to life, as the American construction program devoured massive quantities of cement, crushed rock, sediment, and landfill to construct the large bases. The U.S. military acquired tens of thousands of acres of land on which to build these facilities and to establish rock quarries, uncovered storage, staging areas, and rights-of-way. At year's end, the consortium's workload had expanded by 600 percent, and the value of the construction project more generally by 1,000 percent. In February 1966, the navy's officer in charge of construction (OICC) cautioned, "We've only really begun to fight the construction side of the war."[36]

The RMK-BRJ responded to the demands of war remarkably quickly, organizing hundreds of projects at dozens of sites over the whole of southern Vietnam. Throughout 1965, as the pace of construction work quickened, the consortium embraced its role and grew with these demands by expanding its workforce to more than twenty-four thousand, crowning its executive staff in Saigon with MK's vice president for foreign operations Lyman Wilbur as "resident partner" and acquiring or placing on order $110 million in equipment. Project volume had mushroomed to $12 million of work-in-place per month (WIP). The consortium's executives and engineers continued to marvel at the sheer magnitude of the transformation of southern Vietnam. The scale and pace of the work exceeded anything any one of the companies had ever experienced. The equipment requirements alone in Vietnam surpassed all the equipment owned by MK worldwide, including its subsidiary companies. Executives looked forward to at least another year of growth at or even above the rate achieved so far.[37] They and the navy OICC

---

requirements for each, see Memorandum for the Assistant Secretary of Defense (International Security Affairs), 23 September 1965, NSF, Komer-Leonhart File, box 20, LBJL.

[36] "Construction Escalates in Vietnam," 11.

[37] "Viet Nam: Building for Battle, Building for Peace," *The Em-Kayan*, September 1966, 8–11, *RMK-BRJ Papers. Diary of a Contract*, 77, 87–89, *RMK-BRJ Papers*. H. W. Morrison, "Chairman's Memo: Productive 1965 Is Pacesetter for 1966," *The Em-Kayan*,

had forecast correctly: construction in Vietnam continued to expand exponentially during 1966 and beyond.

There was still no way to guarantee that the sudden development of a vast military infrastructure would mean victory for the United States. On its own, it could not yield an independent Vietnam below the seventeenth parallel. Nor was this the aim; military escalation was not state building, and few believed otherwise. Very few official tours and observation trips involved state-building or economic initiatives as the centerpiece. Instead, military preparedness now occupied the attention of officials back in Washington. A day before Secretary McNamara's visit to the site at Cam Ranh Bay in the first few weeks of the project, Chester Cooper warned an overzealous colonel against mentioning parade grounds and officers clubs soon to be erected at the site and suggested instead that he stick to the military utility of the work in his presentation to the secretary. The colonel, who later thanked Cooper for saving him from "professional suicide," apparently did not understand the seriousness of the escalation being programmed during the late summer and into the fall of that year.[38] McNamara informed the president in late July that the kind of escalation he envisioned to prevent certain and rapid defeat could cost $12 billion through 1966, involve substantially more American combat forces, and require a call-up of reserves.[39] Johnson managed to put off a reserve call-up for a while. But the cost of the project continued to soar along with its rapid Americanization.

The objective now centered on military and, at the same time, diplomatic victory. The credibility of the United States was on the line in Southeast Asia. In large measure, U.S. credibility prevented the full consideration of real alternatives to, as well as the implications for, military escalation in Vietnam.[40] What would the world think, friend and foe, if the United States abandoned its commitments? Not only would it embolden Cold War enemies, officials believed, it would also

May 1966, 1, *RMK-BRJ Papers. 1966 Annual Report, Foreign Operations, RMK-BRJ Papers.* "Construction Escalates in Vietnam," 12.

[38] Chester Cooper, *The Lost Crusade: America in Vietnam* (New York: Dodd, Mead, 1970), 282–83.

[39] See, e.g., the notes of a very interesting and insightful discussion in "Notes of Meeting," July 22, 1965, *FRUS, 1965,* III:209–17. "Supplemental Military Procurement and Construction Authorizations, Fiscal Year 1966," 6–7.

[40] Paper prepared by the Assistant Secretary of Defense for International Security Affairs (McNaughton), March 10, 1965, *FRUS, 1965,* II:427–32.

make friends less than resolute in the global struggle. Even though costly beyond its relative importance to American national security interests and failing, the project in Vietnam continued because American credibility in the Cold War made alternatives unthinkable. A military victory in Southeast Asia certainly would erase all doubts. But such an outcome seemed hopeless, especially in the short term. Administration officials, far too shrewd to place all of their eggs in one basket, extended a carrot around the same time they began overt escalation into war. That carrot, containing a promise of large development aid for the region, might produce a willingness among Hanoi officials to begin talks and allow the United States to move away from the kind of large-scale warfare that at this point seemed imminent. Aside from this aim, it might provide some basis for successfully manipulating the war, or at least perceptions of it.

"THE WORKS OF PEACE":[41] THE MEKONG DELTA AND THE POLITICS OF WAR

That Lyndon Johnson began to consider, and even formally extend, an offer to avoid war in late spring 1965 initially seems at odds with the ramping up of the direct American military role and the related construction of an integrated military infrastructure. At the least, it was very costly and inefficient to put in motion years of construction projects, while seeking an avenue to peace that would make them unnecessary. The offer itself, unveiled during a speech at the Johns Hopkins University shortly after the administration began the Rolling Thunder campaign, was grandiose, visionary, and rather statesman-like for a president who had yet to reveal that side of his foreign policy. Lyndon Johnson remained a committed anticommunist liberal and, like his predecessors, relied on the force of American economic, technological, and military power to project this feature of the nation's foreign policy agenda.[42] In this context, offering officials in Hanoi a peaceful solution

---

[41] "Peace without Conquest," Remarks of the President at the Johns Hopkins University, Baltimore, April 7, 1965, Statements of Lyndon B. Johnson, box 143, LBJL.

[42] Lyndon Johnson's administration soon distinguished itself by a crude invasion of the Dominican Republic in late April in response to the collapse of the Santo Domingo government and allegations of communist machinations to take power there. After Johnson boldly lied to a group of reporters to justify American intervention, McGeorge Bundy justified the president's remarks, saying, "Those weren't lies.... He was building up,

seemed surprising. The offer, however, and the diplomatic move more generally, had in fact been in the offing for quite a long time and only thinly masked motives other than a "peace without conquest."

For some time, the president had been aware of an alternative course for the development of Vietnam. On a visit to Southeast Asia as vice president in 1961, an official with the United Nations (UN) economic commission for Asia introduced him directly to the early stages of a scheme to develop the whole of Southeast Asia using the vast Mekong River. Exposure to the project conjured for Johnson images of his own government developing the back country of the United States, of harnessing the power of nature and putting it to work bettering the lives of the poor. Following the presentation, Johnson offered excitedly that he was "a river man": "All my life I have been interested in rivers and their development."[43] Johnson continued to collect updates and advice from aides and from friends on the project after 1961.

In fall 1963, he received from a close personal friend a letter of advice urging the same kind of solution to the growing crisis in Vietnam. An article attached to the letter discussed the problems of poverty and backwardness related to underdevelopment. The article's author, Arthur Goldschmidt, described a region whose backwardness persisted alongside agricultural abundance; as its raw materials were traded away to bring in much needed finished goods, its people lacked any savings, the region possessed little in the way of a modern infrastructure, and it remained essentially a colony in economic terms. The region thus described was not in Asia, Africa, or Latin America: it was the U.S. South. But the South did not remain mired in it own backwardness and poverty. Conditions there changed dramatically, but only when the federal government reached down and began to pick the South up and develop it. As Goldschmidt compared this change within the American South to the underdeveloped nations of the world, he found in it a good example to be repeated. As he concluded, "The rich nations of the world will have to do for the poor nations what the Federal Government of

'argufying'; he was certainly going beyond the truth, but that's not the same as lying." See Woods, *Fulbright*, 376–82.

[43] Lloyd Gardner, *Pay Any Price: Lyndon Johnson and the Wars for Vietnam* (Chicago: Ivan R. Dee, 1995), 52–53. Nguyen Thi Dieu, *The Mekong River and the Struggle for Indochina: Water, War, and Peace* (Westport, CT: Praeger, 1999), 104.

the U.S. did for the South."[44] Lyndon Johnson agreed with what he had read, answering, "We are in a better position to handle some of the problems of the developing countries because of the problems we faced so recently in developing our own."[45]

Johnson's faith in economic development and in the ability of government to bring it about has been written on extensively elsewhere and forms the very basis of any understanding of his politics. As historian Lloyd Gardner has written, "Johnson's whole career *was* the politics of economic development."[46] As president, his domestic agenda centered on economic uplift for millions of marginalized Americans. Not surprisingly, he carried this vision of the role of government and of combating poverty and ignorance through modernization into other facets of his presidency. In early May 1964, one State Department official recommended to Bundy that the United States move in this direction on Vietnam by "reactivating the Mekong Valley development scheme." Among other benefits, it "would help overcome the backlash features of our actions and ... put us in a far better posture before public opinion." A few weeks later, presidential aide Douglas Cater concurred and suggested the Mekong Project could "provide heartening evidence to the people of that region of a project to bring future bounty rather than bloodshed."[47] Here was an angle the president could appreciate. Not only did the very idea of a vast river development project resonate with him for personal and political reasons, but that it could also serve to blunt criticism of American aggression only enhanced its appeal. Though initially cool to the ideas of modernization and "nation building" in Vietnam, Johnson was ready to include some of these measures, albeit for his own peculiar reasons.

With criticism of Rolling Thunder mounting both at home and abroad, McGeorge Bundy suggested the president deliver a speech that

---

[44] Arthur Goldschmidt, "The Development of the U.S. South," *Scientific American*, 209, no. 3 (1963): 225–32.

[45] Letter to "Dear Tex" from Lyndon Johnson, September 24, 1963, White House Central File (WHCF), Confidential File, box 167, LBJL.

[46] Gardner, *Pay Any Price*, 193, emphasis in original.

[47] Memorandum from Marshall Green to Mr. Bundy, May 29, 1964, NSF, CF, VN, box 53, LBJL, 2–3. Memorandum from Marshall Green to Mr. Bundy, May 30, 1964, NSF, CF, VN, box 53, LBJL. Memorandum to the President, June 9, 1964, NSF, CF, VN, box 53, LBJL.

would explain United States intentions and allay fears that the campaign inaugurated in early March was bombing for bombing's sake. The president agreed, but wanted more. The speech would need to contain a bold statement of America's purpose in Southeast Asia. What was needed, Johnson believed, was the kind of address that would go beyond putting to rest concerns of the use of American power and on to restore faith in America's benevolent intentions. In working out the final details of the address during the latter part of March, presidential aide Jack Valenti inserted a billion-dollar offer of development aid, an offer that dovetailed neatly with Johnson's thinking. Surely such a grand gesture on the part of the administration would give pause to critics everywhere.[48]

On the evening of April 7, 1965, Lyndon Johnson spoke before a television audience at Johns Hopkins University to offer his rationale for recently ramped up American military presence in Vietnam and to tell the world of U.S. intentions to come to the aid of the people of Southeast Asia in a bold new way.[49] In a speech receiving considerable domestic and international attention in the days and weeks that followed,[50] the president suggested the whole area be developed and modernized as an alternative to continued war.

The speech was designed to encourage those in Hanoi to agree to stop warring and to take part in the development of the region, and also to put a good face on the new American measures implemented since February, including sustained aerial bombardment and combat troops. In short, the administration needed to shift responsibility for continued war, particularly that part of the war for which it was responsible, toward Hanoi. The speech characterized the people of Southeast Asia, many millions of them, in the familiar way: "each day these people rise at dawn and struggle through until the night to wrestle existence from the soil. They are often wracked by disease, plagued by hunger, and death comes at the early age of 40." Southeast Asia was indeed a

---

[48] Mr. Valenti's Notes on the Johns Hopkins Speech, Statements of Lyndon B. Johnson, box 143, LBJL.

[49] The television audience was an estimated 60 million. In addition, the administration airdropped the speech over all of Vietnam.

[50] "President Makes Offer to Start Vietnam Talks Unconditionally: Proposes $1 Billion Aid for Asia," *New York Times*, April 8, 1965. "LBJ Offers 'Unconditional' Viet Talks but Stands Firm on U.S. Commitments," *Washington Post*, April 8, 1965. *PP*, III:355–56.

4. President Johnson delivering his "Peace without Conquest" speech at Johns Hopkins University, April 1965.

place of misery. The contrast between their world and that of the developed Western nations could not have seemed starker. All parties could begin the work to reverse these conditions immediately, if only the Vietnamese in Hanoi wished it so.

To lift the people out of poverty and ignorance, "to replace despair with hope, and terror with progress," Johnson promised $1 billion in aid from the United States.[51] That billion, and hopefully more from other nations, would be put to use as part of a program to harness the awesome power of the Mekong River and to put it to work bettering the lives of ordinary people. Through a series of dams and dikes, offered the president, "the vast Mekong River can provide food and water and power on a scale to dwarf our own TVA [Tennessee Valley Authority]." Modernity and a better life for rural people would be brought to the hinterlands of all of Southeast Asia, just as the U.S. government had done in the Mississippi valley during the Great Depression. The possibilities were inspiring:

The wonders of modern medicine can be spread through villages where thousands die every year from lack of care. Schools can be established to train people in the skills needed to manage the process of development. And these objectives, and more, are within the reach of a cooperative and determined effort.[52]

This program, to which Johnson pledged the United States to contribute such a staggering sum, was under the auspices of the UN's Economic Commission for Asia and the Far East (ECAFE) and had actually been under way for nearly seven years.[53] The ECAFE's Mekong Delta project had already conducted numerous surveys and observation trips, and detailed planning was well under way for a system of dams and dikes stretching throughout the delta. The project involved the energies of experts and technicians from twenty nations and eleven UN agencies, who had made available close to $30 million.[54] The American contribution to this effort to date, as Jack Valenti pointed out to Johnson, added

[51] "Peace without Conquest," April 7, 1965, Statements of Lyndon B. Johnson, box 143, LBJL.
[52] Ibid.
[53] United Nations Office of Public Information, Economic and Social Unit, March 1965, WHCF, Confidential File, box 167, LBJL.
[54] "One Johnson Plan is Now Underway," New York Times, April 8, 1965.

up to "less than the cost of four days of military aid" to Saigon.[55] The United States was now on board but would have to play a much larger role to be taken seriously.[56]

Those involved with the project also knew that part of the inspiration for the American president's address grew out of a mix of political considerations.[57] In part, it stemmed from the seventeen-nation appeal following the Belgrade Conference in March and calling on all parties to stop the fighting in Vietnam and to begin negotiations.[58] This added international pressure, coupled with domestic pressure from Congress and the public, and with Johnson's desire to keep a tight lid on evolving Vietnam policy, heavily influenced the decision to draft the speech as well as its specific content.[59] Beyond these immediate political and diplomatic concerns, the administration never really believed that such an approach would bring Hanoi officials to negotiate, nor would it bring the insurgents of the National Liberation Front (NLF) to heel. For one thing, those responsible for drafting the address were careful not to concede anything of substance. For example, Johnson made clear that the objective of the United States was to bring about "the independence of *South* Vietnam," even though the effort to build that state had run to ground over the previous year, and officials in Hanoi had never accepted the idea of a separate southern state. The president and his advisors knew also that the Vietnamese in Hanoi would never negotiate with such a restriction in place. Furthermore, the president committed only to "discussion or negotiation with the *governments* concerned," removing any possibility of NLF participation in a final settlement.[60] North Vietnamese premier Pham Van Dong the next day released a four-point outline of his own government's requirements for talks. They included, not surprisingly, U.S. military withdrawal, recognition of Vietnamese

---

[55] Report to the President from Jack Valenti, March 29, 1965, WHCF, Confidential File, box 167, LBJL.

[56] At a press conference the next day, the president cautioned that the offer contained in his speech was only an idea, not a plan. See Press Conference No. 41 of the President of the United States, April 8, 1965, NSF, CF, VN, box 200, LBJL.

[57] "Johnson's Speech Viewed as Bid to World Opinion," *New York Times*, April 8, 1965.

[58] Johnson, *Vantage Point*, 132–33.

[59] On the domestic pressure, see Melvin Small, *Antiwarriors: The Vietnam War and the Battle for America's Hearts and Minds* (Wilmington, DE: Scholarly Resources, 2002), 21–30.

[60] "Peace without Conquest," emphasis added.

sovereignty, and independence in accordance with the 1954 Geneva Accords, and the participation of the NLF.[61] Neither side could recognize the other's requirements for talks. This impasse surprised no one.[62]

Despite obvious limitations, the speech, if only briefly, earned the praise of the American press and public and of international skeptics.[63] The administration enjoyed a temporary respite as it was being given the benefit of the doubt in a number of important quarters. International opinion shifted overnight as the UN secretary-general embraced the opportunity for peace and wrote Johnson, calling the speech "positive, forward-looking and generous." The considerable volume of mail to the White House changed markedly from five to one against U.S. policy in Vietnam to four to one in favor immediately following the speech. The *Washington Post* called the move "a major offer" and "a new departure" in U.S. relations with Vietnam.

Nevertheless, nothing much came of the proposal for $1 billion in aid, nor from the grand scheme to begin negotiations. While the administration appointed high-profile international financier Eugene Black to head the effort and provided rhetorical support, the U.S. effort in the development project never bore fruit. Within a month, the luster had worn off the president's Mekong initiative as the old criticisms resurfaced. Republicans in Congress had earlier chided the president's offer, asking, "Do you buy freedom for a humble people with a billion-dollar package?"[64] It soon became apparent that the aid money would not materialize, that there would be no freedom for the humble people of Vietnam, and

---

[61] *FRUS*, 1965, Vietnam, II:544–45. For early reaction around the world, see also Memorandum for Mr. Bundy, April 6, 1965, NSF, CF, VN, box 200, LBJL.

[62] Although it disappointed some like George Ball, who lobbied the president to consider the Four Point response from Hanoi an opening and a basis for talks. On the other hand, he was not surprised when Hanoi interpreted an American bombing pause in May as a "deceitful maneuver to pave the way for American escalation." See Memorandum from the Under Secretary of State (Ball) to President Johnson, April 21, 1965, *FRUS*, 1965, II:582–92. George Ball, *The Past Has Another Pattern* (New York: W. W. Norton, 1982), 404.

[63] Memorandum for the President from McGeorge Bundy, April 10, 1965, Statements of Lyndon B. Johnson, box 143, LBJL. See Editorial Note, *FRUS*, 1965, II:543–44.

[64] "Generous Peace – or Just War?," *New York Times*, April 9, 1965. "LBJ Offers 'Unconditional' Viet Talks but Stands Firm on U.S. Commitments," *Washington Post*, April 8, 1965. "Democrats Hail Johnson's Talk; G.O.P. Sees Move to Buy Peace," *New York Times*, April 8, 1965.

war would continue to shove any move toward a peaceful settlement to the margins. By the end of the summer, the president had already made the decisions that would turn his Vietnam "trilemma," as John McNaughton termed it, into a major war involving well over a quarter million troops. Though successful in the short term, the president's speech and the development initiative more generally did not change the complexion of the conflict. The administration had not waited around to figure this out; escalation still raced ahead.

The massive construction project under way for months now and aimed at turning southern Vietnam into a web of defensible military outposts continued. As mentioned, Congress authorized around $2 billion for spending on a war there during the year.[65] In August, the two-firm consortium given responsibility for the transformation of southern Vietnam doubled its reach and resources by adding two other firms, Brown and Root and J. A. Jones. Planners quickly crafted a scheme for creating a modern integrated military infrastructure encompassing all of southern Vietnam. Lyndon Johnson and those around him placed far greater stock in these options than in any pie-in-the-sky regional development project. The political, social, economic, and military context was far too volatile and complex for such an offer to have any real chance at success. Experts and planners estimated that nothing substantial could be accomplished on the Mekong project anyway for at least a decade. Planning and data collection were far from complete. Of the $1 billion offer, the State Department balked that it was too specific and that there existed "no plan for using it." Chester Cooper of the National Security Council believed it "was a nice, round, dramatic figure" but "clearly beyond the ability of the region to absorb."[66] Furthermore, the United States had made no serious provisions for talks; it had outlined no real program of its own, it had sought no international support for a negotiated settlement, it had not consulted officials in Hanoi, and it had not consulted its own client in Saigon. In fact, the administration had worked vigorously to squelch any of these avenues to a settlement. In

---

[65] A $700 million request in May was followed by the establishment of a special fund, the "Emergency Fund, Southeast Asia," worth $1.7 billion in August. Taylor, *Financial Management*, 19–22.

[66] Dieu, *Mekong River*, 110–11. Mr. Valenti's Notes on the Johns Hopkins Speech, Statements of Lyndon B. Johnson, box 143, LBJL. Cooper, *Lost Crusade*, 273.

the end, Lyndon Johnson's peace and economic development initiative was one of a number of political tools he hoped would allow for escalation and war, without provoking public debate that would detract from his Great Society domestic agenda.

By late summer, the administration decided on escalating the war in an attempt to retain control in southern Vietnam and to maintain its own international credibility. There would be numerous other negotiating initiatives over the next several years. They would all take place under the considerable strain of major war. For the time being, the same questions of legitimacy, reliability, security, and, more importantly for the purposes of this study, economic and political viability remained unanswered, for while the president spoke in grandiloquent terms of Southeast Asian regional development, the United States continued to nurse along a deeply flawed and increasingly dependent client regime in Saigon.

"LONG SINCE ... DEPENDENT ON U.S. AID"

Overall, the aid program failed to meet expectations, at least the expectations that had begun the program. Certainly the advent of major warfare over the whole of southern Vietnam further eroded the possibilities for successful state building. It began to chip away at any gains in the economic realm and even to bring on some new problems. The program continued its shift away from development and toward military preparedness, and though inflation had not yet begun its upward spiral in early 1965, that soon changed. It goes without saying that at this point, the dangers of runaway inflation were taken seriously. Signs of increased military preparedness and greater military aid thus caused concern. Over the four previous years, as the American military presence and the Saigon regime's military forces grew, Saigon's budget deficit also grew by more than 300 percent.[67] During those same years, the money supply increased by 70 percent as the regime printed new money to finance its growing deficit. This deficit spending became much greater beginning in 1965 and after.[68] Economic growth in military construction

---

[67] The regime's budget deficit grew from VN$4.7 billion to VN$15.9 billion for the period.

[68] The money supply grew by nearly 70 percent in that year alone. For monthly and annual money supply information, see "Monthly Money Supply Data," NSF, Komer-Leonhart

and related preparations served to dampen inflation temporarily only because AID officials purposefully augmented the import side of the program to "sop up" excess money. Recorded economic growth reflected this shift. Industrialization actually slowed, with fewer than two dozen new factories built in southern Vietnam since 1954, and most of those completed during this period had been planned in past years.[69] AID's comprehensive final report found that by 1964, "the country had long since become dependent on U.S. aid."[70]

The influx of tens of thousands of U.S. forces exacerbated these economic problems. Large numbers of troops brought with them greater demand for a range of consumer goods. By year's end, U.S. troop levels stood at more than 185,000, up from just over 23,000 at the end of 1964. The effect on the economy, as the AID later pointed out, was "almost wholly inflationary." Escalation also strained the economy in other ways. Pressure mounted, for example, as the private contractors sought translators, carpenters, bricklayers, divers, truck drivers, and thousands of Vietnamese laborers in general. Within a year, this ramped up U.S. effort employed 142,000 Vietnamese and third country nationals, up from just a handful in the early 1960s. These figures do not begin to account for the unofficial employment levels – including taxi drivers, restaurant waitstaff, valets, car washers, laundry workers, bartenders, musicians, bar girls, and others catering to the U.S. presence. Furthermore, their employment on or connection to American bases and other military infrastructure took them away from production for a Vietnamese economy. The forces supporting the regime also expanded to more than 510,000 by the end of 1964.[71] All of this required greater expansion of the importation side of the aid equation and the concomitant shrinking of internal production.

The regime could not hope to raise sufficient revenue to accommodate these changes. By 1965, domestic taxes still accounted for a paltry

File, box 6, LBJL. "Weekly Economic Indicators for Republic of Vietnam," January 27, 1966, NSF, Komer-Leonhart File, box 6, LBJL, 7.

[69] Douglas C. Dacy, *Foreign Aid, War, and Economic Development: South Vietnam, 1955–1975* (New York: Cambridge University Press, 1986), 8–10. Not surprisingly, textiles showed the most expansion in this period, while other industries, such as paper, ceramics, and bicycle parts, remained very limited. *USEASV*, II:541–43. USOM, *Operational Report*, 1963–1964, 73.

[70] *USEASV*, I:106–7.

[71] Ibid., 108–9.

7 percent of gross national product. For whoever made up the regime in Saigon, generating sufficient revenue apart from the American aid program to pay for even the rudiments of government proved an impossible challenge. As U.S. military aid grew, the problem became less and less solvable. Southern Vietnam exported next to nothing, and it imported hundreds of millions of dollars worth of commodities and war-related materiel each year. Imports grew rapidly beginning in 1965 and skyrocketed over the next several years. The two-year period following escalation was, according to the AID, "unlike anything ever experienced by an underdeveloped country. An enormous foreign presence was superimposed on a small, basically rural economy in a short time span." At least one rather odd outgrowth of this phenomenon was "far-reaching economic distortions," alongside "a substantial degree of prosperity" for some.[72] Fixing a foreign exchange rate that would be both accurate and beneficial to exporters simply was not possible. Certain of the men within the regime and a relative few importers continued to reap windfall profits from these arrangements, which guaranteed against any substantive changes. The regime's chief revenue source, not surprisingly, remained the American aid program and a lopsided currency exchange rate.

Also in 1964, Vietnam's population remained overwhelmingly rural, some 80 to 85 percent. The American presence and large-scale warfare had not yet had the impact they would have in a few short years. Saigon, the largest city in the south, still claimed only around 1 million inhabitants, and much of this growth occurred during the post–Geneva Conference period.[73] All other urban areas combined were far smaller. Rice production had in large part been restored to levels attained prior to the French war of 1946–1954, and the Vietnamese actually exported some of the crop, although insurgents had at the same time begun to seriously interdict its transport to urban markets.[74] Increased rice production was

---

[72] *USEASV*, I:107 and 110. The level of imports was, to as great an extent as was possible, calculated on the basis of the Saigon regime's budget deficit forecast for the coming fiscal year.

[73] Population figures are, for the most part, estimates, and as such, they vary significantly. The population of Saigon given by AID for 1964 is less than 1 million. The figure given by a RAND study is 1.4 million. See *USEASV*, I:106, and "U.S. Economic Assistance in Vietnam: A Proposed Reorientation," A Report Prepared for the Agency for International Development, RAND Corporation, July 1964, NSF, CF, VN, box 195, LBJL, 15.

[74] *PP*, III:444.

also offset by a trade deficit of nearly $200 million. Exports amounted to only around 15 percent of imports for 1964.[75] Industry remained very limited and overwhelmingly state-owned. Foreign investment was also quite limited, in part due to the regime's nepotistic and parochial policies, but equally or even more so due to the continued political instability and lack of security. The uncertainty following the removal of Diem proved a particularly important factor in stalling all other efforts aimed at reform and development. Numerous programs were shelved and/or ignored as aid resources moved to remedy the most pressing problems with the experiment. Not surprisingly, those problems centered on military solutions to security problems and political illegitimacy. Certainly not new trends, American experts and economic advisors had warned for years of these very obstacles. Nevertheless, by early spring 1965, policy makers in Washington determined that, given the formidable difficulties then prevailing in Saigon and the countryside, the only alternative to American withdrawal from Vietnam was a greater American military presence and wider war.

CONCLUSION

As Washington officials surveyed the project in southern Vietnam in late 1963, it immediately became clear that something dramatic would have to be done to prevent total collapse in Saigon. Over the next several months, political coups followed one upon the other, creating even greater instability. The whole program in Saigon was without purpose and without effective guidance. The Americans looked on with alarm, unable to adequately control a volatile and rapidly changing situation. Meanwhile, the economy was in tatters. Political fluidity prevented any progress on this front. The tax system remained arbitrary, limited, ill-enforced, unfair, and relatively unimportant given the nature and size of the American aid program. The CIP arrangement continued to stifle home production. Yet the aid program, and its substantial increase, became all the more necessary through 1964 and into 1965 to allow for a greatly expanded military/security budget and still keep inflation at

---

[75] The rice surplus for export was around forty-eight thousand metric tons for 1964. That is the last year for any export of rice due to the expanded war. It is also the year in which PL-480 food imports from the United States began to make up for these shortfalls in domestic production. See *USEASV*, II:359. Dacy, *Foreign Aid*, 83.

bay. The efforts outside of Saigon also failed to yield any meaningful and long-term dividends as the countryside teemed with forces opposed to the American-sponsored political system there. The insurgency had thoroughly overrun and decimated the strategic hamlet pacification program. That opposition, loosely fronted by the NLF and aided by Hanoi, gained in popularity and in fighting capability. As American officials, themselves groping about for any solution, settled on greater military force, they seemed only to be perpetuating these problems.

In short, the effort to build a viable state infrastructure in southern Vietnam continued to crumble. The decisions taken in Washington from spring and through summer of 1965 faced this reality squarely. Militarization and the Americanization of the war were measures to compensate for it, not correct it. The president dispatched Secretary McNamara to Saigon in July for another assessment of the needs there, and the latter reported the situation was "worse than a year ago (when it was worse than a year before that)."[76] Never mind state building – the territory below the seventeenth parallel would have to be defended, rather than lost to the enemy. Even the best of the news out of Vietnam now did not point to either a quick or sure victory, a term made much more ambiguous over the previous couple of years. Members of the president's own party also began to call into question, albeit slowly, the very basis of Cold War liberalism and the direction of the containment doctrine. Maybe the commitment was not worth the cost after all. Or maybe Johnson's handling of the nation's Cold War foreign policy was the problem.[77] Amid a rising tide of domestic and international criticism, the Johnson administration continued to escalate the conflict to stave off rapid and complete failure.

From Johnson's perspective, the alternative – withdrawal – remained unthinkable. It might be perfectly fine for the intellectuals and the "flea

---

[76] McNamara presented the president with the now-standard three options for Vietnam: withdrawal, stay the course, or rapid escalation. He also concluded what was a truly sobering, depressing assessment by writing, "The course of action recommended in this memorandum...stands a good chance of achieving an acceptable outcome within a reasonable time in Vietnam." Memorandum from Secretary of Defense McNamara to President Johnson, July 20, 1965, *FRUS*, 1965, III:171–79.

[77] Robert David Johnson, "The Origins of Dissent: Senate Liberals and Vietnam, 1959–1964," *Pacific Historical Review* 65, no. 2 (May, 1996): 249–75. This is the period, too, when J. William Fulbright and Johnson parted acrimoniously. See Woods, *Fulbright*, 384–92.

bite professors" to consider a broad range of options; they were not charged with creating the policy and dealing directly with events.[78] To simply withdraw from Vietnam and admit defeat, Johnson believed, would kill his party and create a destructive rent in American political life. He compared his situation with that of Harry Truman and his "loss" of China and concluded that the latter's "problems were chickenshit compared with what might happen if we lost Vietnam."[79] Aside from the hyperbole, Johnson did believe that his own credibility, and that of his nation, was on display in Southeast Asia. He also believed that the United States shouldered a unique responsibility for the people of the third world. Nor was the president alone. Key advisors, over and over again, supported this appraisal.

From late 1963 through 1965, the United States moved from an ailing aid and assistance project in Southeast Asia to direct military intervention and large-scale base building and major war. Policy makers found themselves unable to bring about a military or political victory. The handful of Vietnamese, mostly military figures, from which the administration attempted to craft a government seemed incapable of pulling one together. Ultimately, officials decided that could no longer be allowed as an obstacle. As Henry Cabot Lodge, appointed ambassador in Saigon again in summer 1965, lectured during a late July meeting, "There is no tradition of a national government in Saigon. There are no roots in the country. . . . There is no one who can do anything." Sounding very much like the president of a few months earlier, he suggested, "We have to do what we think we ought to do regardless of what the Saigon government does."[80]

The resulting impasse culminated in an American takeover of the project and the rapid physical transformation of southern Vietnam. Private contractors responsible for the building up of a modern, integrated military infrastructure had, through their efforts, slowly begun to make it possible to defend the area. Over the next couple of years, the United States remained committed to this approach for solving its growing crisis in Southeast Asia. In the process, officials began inventing

---

[78] The term *fleabite professors* is McGeorge Bundy's. See Small, *Antiwarriors*, 24.
[79] Doris Kearns Goodwin, *Lyndon Johnson and the American Dream* (New York: Harper & Row, 1976), 252–53.
[80] Notes of a Meeting, July 21, 1965, *FRUS*, 1965, III:189–97; quote is on 193.

a different kind of Vietnam, one capable of accommodating full-scale war, many hundreds of thousands of troops, and large-scale population movements; one also without a legitimate government, without legitimate political institutions, and without a modicum of social cohesion and stability. These problems only grew more pronounced over the next few years.

7

THE PARADOX OF
CONSTRUCTION AND
DESTRUCTION: SOUTHERN
VIETNAM, 1966–1968

During the roughly two-year period between the beginning of 1966 and the early weeks of 1968, the United States faced many of the shortcomings of its state-building program very directly. It was not simply a matter of choice. Circumstances forced the Johnson administration to face the very real limitations on its power to influence events. Frustration over these limitations had already led to a greater reliance on military power and, ultimately, full-scale war. The United States continued to rely on an expanded military presence as the best hope to save its credibility in Vietnam. The Vietnam Builders engineers continued building and expanding the large-scale infrastructure projects to accommodate these objectives. The level of infrastructural development deemed necessary was in fact not sufficiently in place until late in 1967. The great paradox was that these latest physical transformations of the southern Vietnamese landscape further undermined the larger objectives, while they made possible a wider and more efficient war.

The expanded violence, dislocation, and general chaos made possible by this construction had, by the late 1960s, not only seriously undermined the effort to piece together a stable state infrastructure, but had also disrupted the Vietnamese countryside as well. By 1968, the war's destruction had turned many hundreds of thousands of rural Vietnamese into refugees. In enormous numbers they fled first from the war in the countryside into urban environments in a kind of forced urbanization that further exposed the inability of the cities to accommodate the rising numbers. Some flowed back again out of the cities; some flowed into the system of encampments designed to receive the flood of refugees and provide protection and security. The system of relief was only ever able to militate against these effects of war for a small minority of the refugees. This failure perpetuated the sense of alienation and resentment between the people and representatives of the regime in Saigon.

Expanded warfare also further exacerbated years-old economic woes. The economy became, even more so than in past years, reliant upon the upwardly spiraling American aid program. The Commodity Import Program (CIP) mushroomed, and with it, continued windfall profits for importers. These growing programs nurtured a web of graft and cronyism that shocked participants, observers, and investigators. The exchange rate also provided substantial profit-taking opportunities and resulted in a bonanza of currency speculation and capital flight, preventing any meaningful level of internal investment. Hoarding goods to drive up prices, currency speculation, the black market, a suspect import licensing system, payoffs and kickbacks, and general waste and inefficiency came to characterize the economy of southern Vietnam. Even before the Tet Offensive of early 1968 forced a reassessment of prospects in southern Vietnam, the state-building mission had encountered its own contradictions.

"RMK-BRJ IS CHANGING THE FACE OF SOUTH VIET NAM"

"Motor grader operators work with loaded carbines at their sides; ... scrapers cut roads across the shadows of hastily prepared gun emplacements; a lean tanned construction superintendent waxes enthusiastic over the future while helicopters stutter overhead looking for enemy guerillas." This is the way veteran correspondent and photojournalist Paul B. Harder described all of the building activity in southern Vietnam in 1967. Detroit Diesel Engine sent him to Vietnam precisely to capture, in both writing and photography, this activity. His experience with numerous other building projects in countries around the world qualified him to assess the "scope and complexity" of the state-building effort under way all across Vietnam for the magazine's readers (and to showcase much of that company's equipment then in use in Vietnam). Though seemingly contradictory, the rapid and large-scale buildup of the physical infrastructure over all of southern Vietnam continued in tandem with the widespread destruction already described. After recognizing the inherent "paradox" of this simultaneous construction and destruction, Harder applauded the immense construction effort undertaken by the private contractors. The campaign to build the new and modern American-built infrastructure also came in for high praise, and the writer concluded that the experience was "a fair commentary on the Free World's [sic] military effort that much of the physical and human investment being pumped into Vietnam today will help hasten the day of realization [development]."[1] Harder's photojournalism filled more than twenty pages with innumerable details of the construction process, of the enormous costs, of the inherent difficulties of building in such an environment, of the danger of the work, and so on. The reader searches in vain, however, for any sustained depiction of the destruction brought on by elements of the same mission as that containing the consortium and other military construction units.

The reporter's preoccupation with and enthusiasm for the sheer magnitude and ingenuity of the building projects mirrors the perception of the construction engineers, military officers, and policy makers as well. One of the reasons the paradox of construction and destruction ran parallel everywhere in southern Vietnam without arousing much interest beyond congressional investigative committees is precisely because the military effort garnered so much attention. Officials and policy makers monitored that effort and used it to measure success. Secretary McNamara and Robert Komer, to name but two, showed their keen interest in the buildup of ports and airfields and in ending the congestion that jammed up the flow of war materiel. As Secretary McNamara told the Senate committee members in 1966, to wage war "in a country of this sort requires the construction of new ports, warehouse facilities, access roads, improvements to highways leading to the interior of the country and along the coasts, troop facilities, hospitals, completely new airfields and major improvements to existing airfields, communications facilities, etc." The overall system of funding also favored the military and related programs. Congress authorized $1.4 billion for construction in Vietnam, for example, in the 1966 military budget, while the issue

[1] Paul B. Harder, "Vietnam – Paradox of Construction and Destruction," *Power Parade*, 1967, 1.

of refugees, the most visible manifestation of the destruction, received $22.5 million, of which all but $3 million was actually designated for Agency for International Development (AID) salaries, equipment, and logistics.[2] The Vietnam Builders spent lavishly with little oversight, principally because that effort made the war possible. And the war, policy makers believed, was the only way to stay on in southern Vietnam and to avoid having to face the failure of the project.

That the project would turn out to be a failure was not obvious in 1966. This is particularly clear when viewed through the lens of the contractors and amid the whirlwind surrounding their activities from 1966 through 1968. Indeed, the Vietnam Builders, the name adopted early in 1966, established themselves as a relatively permanent fixture within Saigon and within the larger American mission. Over the year and a half extending from January 1966, the Builders put in place $670 million of construction projects, compared to $130 million over the whole of the previous four years.[3] Along the way, the consortium integrated itself into Vietnam in much the same way as the American military forces. These American engineers share with their equals from the civilizing projects in the Philippines to the technomilitary triumphs of the Persian Gulf War an omnipresent enthusiasm and unwavering faith in the power of American technology and expertise. They continued to believe, right

---

[2] See "Supplemental Military Procurement and Construction Authorizations, Fiscal Year, 1966," Hearings before the Committee on Armed Services and the Subcommittee on Department of Defense of the Committee on Appropriations, U.S. Senate, 89th Cong., 2nd sess. (Washington, DC, 1966), 4, 12. See also "U.S. Apparatus of Assistance to Refugees throughout the World," Hearings before the Subcommittee to Investigate Problems Connected with Refugees and Escapees of the Committee on the Judiciary, U.S. Senate, 89th Cong., 2nd sess. (Washington, DC, 1966), 55–56.

[3] The Vietnam Builders' *Diary of a Contract*, 135, *RMK-BRJ Papers*, recorded that the year 1966 was "as wild a period as any human being can imagine. Thousands of people were arriving from the United States, South Korea, the Philippines and 27 other nations; tens of thousands of South Vietnamese were hired and taught a construction trade; hundreds of thousands of tons of materials and equipments were off-loaded over the beach and delivered to depots, which were themselves in the process of being built; airfields, ports, pipelines, barracks, hospitals, ammunition dumps, storage areas, roads – in fact, every type of useful facility known to man had to be built for the military services. Not the least of the problems being faced was building the base for the contractor's own operations – camps, maintenance shops, warehouses, etc. These competed for the labor, materials and time which the soldiers, sailors, airmen marines understandably felt were there to fulfill their own urgent needs. In short, it was a period of 20-hour days, 7-day weeks, frayed nerves, deadlines, shortages and magnificent achievement."

up until the expiration of the contract in 1972, that their work would engineer a victory for the United States in Vietnam.[4] The monetary value of the projects really only tells a part of the story.

From its office headquarters complex in the heart of Saigon, the Builders began publishing a newspaper titled simply the *Vietnam Builders* in the spring in both English and Vietnamese, with a combined circulation of forty-six thousand. Its pages carried stories of construction projects under way, of budgets and costs, and of military adventures. The paper also ran regular human interest and entertainment features from local dances to the RMK-BRJ softball league games between the all-Filipino "barefoot boys," and better equipped American air force and navy teams. The former soundly defeated the American teams even without shoes and proper equipment.[5] The paper regularly ran congratulatory and complimentary comments from both American and Vietnamese political and military officials. Its essays, articles, and commentaries were notably positive, upbeat, and even fun. The paper contained scarcely a mention of the war's destruction in the countryside, and its violence shows up only episodically. Its pages contained no discussion of the politics of war and offered no forum for airing differing views on the various aspects of the war then being hotly contested back in the United States. These matters lay beyond the purpose of the paper.[6] The *Vietnam Builders* served to connect the Builders with readers and the readers to each other as a vital part of the life of the American mission in Saigon and in southern Vietnam. Contributors from Vung Tau, Ban Me Thuot, and Qui Nhon to Phan Rang, Rach Soi, and Cam Ranh

---

[4] Michael Adas, *Dominance by Design: Technological Imperatives and America's Civilizing Mission* (Cambridge, MA: Harvard University Press, 2006), chaps. 3 and 7.

[5] *Diary of a Contract*, 139, 143. *Vietnam Builders* 1, no. 15 (1966): 8.

[6] Although, at the same time, MK's chairman, H. W. Morrison, sharply criticized those at home who spoke out against the war in Vietnam. In July 1966, he wrote in the company's magazine of "a certain few people in our own country [who] erode the morale of our fighting men and weaken national resolve by their words and deeds." He continued, "How disconcerting it is that television and newspapers tend to give continuing prominence to the actions of a few headline-seeking students and vociferous politicians, thereby depicting our nation to people abroad as a land divided of purpose and direction. It is a sad commentary, indeed, when one bearded student who burns a draft card can receive the full attention of news media while millions of true Americans must go unnoticed because they are so uninteresting, so old-fashioned and so righteous that they still fly the flag and would willingly lay down their lives for their country." H. W. Morrison, "Subject: Steadfast America Can Win in Viet Nam," *The Em-Kayan*, July 1966, 1.

all provided the stories that came together in the pages of the *Vietnam Builders* in a way that communicated much more than the "news." They helped to create the sense of harmony and united effort that U.S. policy makers back in Washington regularly emphasized in their own explanations for why there was a war to be fought in Vietnam.[7]

The creation of such an atmosphere likely also served well a workforce quickly cobbled together and consisting of Americans, Vietnamese, Koreans, Filipinos, and hundreds of other third country nationals. A consequence of harsh work conditions, low pay, long hours with no overtime, and job hazards, one of the most difficult challenges lay in keeping an adequate number of workers in the field. Inflation also far outpaced wages, making it more difficult to attract skilled workers. A Vietnamese worker's pay scale, for example, was based on the 1957 schedule and did not reflect the considerable inflation during the period. The Builders even inaugurated their own program for training Vietnamese students in the skills needed for construction, sending the first 219 off to various job sites as part of the six-week program in 1966.[8] At its peak, the consortium's workforce numbered slightly more than fifty-one thousand, with around forty-seven thousand Vietnamese, Koreans, Filipinos, and others, and four thousand Americans overwhelmingly as supervisors and managers. Within these numbers, however, this workforce changed a great deal. Over the life of the contract, the Builders employed between 180,000 and 200,000 Vietnamese.

Some among the Americans blamed this volatile working environment on the shortcomings of the natives themselves. One journalist offered that the Vietnamese were "small men" and they "often weigh only 90 lb or so, and look like children at the wheel of a big bulldozer or truck. Some are strong enough for only four or five hours a day of such work." Apparently, part of the difficultly in maintaining an adequate workforce stemmed from the lack of stamina among the locals. The article, however, offered no explanation for how the same Vietnamese

---

[7] A few titles illustrate the point: "Barber Remembers the Mane; Meets Former Patrons in VN," "Curfew Curtails OGN Gala Dance," "'King' Khang: Top VN Surveyor," all in *Vietnam Builders* 1, no. 15 (1966). "R. Adm. Husband Praises OICC-Joint Venture Team," "Project No. 1 – It Needs Your Help," "Qui Nhon – Another Port Ready for Business," "VN Employee, 52, Performs Aquabatics for Saigon River Marine Projects," all in *Vietnam Builders* 1, no. 19 (1966).

[8] "RMK-BRJ Starts Student Co-Op Training Program," *Vietnam Builders* 1, no. 15 (1966): 1.

ever became such efficient and productive farmers in this climate that exhausted the American soldier.[9]

A high rate of turnover, the demands of the work, and the fluidity of a war environment in general gnawed away at cohesion and unity of purpose that the private contractors relied upon in their constant race to make deadlines and increase the pace of work on hundreds of simultaneous projects across southern Vietnam. Some of the most troubling labor unrest, which the Builders' own self-evaluation termed a "minor civil war," began not out of grievances between labor and management, but out of the general opposition to the regime.[10] Despite these and other considerable obstacles, the Builders benefited from a large pool of labor. Because of the very limited nature of Vietnamese home production and industry, these laborers were unlikely to be siphoned off to other attractive industry and/or factory jobs locally. Ironically, had the earlier efforts to build a native economy and industrial base succeeded, this large number of workers would not have been available. On the other hand, they would not have been necessary either. Nevertheless, Builders' management understood the need to attract workers given the omnipresent war climate.[11] The creation of its own subculture no doubt aided in this. It also helped the consortium to ease thousands of American workers into the very different environment of construction work in Southeast Asia.

That work environment was busier and the activity more frenetic than ever in 1966. Despite all that had been built up during the second

---

[9] *Diary of a Contract*, 148, 153. "Work Increases as War Expands," *Engineering News-Record*, May 13, 1965.

[10] The documentary record is replete with references to the perennial problem of insufficient labor in both numerical terms and in terms of quality. There are, in addition, a number of references to strikes, riots, and insurgent activity among workers, which disrupted the construction process. See, inter alia, "Evaluation of Contractor's Performance," 1 April 1966–30 September 1966, *RMK-BRJ Papers*, III-b-1, VI-c-1 to VI-c-4. *Jones Construction Centennial: Looking Back, Moving Forward* (Charlotte, NC: Laney-Smith, 1989), 154. "U.S. Ally in Vietnam: Civil Works," *Engineering News-Record*, May 5, 1966.

[11] The average Vietnamese carpenter, for example, earned twenty-five piasters per hour (about thirty-three cents). As part of the drive to reduce the size of the workforce and to increase the number of Vietnamese supervisors to replace Americans, RMK-BRJ General Manager Jim Lilly began a training program to teach skills and offer incentives to particularly talented and hardworking Vietnamese. They could, potentially, double their pay in twenty-four weeks after passing a series of evaluations and tests. Lilly was optimistic, pointing out that the program would be "more extensive than the entire craftsmanship development program of the state of California." "VN Incentive Program Launched," *Vietnam Builders* 1, no. 19 (1966): 1.

half of 1965, it was really just the beginning of a much greater construction project. Engineers forecast the requirements in terms of equipment, manpower, capital, and time based on the support needed for around two hundred thousand American troops. No one yet imagined building to accommodate over one-half million. Even at this still limited level, however, construction achieved a pace of $1 million of work-in-place per day by late summer. The contractors expected to (and did) achieve $40 million of work-in-place per month in the fall. To compound the difficulties, southern Vietnam still lacked the infrastructure to handle the barrage of equipment and supplies necessary to carry out that construction. As MK's own monthly publication announced in August 1966, "logistical problems are enormous, for virtually everything has to be shipped in – and in prodigious quantities." The lack of adequate airfields and of ports in particular made the buildup for war all the more challenging. Military planners expected the engineers to build a modern national infrastructure to accommodate hundreds of thousands of troops and major war, and yet, the very fact of limited or absent infrastructure sharply restricted their ability to do so.

Projects required, for example, close to 150 million board feet of lumber, 3,600 prefabricated buildings, 11 million pounds of nails, 750,000 sheets of plywood, and 98 million pounds of asphalt, plus nearly 2,000 trucks and tractors, just to name a very few of the much needed materials.[12] Construction materials competed with an increasing flow of commodity aid, food aid, military aid, and all other imports for limited dock space, deep-draft berthing, and airfields. Once the needed materials did arrive, a reliable transportation system would have to then disperse the right supplies and equipment to the right job site out of the many hundreds then under way.[13] The Builders also required the simultaneous construction of their own camps, demanding still more resources of labor, time, materials, and a system of efficient and rapid supply.[14]

---

[12] "Construction of Military Facilities by RMK-BRJ Is Changing Face of South Viet Nam," *The Em-Kayan*, August 1966, 12–13. To date, the Builders had paved 1,260 acres in airfields alone, imported 1,628 miles of water pipe, and poured enough cement monthly to pave thirty-five miles of four-lane highway. Chairman's Memo, "Subject: Impressive Achievements in South Viet Nam," *The Em-Kayan*, December 1966, 1.

[13] *Diary of a Contract*, 148, 154.

[14] Recognizing these difficulties, and also, the unprecedented burdens of construction in southern Vietnam, the U.S. Navy negotiated with the Builders a substantial change in the contract arrangement. In May 1966, the contract changed from a cost-plus-fixed-fee

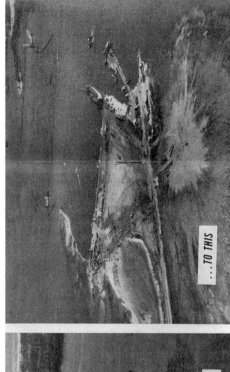

FROM THIS . . .

. . . TO THIS

DREDGES CREATE VIET NAM 'SEAPORT' AT PERFUME RIVER MOUTH

5. Left-hand image shows a tiny spit of land at the mouth of the Perfume River near central Vietnam before large-scale development. Right-hand image shows some subsequent development, with dock space for ships and lightering facilities. The RMK-BRJ brought in 1.5 million cubic yards of fill to create this sixteen-acre site. At the time of this photo, 1969, the site was still under heavy construction.

In May, the Builders began the initial work for a large new project fifteen miles northeast of Saigon at Long Binh, where Highway 1 intersected Highway 15. The project called for "a mammoth camp" to "house the military forces which were in Saigon – another step to relieve the ever-increasing inflation." Large numbers of American troops in and around Saigon only exacerbated the growing problem of inflation brought on by the war. This "instant city" at Long Binh, at an estimated cost of well over $60 million, would relieve some of that economic pressure. Planners designed the new base as an army headquarters consisting of 475,000 square feet of barracks, 20,000 square feet of commercial structures, 15,000 square feet of mess facilities, and 420,000 square feet of administrative buildings.[15] The new base required 6 million board feet of lumber, the removal of 1,200 acres of heavy first-growth jungle, the building of 180 miles of roadways and streets, the erection of 3,500 buildings, two dozen helicopter pads, and barracks for between 40,000 and 50,000 troops. The Long Binh facility covered twenty-five square miles and functioned as an important element in the overall military infrastructure linking together otherwise distant and disparate parts of southern Vietnam.[16] When completed, the complex served as a hub for the region. Its supply depot, the largest of four major centers, supplied the II, III, and IV Corps Tactical Zones covering the majority of the territory below the seventeenth parallel.[17] This new modern military

type to a cost-plus-award-fee (CPAF) type. The CPAF contract provided extramonetary incentive to the contractor to complete projects quickly and retain a high degree of quality. The CPAF contract outlined the following categories for evaluation of work: (1) quality of work, 15 percent; (2) management, 30 percent; (3) performance, 40 percent; (4) cost, 15 percent. Supplemental Agreement No. 3 to Contract NBy 44105, May 25, 1966, *RMK-BRJ Papers*. Letter from Officer in Charge of Construction, Naval Facilities Engineering Command (OICC) to the Vietnam Builders, January 23, 1967, *RMK-BRJ Papers*. Letter from R. K. Woodhead, San Bruno Office, Contract Changes, September 22, 1966, *RMK-BRJ Papers*. The CPAF contract worked in the following way: in addition to a fixed fee negotiated for each individual project, the Builders could earn an award up to four-ninths of the fee. As an example, a specific project out of many contracted for in 1966 cost $57 million. The base fee for the job was $975,000, and the maximum award fee was $433,000. Thus the maximum payment for this particular job stood at $1.4 million.

[15] Paul Harder, "Long Binh – Out of the Jungle an 'Instant City,'" *Power Parade*, 1967, 2–4.

[16] Ibid. "Long Binh: New Military 'City' in Viet Nam," *The Em-Kayan*, June 1967, 3–5. *Diary of a Contract*, 278–83.

[17] The American mission had already subdivided southern Vietnam into four tactical zones. They were I Corps in the northern part of southern Vietnam, II Corps for the area north

6. Morrison-Knudsen's magazine, *The Em-Kayan*, captioned this photo, "Warehouses, billets and wharves take shape at Saigon Army Logistical Depot," 1966.

base, like a number of others, was not a part of the initial planning
but became necessary as the war and the construction progressed and
expanded. The rapid pace of the expansion meant that the construction
needs simply could not be accurately estimated.

Likewise, the port facilities at Saigon, even though somewhat
expanded by late 1965, ultimately could not handle the growing flood of
goods. The port was now one of the busiest in all of Asia, drawing com-
parisons to China's international port at Shanghai. The volume of commercial, military, AID, and other materials had expanded so rapidly and
to unforeseen levels that it threatened to bottleneck the whole project
and cause critical delays.[18] By design, Saigon's port facility could handle

of Saigon, III Corps around Saigon, and IV Corps in the Mekong Delta. Carroll H. Dunn,
Base Development in South Vietnam, 1965–1970 (Washington, DC: Department of the
Army, 1972), 117.

[18] Memo from Saigon to AID/Washington, Summary of Port Statistics for 1966, August 1,
1966, NSF, Komer-Leonhart File, box 20, Lyndon B. Johnson Library (LBJL).

only about 1.5 million tons of cargo per year. In November 1965 alone, the port received 218,000 tons of cargo. As the buildup continued into 1966, cargo through this one port averaged a staggering rate of 5 million tons per year. Over 120 ships waited weeks, and sometimes months, for space to off-load. Others were off-loaded by lightering barges that could then take advantage of shallow draft to off-load cargo at other facilities or simply along the shore. As a journalist recounted the situation in 1967, "there are about 1,000 barges, junks and sampans – every estuary of the Saigon river is clogged with them – laden with imports that date back as far as last April, with their owners collecting rentals they never dreamed of." The general chaos and confused nature of this delivery arrangement also nurtured a growing black market for the whole range of American imports. Pilferage of goods, something everyone from AID to the Vietnam Builders complained of, became a constant problem. The hundreds of barges lined up four or five abreast on one side of the river and loaded with such American goods as motor scooters, canned foods, transistor radios, and medical supplies were referred to wryly as "Charlie's warehouses" because of the easy access provided to the insurgents or to anyone else. By November 1966, cargo into Saigon had risen to over four hundred thousand tons per month, and much more was on the way.[19] Nor was the experience at Saigon unusual. The ports at Quang Ngai, Qui Nhon, Nha Trang, Da Nang, and Cam Ranh Bay all saw imports increase threefold by early 1967. The port system needed, in addition to a Herculean effort to just build more, additional trained workers, much tighter security, greater oversight, more warehouse and storage facilities, and much greater coordination between all the port users. Amid criticism over what seemed like a total lack of planning and the failure to anticipate such problems, Robert Komer and others in the American mission hurried the process of port expansion.[20]

---

[19] Letter from the Port of New York Authority, Austin J. Tobin, to Walter Stoneman, AID, February 9, 1967; Memorandum for the Assistant Secretary of Defense (International Security Affairs), September 23, 1966, NSF, Komer-Leonhart File, box 20, LBJL. Helen D. Bentley, "Port Snarl Imperils Viet Economy," *Baltimore Sun*, February 2, 1967. Memorandum from General William C. Westmoreland to Commander in Chief, Pacific, May 29, 1966, NSF, Komer-Leonhart File, box 20, LBJL, 2.

[20] Ibid. Bentley, "Saigon Port Jam Called Worst Ever," *Baltimore Sun*, January 19, 1967, and "Congestion, Corruption Strangle Saigon," *Baltimore Sun*, February 6, 1967. Memorandum for: The Honorable Robert W. Komer, February 8, 1967, NSF, Komer-Leonhart File, box 20, LBJL.

7. Construction photo from 1967 showing a fleet of Vietnamese-owned sampans delivering sand for fill of the marshy area around the massive new Saigon port complex.

That expansion effort was under way in numerous ports simultaneously by mid-1966. Plans to improve the facilities at Saigon included construction of all new deep-draft berthing and related docking facilities. In late 1966, the Builders finished the initial phases of a major renovation of the port with Quay #1 and Wharf #1. Both of these docks soon provided deep-draft berthing and modern dock space the equivalent of several city blocks in length. The navy handed Quay #1 over to the U.S. Army in October, and Wharf #1, completed in November, catered to Vietnamese naval vessels.[21] The Builders also raced ahead on the remaining phase of the renovation project just upstream from these other facilities.

This expansion and modernization of the port involved the creation of a whole new facility about two miles upstream from the Saigon docks. Named Newport, these docks would be isolated from the hectic and overcrowded activity at Saigon, yet connected to the Long Binh base by high-speed Route 1A, and close to the air terminal at Tan Son Nhut. Newport, which opened for deep-draft vessels in January 1967, sat on a

[21] "Quay Helps Ease Saigon Port Congestion," *The Em-Kayan*, January 1967, 3–5.

Quay Helps Ease Saigon Port Congestion

8. Unloading of a military ship transport (MST) at the newly opened Saigon Quay, January 1967.

one-hundred-acre site and provided twenty-four hundred feet of deep-draft berthing space, hundreds of thousands of square feet of covered storage/warehouse space, its own power plant, and maintenance and repair facilities; it was the culmination of, according to *The Em-Kayan* magazine, "the transformation of wasteland into a major harbor facility."[22] The job involved the reclamation of approximately sixty acres of swamp that at high tide were completely submerged. It called for transforming a substantial portion of the shoreline just below the Bien Hoa Highway bridge over the Saigon River. Hundreds of thousands of cubic yards of fill, the equivalent of thirty-eight acres, had to be brought in to stabilize the ground. At one time, six floating pile drivers worked feverishly sinking hundreds of iron pilings, the equivalent of thirty-eight miles in length, more than one hundred feet into the riverbed. Two thousand tons of cap beams and stringers were then set atop the piles, and

[22] "Ships Berth at New Saigon Port Complex," *The Em-Kayan*, April 1967, 1–3.

dozens of massive, prefabricated concrete slabs were brought into place by barges. The ramps for "LSTs" (landing ship, tanker) were completed and handed over in October 1966. The deep-draft berths required an additional forty acres of fill and months of ten-hour days and seven-day weeks. This section of the project, "increment 2" in contractor parlance, consisted of four deep-draft piers to be completed at about two-month intervals, each providing 620 feet of dock space. Newport officially opened in July 1967, although its new barge, LST, and deep-draft berthing facilities had been in use for months.[23] The largest single port project, Newport relieved the heavy congestion at the Saigon terminal by shifting the burden of U.S. military ship traffic upstream. Port congestion had, in fact, aroused the interest of officials in Washington for some time. Policy makers understood that limited port space sharply restricted their ability not only to carry out a military buildup, but also to sufficiently augment the commodity and food aid side of the program to offset that buildup and the depredation caused by continuing war. Engineers estimated the Newport facility alone increased the capacity of the Saigon port system by 100 percent. Overall, the massive construction meant that Saigon could simultaneously discharge 50 percent more ships than at the end of 1965.[24]

Only three miles from downtown Saigon, the Tan Son Nhut airfield, the principal hub of air traffic since 1954, also underwent significant expansion and renovation at this time. More than simply an airfield, the

---

[23] *Diary of a Contract*, 261–63. Paul Harder, "Newport – Relief for a Massive Shipping Headache," *Power Parade*, 1967, 6–8. "Newport Getting First Deep-Draft Pier," *Vietnam Builders* 1, no. 24 (1967): 4. Letter to RMK-BRJ from OICC, Subject: Contract NBy-44105, Construction of Facilities and Related Services in Support of U.S. Operations in Southeast Asia Area, March 27, 1967, *RMK-BRJ Papers*. The Builders' newspaper gushed at the opening, "All traces of girlhood were gone – the unsightly gap-tooth piling and the distressing dental-brace reinforcing steel. The 'bride' upon whom so much care and affection was lavished for 13 months, had become a very attractive young woman." "Newport Becomes a Reality – Officially," *Vietnam Builders* 2, no. 6 (1967): 1.

[24] I have arrived at an increase of 100 percent for the port overall by estimating the port's capacity prior to the completion of Newport at three hundred thousand tons per month. In November 1966, the port received 415,000 tons, and in January 1967, 267,000 tons. My estimate is based on a compromise between these figures. The port's capacity after completion of Newport increased to six hundred thousand tons per month. "LBJ Keenly Interested in Newport Progress," *Vietnam Builders* 1, no. 19 (1966): 1. Memorandum for: The Honorable Robert W. Komer, February 8, 1967, NSF, Komer-Leonhart File, box 20, LBJL. John Prados, *The Hidden History of the Vietnam War* (Chicago: Ivan R. Dee, 1995), 107.

9. A barge-mounted crane drives pilings for expanded berthing and dock space in Saigon River, 1966.

Ships Berth at New Saigon Port Complex

10. A 1967 aerial view of the massive Saigon port complex, called Newport, under construction.

11. Vietnamese working in the foreground, while a landing ship, tanker (LST) off-loads at a new shallow-draft facility in the background, spring 1967.

Builders helped to transform Tan Son Nhut into a modern air complex and a main army headquarters base. The project involved an expansion of the aircraft parking apron, nine thousand feet of new taxiways, a new ten-thousand-foot runway parallel to the existing one and capable of landing jet aircraft, construction of a communications center and telephone exchange, new hangars, extensive road repair and construction, a renovated system of drainage, new maintenance and repair facilities, an independent power plant, an ammunition depot, barracks and dormitories, sewage treatment facilities, and a chilled water distribution system.[25] As an airfield, Tan Son Nhut handled a volume of air traffic comparable to the world's busiest commercial airports. Officially dedicated in June 1967, the new parallel jet runway made possible 45,000 takeoffs and landings every month. This volume consisted largely of military traffic, although commercial liners, such as Pan American, Air

---

[25] Letter from OICC to RMK-BRJ, Subject: Contract NBy-44105, March 18, 1967; Letter from OICC to RMK-BRJ, Subject: Contract NBy-44105, March 28, 1967; Letter from OICC to RMK-BRJ, Subject: Contract NBy-44105, March 31, 1967, *RMK-BRJ Papers*. *Diary of a Contract*, 197–202. Paul Harder, "Tan Son Nhut – A Modern Jet Port for Saigon," *Power Parade*, 1967, 12–14.

France, Air Vietnam, Japan Airlines, and Thai International, regularly came and went as well. Although by far the largest, the Tan Son Nhut airport became only one of five equipped with parallel jet landing strips and thus capable of heavy military traffic. The other airfields were those at Da Nang, Phan Rang, Chu Lai, and Cam Ranh.[26]

Commonly referred to as the "Little Pentagon," the Tan Son Nhut base also aimed at "getting the dozens of MACV [Military Assistance Command, Vietnam] offices now scattered throughout Saigon under one roof."[27] Once accomplished, the center would serve as a major element in the overall "Saigon complex" consisting of the new port facilities (Newport), the large Bien Hoa air base, the massive base of Long Binh, the LST ports at Vung Tau and Can Tho, and numerous other smaller installations and facilities and involving many tens of thousands of service personnel.[28] In this sense, the completion of work on the base in 1967 represented a crucial step in the larger plan to create a modern, national military infrastructure that would link the disparate parts of southern Vietnam and render them defensible. Tan Son Nhut, like the Newport project, was, however, only regional. Other major military centers mirroring those in the delta region were simultaneously under construction to the north.

The Builders hurried to complete work on a large-scale port facility 180 miles northeast of Saigon, in the second Corps Tactical Zone, or II Corps. The Cam Ranh Bay had for years been considered one of just two substantial ports of southern Vietnam. And though much smaller than the southern point of entry, Cam Ranh was the only other port with any deep-draft capability prior to major escalation. The Cam Ranh peninsula, situated about halfway up the coast of southern Vietnam, is strategically located and U.S. military planners recognized its potential just as had the French so many years earlier.[29] The Builders had actually carried out substantial work at the port since the earliest days of the

---

[26] "Another Jet Runway at Saigon's Doorway," *The Em-Kayan*, July 1967, 8–10. "Another 10,000-Foot Runway at Bien Hoa," *The Em-Kayan*, March 1968, 8–10.

[27] "'Little Pentagon' Is Refresher Course for MACV Project Superintendent," *Vietnam Builders* 1, no. 24 (1967): 2.

[28] Dunn, *Base Development*, 68–69.

[29] The Cam Ranh peninsula, extending out eighteen miles and only one to five miles in width, offered an ideal refuge and port for oceangoing vessels. The French in the nineteenth century, the Russians during the Russo-Japanese War of 1905, and the Japanese during World War II all made use of this port. *Diary of a Contract*, 59.

contract. However, that work had been quite limited relative to the demands for construction that followed. After a lull in construction activity there following the summer of 1964, work resumed, and the number and scope of the projects associated with the new complex at Cam Ranh expanded rapidly following the Johnson administration's decision to escalate the war a year later.[30]

The hurriedly constructed "interim air base" had to be considerably expanded. The expansion would now include a major air base, logistics depot, and port facility. What had begun as one project soon swelled to twenty separate jobs, most of them under way simultaneously. A naval small boat facility, a barracks/dormitory, a large area of covered storage and warehouse space, petroleum/oil/lubricant (POL) storage facilities, and a large ammunition depot, among other things, had to be built. The job involved moving more than 3 million cubic yards of earth to build up the area for runways, aprons, taxiways, and buildings related to the airfield alone. Workers split into shifts and worked twenty-four hours per day on port improvements. Dredges simultaneously removed millions of cubic yards of material to make way for deep-draft traffic. Within eighteen months of initiating renewed construction, Cam Ranh had been transformed from endless acres of "unbroken sand dunes" into a modern, world-class air and sea terminal. The complex now boasted a modern jet airstrip, substantial deep-draft berthing facilities, ample warehouse space, many miles of new roads, including a new causeway, and numerous other assets.[31] The expansion program made it possible for the Cam Ranh complex to serve a wide area encompassing Nha Trang to the north, Ban Me Thuot much deeper in the interior, Phan Rang to the south, and all points in between.

Farther north, more than 350 miles from Saigon and centered in I Corps, the Builders had been at work on the port at Da Nang for several years, even before that first contingent of U.S. Marines splashed ashore there in March 1965. Because the war continued to expand, so, too, did the demands on port capacity and speed at Da Nang. Military commanders saw this port as crucial in pacifying the northern part of southern Vietnam just below the seventeenth parallel. Consequently,

---

[30] *Diary of a Contract*, 115–16.
[31] "Viet Nam: Building for Battle, Building for Peace," *The Em-Kayan*, September 1966, 8–11. *Diary of a Contract*, 226–33.

VIET NAM♦ BUILDING FOR BATTLE BUILDING FOR PEACE

12. A dramatically transformed Cam Ranh Bay in 1966. *The Em-Kayan* magazine captioned this image, saying, "Once a lonely stretch of sandy beach, ships unload at port development that will provide South Viet Nam's future economy with one of the best commercial shipping facilities in Southeast Asia." Photo taken in 1966.

construction there surged again after 1965. An expanded port and airfield would allow for the introduction of troops and supplies on a sufficiently large scale. Operations there took on the now familiar formula for base construction: expanded storage, always in short supply, dredging coupled with pier construction for deep-draft berthing, heavy fill operations to build up the land, POL storage, a ten-thousand-foot asphalt landing strip and related facilities, three power plants, miles of roads, and a new seventeen-hundred-foot-long bridge. The work in the area was extensive, requiring the labor of 570 American personnel, 1,000 third country nationals, and 8,100 Vietnamese.

Planners split the facility into Da Nang West and Da Nang East, requiring duplication of numerous jobs and assets. A sprawling base divided by the Da Nang River, each wing required its own system of electric power generation. Construction work on both sides competed for resources of men and equipment. Opposition to the war and to the

13. Vietnamese workers employed by the RMK-BRJ operate concrete paving equipment on Da Nang airfield construction project, 1966.

Saigon regime also complicated the construction work as the Builders' workforce evaporated during a particularly acute crisis in May 1967, forcing a temporary halt on all work. Nevertheless, the Builders met the construction demands and created another modern military complex just one hundred miles from the Demilitarized Zone.[32] By early 1968, the base supported two-thirds of the navy's entire strength in Vietnam, along with the seven thousand air force personnel in I Corps, most of which were in Da Nang. Once operational, this complex supported more than eighty thousand troops.[33]

The five projects at Long Binh, Newport, Tan Son Nhut, Cam Ranh Bay, and Da Nang represent a little less than half of the whole construction program for southern Vietnam.[34] With a combined value of

[32] *Diary of a Contract*, 51–54, 107–9, 211–21. Paul Harder, "Da Nang – Southeast Asia's Finest Air-Sea Terminal," *Power Parade*, 1967, 10–11. "Danang – World's Busiest Airport?," *Vietnam Builders* 1, no. 15 (1966): 1.

[33] Dunn, *Base Development*, 68.

[34] At least in monetary terms, these projects represented less than half the value of all work put in place during the life of the contract. There were literally hundreds of large construction projects under way simultaneously all over southern Vietnam. See, e.g., Letter from Brown & Root to MK, Raymond, J. A. Jones, March 1, 1966; Letter to MK, Raymond, Brown & Root, J. A. Jones from R. K. Woodhead, Project Manager, September 22, 1966; Letter to Raymond, MK, Brown & Root, J. A. Jones, Subject: Contract NBy-44105, March 28, 1967; Letter to Raymond, MK, Brown & Root, J. A. Jones, Subject: Contract NBy-44105, March 30, 1967, *RMK-BRJ Papers*.

more than $790 million, these five stand out for their scope and scale.[35] They also vividly illustrate the objectives of the buildup. The construction of these massive bases, airfields, and ports allowed for the influx of an unprecedented volume of military materiel, troops, commodity, and other aid. A vast road network crisscrossing more than one thousand miles served to connect them in a matrix stretching from Phu Bai in the north to the POL storage facility at Soc Trang deep in the Mekong Delta. These five projects combined with all the rest, though sometimes couched in terms of their ultimate value to the state of South Vietnam, were necessary because the effort to build that state had met with failure over the previous decade. Builders, military planners, and political officials alike, at one time or another, touted the construction for its contribution to southern Vietnam's economic development, modernization, and eventual independence. The chief obstacle to the entire effort, it should be clear, had to do with the critical lack of infrastructure of every kind. The kind of infrastructure being put in place was explicitly military and did not aid in the development of an independent southern state. Building a vast network of modern military bases certainly allowed for the infusion of far greater military aid than would otherwise have been possible. Those bases and the larger war they made possible, however, also created considerable chaos in social, political, and economic terms.

The larger bases detailed here do not fully represent the magnitude of the construction. Many others competed for materials and labor, and their costs ran into the many millions. The great air base at Bien Hoa, for example, became a full-service facility, complete with its ten-thousand-foot jet landing strip, ammunition depot, POL storage, barracks, and a cost of $80 million. Similarly, the large, modern military installations at Pleiku, Qui Nhon, Vung Tau, and Nha Trang all required dozens of miles of road construction, prodigious quantities of labor and resources, the elimination of hundreds of acres of jungle, and a huge volume of supplies of all kinds to keep them operational. They combined for a total cost of nearly $200 million. Other projects included those at Cat Lo, Can Tho, Soc Trang, Phan Rang, Phu Cat, Ving Long, Rach Gia, My Tho, Ban Me Thuot, and An Khe. These projects required the establishment of

---

[35] *Combined Completion Report, Basic Report, 1962–1972*, schedule XIII, 3 of 3, *RMK-BRJ Papers*.

14. Workers inventory RMK-BRJ equipment on hand, "Saigon Island Depot," 1968.

huge rock quarries in southern Vietnam to obtain the millions of tons of rock needed for roads and fill and the acquisition of many thousands of acres on which to build bases, and as rights-of-way. The Builders, during the life of the contract, moved 91 million cubic yards of earth, used 48 million tons of rock product, nearly 11 million tons of asphalt, poured 3.7 million yards of concrete (enough to have built a wall two feet wide and five feet high completely around southern Vietnam), and moved an average of more than five hundred thousand tons of goods every month. The U.S. Navy and the Builders valued the construction put in place across southern Vietnam at $1.9 billion at the completion of the contract period.[36] Certainly, such a mammoth construction program brought in much capital and technology and left a physical infrastructure unparalleled in all of Southeast Asia.

The construction projects just surveyed are significant for reasons other than their sheer scale, however. Their significance also lies in their larger meaning to the thrust of and the specific outlines of U.S. foreign policy. The projects in southern Vietnam are as clear an indication as the historian is likely ever to get of the supreme confidence placed in

---

[36] The contract extended to 1972, though the most intense period of construction was achieved during 1966–1968. *Combined Completion Report, Basic Report*, schedule XIII, 1–3, *RMK-BRJ Papers*. "RMK-BRJ, the Vietnam Builders, 'the Construction Miracle of the Decade,'" *RMK-BRJ Papers. Diary of a Contract.*

these kinds of solutions in the face of insurmountable obstacles. In dealing with those obstacles, the architects of U.S. Vietnam policy came to rely on the power of technology, machines, engineering, and American know-how.[37] The engineers and managers of this program repeatedly characterized their activities and responsibilities in these terms. In 1966, and only about a year into the major military buildup, the contractors saw themselves as "changing [the] face of South Viet Nam" through the construction projects. As late as April 1972, MK's in-house magazine described the "unprecedented construction program" that had created in southern Vietnam "a nucleus of competent builders as well as scores of long-term improvements to assist the nation in its continuing struggle for independence."[38] They and political officials as well remained both markedly proud of and highly confident in their work to bring a solution to this troubled place and a Cold War triumph for the United States.

Only when assessed in full measure does one begin to appreciate why those involved referred to their work as "the construction miracle of the decade." The combined result of these many projects made the defense of a piece of territory possible. Overall logistics capacity, from airfields to sea ports, increased many times over during this brief period. The network of canals and rivers, of roads primary, secondary, and tertiary, also expanded many times over. This expanded capacity made possible the prosecution of a major war. By the middle of 1968, the United States deployed over 530,000 troops. The military forces defending the Saigon regime, the Army of the Republic of Vietnam, numbered 562,000 by the end of 1966. This force level, which needed also to be highly mobile, required an immense and efficient logistics grid. Prior to the construction "miracle," nothing like a modern communications and transportation grid existed below the seventeenth parallel.

The construction program created enough of one to make war possible. The emphasis on preparation for war, however, represented an important shift in the objectives of state building. While southern Vietnam's military-related infrastructure, roads and bridges, ports and airfields became more or less modernized, the war destroyed hamlets,

---

[37] Adas, *Dominance by Design*, esp. chap. 5.
[38] "Construction of Military Facilities," *The Em-Kayan*, August 1966, 12–13. "Building Bridges in South Viet Nam," *The Em-Kayan*, April 1972, 10–11.

villages, and farmland, turned millions of peasants out as refugees, and generally disrupted the countryside in an overwhelmingly agrarian society. The resulting mass movement and forced urbanization exposed the absence of an adequate infrastructure in the urban environments as well. Access to decent housing, jobs and job training, health care and education, and measures to combat poverty and protect against vice and crime were notably absent. Consequently, the flood of refugees became not part of the thriving, generally prosperous life of the city, but an added burden on an already critically burdened social, economic, and political system.

"NOT MUCH MORE THAN A DROP IN THE BUCKET": REFUGEES, PACIFICATION, AND THE "OTHER WAR" IN SOUTHERN VIETNAM

As officials had forecast, expanding to war in Vietnam also raised its visibility at home and placed greater strain on the policy consensus the president had been able to hold together. As one consequence, the period witnessed a leap in the number of congressional investigations into American policy and activity in southern Vietnam. Increasing criticism and pressure from Congress in fact paralleled a burgeoning anti-war movement in the United States. Both houses of Congress carried out numerous investigations covering different aspects of the American mission to Southeast Asia. The investigations quickly piled up and ultimately exposed an alarmingly ineffective aid program and the contradictions that had by now undermined the project in southern Vietnam.[39]

As the war intensified during these years, so, too, did the level of disruption and dislocation. The great majority of the war was carried out below the seventeenth parallel. Frustrated by the continued resilience and pervasiveness of the revolution in the countryside, MACV Commander General William C. Westmoreland decided to go after the insurgency and the apparatus now built up around it consisting of Vietnamese peasants. Military officials surmised that to eliminate the insurgency, it would be necessary to shake it loose from the population

---

[39] See, e.g., the very visible hearings conducted by Senator J. William Fulbright, *The Vietnam Hearings*, with an introduction by J. William Fulbright (New York: Vintage Books, 1966).

from which it drew support. To U.S. planners, this necessarily involved massive firepower, the destruction of much of the village structure of rural society, the elimination of farms, crops, and forests used for sustenance and cover, and the forced removal of hundreds of thousands of people.

The American military force level increased from just fewer than 200,000 by the end of 1965 to more than 385,000 a year later, then to 485,000 in 1967 and to 536,000 by the end of 1968. Throughout, the United States retained an overwhelming technological, economic, training, and equipment advantage. As George Herring has written, "the Americans who fought in Vietnam were the best-fed, best-clothed, and best-equipped army the nation had ever sent to war."[40] General Westmoreland jettisoned the "enclave" concept early on, which would have kept American troops with their backs to the sea, safeguarding U.S. air bases, and engaged those forces in offensive operations out in the hinterland of southern Vietnam. In 1966, American troops carried out what were termed *search and destroy* operations designed to actively seek out pockets of insurgents and engage them wherever they were found. This tactic increasingly involved the troops in the villages and hamlets of rural Vietnam. At the same time, these operations relied on air support from helicopters and B-52 bombers to compliment their movements and engagements. As the physical infrastructure of southern Vietnam expanded along with the military forces, it at last became possible to extend military combat to the countryside. One of the consequences was the generation of large numbers of refugees fleeing combat and a more general movement of people from the rural environment into cities from 1965 forward.[41] This movement of millions of people created grave social instability and seriously challenged the capacity of the American mission and its Vietnamese allies to bring about a legitimate and stable political system capable of governing. Given the regime's obvious weaknesses over the previous years, the added chaos and volatility of a mobile, displaced population made the success of the project ever more unlikely.

[40] George Herring, *America's Longest War: The United States and Vietnam, 1950–1975,* 4th ed. (New York: McGraw-Hill, 2002), 181.

[41] For a detailed description and analysis of the emergence of a serious refugee problem from the perspective of the AID, see *United States Economic Assistance to South Vietnam (USEASV),* II: 824–46.

As early as summer 1965, a Senate subcommittee chaired by Senator Edward M. Kennedy disclosed that the war had resulted in between 380,000 and 500,000 refugees. More than two hundred thousand of those were then being held in "makeshift camps as wards of the state" as there was little infrastructure or plan in place to deal with them. Witnesses testified that the problem would become much more serious over the weeks and months to come.[42] As long as combat increased in intensity and coverage over large areas of rural Vietnam, noncombatants would be compelled to flee for survival or to leave burned-out and bombed-out hamlets. Some fled directly into the system of encampments quickly being built along the coast. Some simply walked to the nearest city and became a part of its growing urban population.[43] Others, particularly orphaned children, were taken in by family or others from their home village. The Saigon regime's Ministry of Social Welfare attempted to receive and catalog displaced persons with only mixed results.[44] Among both the Vietnamese and Americans, thinking on the issue of refugee generation lagged far behind. American officials believed that "the problem of refugees is something that is primarily in the hands of the Vietnamese [Saigon] Government [and] we are satisfied that the refugees are getting at least a minimum of care," according to an official at the U.S. State Department. The AID viewed them largely as a burden on an already strained economic system because, as farmers, they "bring with them no special skills" that would make them useful in the city. The American mission had no funds budgeted for refugee relief and no one assigned to refugee work. As the Senate hearings made public the subcommittee's findings, officials scrambled to piece together a policy to begin to deal with the crisis.[45]

---

[42] U.S. Congress, Subcommittee to Investigate Problems Connected with Refugees and Escapees, *Refugee Problems in South Vietnam and Laos*, 89th Cong., 1st sess., 1965, 14–15, 87.

[43] Louis A. Wiesner, *Victims and Survivors: Displaced Persons and Other War Victims in Viet-Nam, 1954–1975* (New York: Greenwood Press, 1988), 61–65.

[44] U.S. Congress, *Refugee Problems*, 143. The ministry estimated the number of orphaned children, for example, at ten thousand. This figure reflected only those in orphanages and not those taken in by other villages or held in one of the numerous refugee encampments. Officials acknowledged that the latter accounted for the vast majority of orphaned children, but there existed no system to accurately keep track of the growing numbers of refugees.

[45] U.S. Congress, Subcommittee to Investigate Problems Connected with Refugees and Escapees, *Civilian Casualty and Refugee Problems in South Vietnam*, 90th Cong., 2nd

Nevertheless, investigators found little progress in dealing with the still growing population of refugees into 1967 and 1968. There existed no accurate accounting of the flow of people out of war zones into cities and back again. Some Americans close to Saigon believed the regime greatly underreported the problem. Refugees were considered resettled, for example, by simply changing the status of the camp in which they lived from temporary to permanent. Officials running the camps also created phantom refugees by keeping names on the official list of inhabitants who were either dead or no longer present. This deception ensured the uninterrupted flow of monetary and other refugee relief aid from Saigon and the American aid program. Many tens of thousands of the war's victims simply remained beyond the reach of the regime's accounting system. The congressional investigation placed the number of refugees as of December 1966 at more than 1.6 million. The Americans generally believed their Vietnamese ally kept the numbers of refugees artificially low for political reasons. In Saigon, for example, the regime published monthly maps detailing the refugee problem by area. Saigon, without exception, showed zero refugees each month, while in private, officials acknowledged the presence of between three hundred thousand and five hundred thousand in the city. Congressional investigators found many of these living on the streets, in cemeteries, and in hollowed-out tombs.

A 1967 survey revealed the rate of civilian war casualties ran at approximately one hundred thousand per year. Many of those injured and crippled by war received either inadequate medical aid or none at all. There existed no health care system as such for the whole of southern Vietnam. There were too few doctors and hospitals for far too many in need of care. Shortages of trained nurses, social workers, medical supplies, and facilities persisted. The number of cases of cholera in southern Vietnam had increased from a few hundred in 1963 to more than twenty thousand by 1965. One physician investigating the problems reported that "the destruction of villages, the uncontrolled movement of groups of people and the squalid conditions in the camps have

---

sess., 1968, 2, 4. Richard Eder, "U.S. Refugee Plan for Vietnam Set," *New York Times*, August 31, 1965. American officials even approached agencies of the United Nations for help with the crisis. See Richard Eder, "U.S. Seeking U.N. Aid for Vietnamese Refugees," *New York Times*, February 15, 1966.

broken the natural barriers to the spread of disease."[46] A congressional investigation concluded similarly that "the situation in South Vietnam is that there is just too much disease and too great a demand for medical services. Almost every disease known to man is present."[47]

By 1968, an estimated thirty to fifty thousand amputees awaited prosthetics that they would likely never receive. Another fifty thousand or more civilian war victims died each year before reaching understaffed, underfunded, and overcrowded hospitals. Dr. John H. Knowles, superintendent of Massachusetts General Hospital, conducted another study late in 1967 and found the welfare of the Vietnamese people had not been given the priority it urgently needed. He estimated that nearly one-third of the Vietnamese people had tuberculosis, 80 percent suffered from "worms of one sort or another," and the thirty to fifty thousand amputee cases would likely have to wait five to fifteen years for artificial limbs. Knowles also found that the Saigon regime "spend[s] less than one percent of their budget on health services, less than any country – with or without war."[48] Although funding aimed at ameliorating some of these problems did increase, the war increased at a more rapid rate.

The poor conditions inside the refugee encampments themselves also compounded critical public health problems. Those in the camp system often did not receive the promised monetary aid or resettlement allowance. A study of eighteen such camps in 1968 revealed that the schools, medical dispensaries, housing units, and sanitary facilities budgeted for the system had either not been established or were woefully inadequate. Lack of proper drainage and sewage facilities and overcrowding quickly became endemic within the system. One field investigator reported,

We saw women and children crowded into hovels with little or no room to move or sleep, or even breathe. We saw places without water or cooking areas or sanitation facilities which were called model camps. We saw vacant-eyed

[46] U.S. Congress, *Civilian Casualty*, 5–7.

[47] *An Investigation of the U.S. Economic and Military Assistance Programs in Vietnam*, U.S. House, 42nd Report by the Committee on Government Operations, 89th Cong., 2nd sess. (October 12, 1966), 72.

[48] Hedrick Smith, "More Health Aid for Saigon Urged," *New York Times*, September 22, 1967. See also U.S. Congress, *Civilian Casualty*, 5–7.

peasants staring out of dark recesses with nothing but time on their hands. The refugee problem cannot really be understood until one sees the flesh and blood of it.[49]

The overall rate of infection in southern Vietnam mushroomed, as evidenced by the elevated death rate among children less than two years of age from dysentery and pneumonia. In some cases, refugees had not received food allowances, and no work was available for many months. Nearly half identified themselves as farmers and needed no special training to be put to use. Still, they were in the pipeline to be retrained and were in most cases not permitted to return to their land.

Combined, the flood of refugees and civilian war casualties created a grave crisis in the countryside of southern Vietnam that soon engulfed the cities and required far greater resources than anyone had forecast. Despite having increased the aid and personnel devoted to receiving and assisting refugees, AID director William Gaud told Kennedy's subcommittee, "The fact of the matter is that the health problem is so enormous that everything that we have done to date is really not much more than a drop in the bucket. . . . In terms of providing adequate facilities, you might . . . say we have scarcely scratched the surface."[50] And the problem only grew in magnitude. On the eve of the Tet Offensive of early 1968, analysts estimated the number of uprooted Vietnamese had grown to approximately 4 million, or one out of four Vietnamese below the seventeenth parallel.[51]

Despite the growing crisis, officials continued to downplay the extent and the implications of the problems associated with so many uprooted people. Reluctant even to admit that the stepped-up war itself generated large numbers of refugees, they explained this rise as a consequence of insurgent "terror," of fighting between the insurgents and the Americans and their allies, and of lesser opportunities in the countryside and greater opportunities in the city. During the Senate subcommittee's 1966 hearings, for example, AID director William Gaud testified that the refugee situation "developed very rapidly as a result of the military situation in Vietnam." Chairman Kennedy interrupted to observe, "You are our

---

[49] See U.S. Congress, *Civilian Casualty*, 11.

[50] U.S. Congress, *U.S. Apparatus of Assistance to Refugees throughout the World, Hearings before the Subcommittee to Investigate Problems Connected with Refugees and Escapees,* 89th Cong., 2nd sess., 1966, 41.

[51] U.S. Congress, *Civilian Casualty*, 2–10.

first witness from AID who has related the increase of refugees to the military activity," to which Gaud responded, "I am?"[52]

The presence of so many refugees was ultimately considered "voting with the feet." Vietnamese peasants were choosing the American-backed regime over their rural existence and an alliance with the insurgency. Consequently, there remained a basic ambivalence regarding refugee policy. As Robert Komer wrote in a memo in late 1966, "we here [are] deeply concerned by [the] growing number of refugees.... Of course, in some ways, [the] increased flow of refugees is a plus" because it helped deprive the insurgents of a base and sent peasants into the arms of the Saigon regime.[53] The generation of refugees, in the end, served both the regime and the refugees themselves, according to some who, like senior advisor on pacification James May, believed "the refugee camps bring the people in closer to the urban centers, where they can have modern experiences and learn modern practices. It's a modernization experience."[54] While this argument had some merit insofar as the generation of refugees siphoned off the insurgents' base of support, it ignored an even more troubling reality.

Millions of Vietnamese peasants came to reside in the refugee camps not out of choice, but as a matter of survival. In some instances, they were purposefully driven out by the U.S. military to deny the insurgents sanctuary within a particular village. Many were also driven out following firefights that destroyed their villages and left them no place to go. When surveyed, the vast majority of refugees in some twenty-five camps said they had been brought there by the Americans or fled for fear of American aircraft and artillery.[55] In any case, the war separated many hundreds of thousands from their homes and families, their farm lands, and their ability to carve out a living for themselves and their

---

[52] See U.S. Congress, *U.S. Apparatus*, 49.

[53] *The Pentagon Papers: The Defense Department History of United States Decisionmaking on Vietnam*, Senator Gravel ed., vol. II (Boston: Beacon Press, 1971), 569; hereinafter *PP*.

[54] George M. Kahin, *Intervention: How America Became Involved in Vietnam* (New York: Anchor Books, 1987), 407–08.

[55] U.S. Congress, *Refugee Problems*, 294–95. Address by Senator Edward M. Kennedy, before the World Affairs Council of Boston, on His Recent Trip to South Vietnam, January 25, 1968; U.S. Congress, *Civilian Casualty*, Appendix 2. Allan E. Goodman, *The Causes and Consequences of Migration to Saigon, Vietnam* (New York: Southeast Asia Development Advisory Group, 1973), 152. Wiesner, *Victims and Survivors*, 127–32.

families. Once inside the camps, the lack of adequate medical care, food aid, resettlement allowance, and work, coupled with the corruption at the refugees' expense, demonstrated perhaps more effectively than anything else the incapacity of the regime to adequately care for the rural people. The camps, consequently, bred a sense of resentment toward regime officials as well as the Americans. Furthermore, because little effort was made to distinguish between those Vietnamese actively involved in the insurgency and those who were not, the camps provided optimal recruiting opportunities for the resistance.[56]

The war was quickly altering the landscape of rural Vietnam and profoundly changing what had been the relationship between the people and the environment. No longer a nation of farmers and a leading rice exporter, southern Vietnam had to import nearly 500,000 tons of rice to feed itself in 1966, and 750,000 tons in 1967. By the following year, southern Vietnam had gone from about 15 percent urban to 40 percent urban, increasing the urban population to more than 6 million. In 1974, southern Vietnam was 65 percent urban.[57] Within the state-building context, the creation of a large and mobile population through open warfare was a critical failing of the overall effort. The millions of displaced Vietnamese who would one day make up the citizenry of "South Vietnam" would almost certainly have to once again reside in the countryside and reconstitute that rural infrastructure on which the nation of Vietnam had been built centuries earlier. As that environment increasingly became the venue for large-scale warfare, including crop destruction, widespread use of defoliants and herbicides, and antipersonnel mines, the likelihood that it could be of any value to a new state grew increasingly remote.

At the same time, this volume of people on the move both hindered and aided in the larger effort aimed at the "pacification" of the Vietnamese in the countryside. Pacification, in one form or another, had been a part of the overall effort for a number of years, stretching back to the system of strategic hamlets attempted during the Diem regime's final couple of years. The objectives, according to the AID's official history,

---

[56] See sources in note 14.
[57] Eric Wentworth, "Plan to Help Vietnam Feed Self Fails," *Washington Post*, January 21, 1967. Samuel P. Huntington, "Political Stability and Security in South Vietnam," December 1967, NSF, CF, VN, box 59, LBJL, 21. Marilyn B. Young, *The Vietnam Wars, 1945–1990* (New York: Harper Perennial, 1991), 172–77.

involved establishing security, winning over the people, and then moving into a "more ambitious 'nation building'" phase.[58] Quite simply, pacification of the countryside involved securing and fortifying the villages and hamlets within the provinces, implementing programs to win over the loyalty of the people, and, having met these goals, establishing a legitimate presence for the Saigon regime over the whole of southern Vietnam. Pacification thus called for greater political, economic, and social measures, rather than a strict reliance on military action. Following a spring 1966 conference in Honolulu, this so-called other war received much greater emphasis as officials realized the more conventional war so far had yielded no real dividend in the countryside, where, many agreed, it mattered most.[59]

As Robert Komer, in particular, looked at the problem in the countryside in 1966, he drew some troubling conclusions for U.S. aims. He put the dilemma quite bluntly when he wrote,

We have now reached the point where we must seriously examine the situation we'd confront in [the] event of negotiation combined with a military stand-down on both sides. We would be at a major disadvantage if we had no structure in the countryside adequate to compete with the Viet Cong infrastructure. So a major aim in accelerating pacification is to put the GVN in a better position to compete for the allegiance of the countryside in a situation of military stand-down.[60]

By the late 1960s, the revolution had built an elaborate and enduring infrastructure over the whole of southern Vietnam. As the war's destruction increased during this period, however, control of territory and people became both more important and more difficult.

The insurgency in the countryside struggled to adapt to the increased warfare and pacification efforts. Cadres in My Tho province, for example, tried to reduce the outflow of refugees by encouraging villagers to build "combat hamlets" and remain on the land to resist the regime and the Americans. The revolution's leaders hoped to counter pacification efforts through education, planting thorny hedgerows and bamboo to

---

[58] AID Administrative History, box 1, LBJL, 479.

[59] PP, II:548–60. "Giving a New Thrust to Pacification: Analysis, Concept, and Management," August 7, 1966, NSC, Robert Komer File (1966–1967), box 7, LBJL. This document is also in PP, II:570.

[60] Robert Komer, "The 'Other War' and South Vietnam's Future," United States Information Agency (USIA), NSC, Robert Komer File (1966–1967), box 7, LBJL.

act as fences around villages, building canals and spiked pits, and planting grenades and other weapons. These tactics were accompanied by more stringent policies of taxation and punishment to enforce compliance. The expansion of warfare and pacification meant more difficulties for maintaining the infrastructure of the insurgency, and the increasingly defensive nature of the revolution's strategy also resulted in the diminution in its own developmental projects such as clinics, schools, and improving the infrastructure of the hamlet. The expanded U.S.-Saigon pacification efforts, themselves laced with the rhetoric of "revolution," were a very self-conscious effort to get into the countryside and build a countervailing network. According to historian David Elliott, however, "the greatest problems for the revolution were not being created by clever pacification tactics or 'revolutionary development' cadres, but by the bombing, shelling, and military operations that made it nearly impossible to stay in the hamlets being fought over."[61]

Within weeks of the Honolulu Conference, thousands of Vietnamese and American advisors began training in the techniques of *revolutionary development*, another very purposeful term for pacification. Teams of fifty-nine Revolutionary Development cadres dispersed into the countryside to win over the people by digging wells; building schools; paving roads; providing modern technologies in sanitation, food preparation, health care, and screenings; and generally modernizing the villages of rural Vietnam. Planners, such as the head of the program on the American side, Robert Komer, placed great emphasis on the "revolutionary" nature of the program to undermine the insurgents' claim to revolution. The term also connoted something of the program's aim. Pacification, if successful, would not only transform the village structure of Vietnam, but radically alter the political economy of the people. According to one U.S. statement, the effort "aim[ed] at reconstituting the fabric of Vietnamese society."[62] For pacification to work, the provinces, and hence villages and hamlets, of southern Vietnam would have to become dependent on the Saigon regime as the source of government patronage, largesse, goods, security, political representation, and an array of

---

[61] David W. P. Elliott, *The Vietnamese War: Revolution and Social Change in the Mekong Delta, 1930–1975* (New York: M. E. Sharpe, 2002), II:909–11.

[62] Statement quoted in Samuel P. Huntington, "Political Stability," 8.

services. Traditional village structures of authority, taxation, and law enforcement would be at least substantially weakened, and at most entirely removed. Large urban centers of governmental influence and power would also be the destination of all rural goods. A transportation grid would link the two to facilitate movement in both directions. The new scheme would thus result in a transformed Vietnam, complete with all the requisite physical features of a modern state. Pacification was again couched within the modernization idiom of earlier years, although little evidence exists that policy makers carefully mined those earlier examples for lessons.

The renewed effort was similarly bold and confident of ultimate success. The countryside of southern Vietnam needed to be remade. If properly reformed, modernized, pacified, measured, analyzed, and accounted for, the war in the countryside would bear fruit for the overall project. The American mission needed to make rural Vietnam's complex and variegated features legible and coherent. Development, perhaps especially for the purpose of a broad-based military campaign, meant centralization, coherency, categorization, and an accounting. As anthropologist James C. Scott has written, "contemporary development schemes, whether in Southeast Asia or elsewhere, require the creation of state spaces where the government can reconfigure the society and economy of those who are to be 'developed.' The transformation of peripheral nonstate spaces into state spaces by the modern, developmentalist nation-state is ubiquitous and, for the inhabitants of such spaces, frequently traumatic."[63] Rural Vietnam was that "nonstate" space that needed to be brought into direct contact, and thus under the control, of, the regime in Saigon. Planners, military and other, had long considered this conversion absolutely necessary if the regime was to extend its presence and make it legitimate in the countryside of southern Vietnam. In the context of the Vietnam War, that effort came overwhelmingly from the United States in concert with a frequently changing assortment of Vietnamese officials in Saigon over a number of years. The decentralized, village-based social, political network of Vietnam presented an obstacle to stamping out the resistance and to bringing a central government

---

[63] James C. Scott, *Seeing Like a State: How Certain Schemes to Improve the Human Conditions Have Failed* (New Haven, CT: Yale University Press, 1998), introduction, 187.

to the interior of southern Vietnam. In large measure, this is precisely what the numerous pacification campaigns aimed to do. Although the war in the countryside was primarily conceived of as a problem with a necessarily military solution, this "other war" took on increased importance from 1966 forward. The two efforts became inextricably tied together.

One of the consequences was the generation of large numbers of refugees while, at the same time, expanding the pacification program from village to village in most of the provinces of southern Vietnam. For the military campaign to be successful, it had to engage the "enemy" and either destroy that enemy or send it fleeing the villages and hamlets. For the pacification program to work, those villages needed to be reshaped and secured, their inhabitants identified, named, listed, and accounted for. Some of the villages would have to be destroyed if they harbored high concentrations of enemy and the inhabitants moved somewhere else. Others could simply be fortified in place. Nevertheless, all needed to fit into the larger system of accounting for the war's setbacks and gains, its wins and losses, its enemy and friendly. In one of the most measured wars in the history of warfare, these details were supposed to demonstrate success that was otherwise illusive. Pacification's strategic hamlets, its *Chieu Hoi* (Open Arms), *Chien Thang* (Will to Victory), and *Hop Tac* (Victory) programs, its Revolutionary Development (RD) cadre, and later, its Civil Operations and Revolutionary Development Support all were conceived as tools to both define success and measure it.[64] Without them, to some extent even with them, the campaign to end the resistance could not be assessed. The Hamlet Evaluation System, for example, measured greater and greater numbers of people living in areas considered under the regime's control because its categories counted refugees who had fled other areas of intense combat. As the war decimated the countryside, the devices used to measure the success of pacification continued to turn out good news in the form of growing numbers of people showing up in collection centers under the direct control of the regime and the United States.

---

[64] Richard A. Hunt, *Pacification: The American Struggle for Vietnam's Hearts and Minds* (Boulder, CO: Westview Press, 1995). Pamela A. Conn, "Losing Hearts and Minds: U.S. Pacification Efforts in Vietnam during the Johnson Years," PhD diss., University of Houston, TX, 2001.

This marriage of the military and pacification campaigns was an uneasy one, to say the least. A large military presence and combat activity both served to alienate rural people and undermine efforts to pacify. Refugees fled these hostile environments for greater security elsewhere. They were thus channeled into the system of refugee camps or simply survived by the kindness of friends or family. Pacification efforts under way in villages were undermined in this way. More than once did heavy combat operations destroy a village that had already been the object of much AID attention.[65] People on the move could not be pacified, despite what the measurement devices might suggest. Nor could they be convinced that the regime being supported by the Americans had the wherewithal, not to mention the desire, to see to their needs.

Pacification also suffered the same difficulties encountered by earlier efforts. Funding, staffing, training, and equipment remained inadequate and in short supply. The level of interest waxed and waned among regime officials. Its representatives could not overcome distrust among the people, nor could they overcome the enmity of the insurgents. Thousands were kidnapped or killed. Only about half of all the so-called RD cadres required to carry out pacification ever completed training and went into the field. Actions and operations remained poorly coordinated from one place to the next. Probably the most important single factor, combat operations and the military solution to the problem of security in the countryside, continued to receive the highest priority and the lion's share of funding.[66]

The war in southern Vietnam, with its related generation of hundreds of thousands of refugees, combined with the pacification effort, attempted to make sense of and to come to control the rural environment of Vietnam to a greater extent than had any of the similar efforts

[65] U.S. Congress, *Refugee Problems*, 294–95. AID Administrative History, box 1, LBJL, 490–92. Neil Sheehan, "Vietnam Peasants Are Victims of War," *New York Times*, February 15, 1966.

[66] Memorandum for the President from William Leonhart, December 30, 1966, NSC, Robert Komer File (1966–1967), box 9, LBJL. Max Frankel, "U.S. Expert Reports Vietnam Rural Aid Failures," *New York Times*, April 30, 1967. Robert Erlandson, "Viet Pacification Program Appears in Serious Trouble," *Baltimore Sun*, May 12, 1967. Beverly Deepe, "U.S. Streamlining of Viet Bureaucracy Curbs Infighting," *Christian Science Monitor*, May 13, 1967. Ward Just, "Komer Seen Key to Role for Civilians in Vietnam," *Boston Globe*, May 16, 1967. PP, II:615–23. Wiesner, *Victims and Survivors*, 89, 90–94.

over the preceding fourteen years. It was an unprecedented campaign in scope and ambition. While it certainly yielded dividends from a military/strategic perspective, it also, in retrospect, fatally undermined whatever opportunity had existed to engage the countryside in the state-building project below the seventeenth parallel. Amid near-total disarray and social chaos and saddled with a full-blown public health crisis, southern Vietnam was further than ever from becoming an independent state capable of harnessing the energies of the people and defending its own sovereignty in the absence of American aid. That aid mushroomed to unheard-of levels during this same brief period and threatened runaway inflation, choked off any remaining possibility for encouraging greater private investment and home production, and reined in any semblance of independent political leadership. The war now demanded a greater flow of commodity, military, and construction aid.

The aid program contributed to the problem as it inundated southern Vietnam with an array of consumer goods, equipment, and people. The avalanche of goods and the resulting economic inflation became one of the chief preoccupations of the American mission, officials back in Washington, and congressional investigators. In 1966, the United States sent to Vietnam $793 million in economic aid and $686 million in military aid. This level of aid dropped slightly in fiscal 1967, but rose again to nearly $2 billion for 1968. Merchandise imports alone accounted for $650 million to $750 million of this aid package for each of those years.[67] This influx of troops, equipment, money, and other goods in large quantities critically undermined the building of an internal economic base, even without the flood of people. Officials planned the infusion of large quantities of goods as an anti-inflationary device, and the effort probably kept inflation from spiraling completely out of control.[68] However, it also created many opportunities for corruption, which became rife throughout the aid program. Congressional investigators found that an alarming quantity of aid goods never reached their intended target, but were diverted into the thriving black market that operated as a kind of economy within an economy throughout much of the war.

---

[67] Douglas C. Dacy, *Foreign Aid, War, and Economic Development: South Vietnam, 1955–1975* (New York: Cambridge University Press, 1986), 200. *USEASV*, I:8.

[68] *USEASV*, I:107.

"A NATIONAL SYMPHONY OF THEFT, CORRUPTION, AND BRIBERY"

One of the most critical problems created by the buildup for war related to the personal economy of salaried and wage-earning workers. Vietnamese families found it increasingly difficult to make ends meet after 1965. During the second quarter of 1966, the cost of living soared by 74 percent, compared to just 3.5 percent a year earlier. The cost of food, the most important single cost in a Vietnamese family's budget, rose 70 percent. By 1967, overall price levels had risen 190 percent since the buildup began in mid-1965. This galloping inflation hit civil servants especially hard, but also affected military personnel and other government workers who lived on fixed incomes.[69] Additionally, the United States found it necessary to subsidize the currency by frequently purchasing large amounts of piasters to artificially squeeze the money supply and at least limit some of the damage caused by inflation. The politics of hyperinflation could be as dangerous as any crisis the regime faced. Early in 1966, Ambassador Lodge communicated to top Vietnamese officials that "the economic problem is now top priority."[70] If left unchecked, inflation could spiral out of control and create considerable problems. As one official in Vietnam told a House subcommittee investigating the aid program in 1966, "the price of rice could put a lot bigger mobs in the streets than the monks can muster."[71]

Importantly, those Vietnamese working for the Americans, estimated at perhaps three hundred thousand, enjoyed greater earning power than could be had otherwise. Many other Vietnamese took advantage of the economic distortions and gaps created by the essentially unregulated or poorly regulated U.S. program by becoming involved in the black market, where earnings could be considerably greater. As the economic effects of the war made life more difficult for the people who continued to work within the system, they, too, grew frustrated with and alienated

---

[69] As opposed to private businessmen and workers in the private sector. "Inflation, Income and Incentives in Vietnam," November 1967, NSF, CF, VN, box 58, LBJL.

[70] Telegram from the Embassy in Vietnam to the Department of State, February 16, 1966, in *Foreign Relations of the United States*, vol. IV (Washington, DC: GPO, 1961–1963), 223–27; quote is on 226; hereinafter *FRUS*. Paper prepared by the Assistant Secretary of State for Far Eastern Affairs (Bundy), February 23, 1966, *FRUS*, 1966, IV, Vietnam: 246–55.

[71] *An Investigation*, 25.

from the aims of the project. Economic dislocation and profound distortions created by the aid program and war fed a shadow economy of speculation, smuggling, hoarding, black-marketeering, and outright theft that rivaled the official one. Indeed, those involved in the black market enjoyed not only considerably greater profits, but a more advantageous currency exchange rate and often the tacit approval of, or at least the quiescence of, officials of the regime. Certain of those officials themselves became deeply involved in the corruption of the system. An unidentified U.S. official in Vietnam told congressional investigators "that running parallel with the war is a national symphony of theft, corruption, and bribery." Investigators turned up an alarmingly inefficient and counterproductive aid program. As the war progressed, problems in the program became more pronounced and more difficult to solve than ever. The conclusions of that investigation, which was carried out by the House Committee on Foreign Operations, constituted the most damning indictment by Congress of the overall program to date.[72]

The committee began its thorough investigation early in February. Members and staffers traveled to Vietnam in March 1966 to conduct observation trips to various sites and hold more formal hearings with an assortment of members of the American mission. They questioned officials in the AID mission of the U.S. embassy, the U.S. Information Agency, and the U.S. military. In Vietnam, they observed the port facilities at Cam Ranh Bay, the pacification system at a variety of specific locations, police training facilities, and the refugee relief program around Vung Tau and collected statements, both official and unofficial, from scores of people on virtually every aspect of the U.S. program. They held additional hearings in Saigon, Bangkok, Taipei, and Hong Kong. After returning to Washington, the committee held another set of hearings with American officials stretching from July to August. The investigation was, as the committee claimed, "the first comprehensive congressional report ever written on the U.S. AID program in Vietnam."[73] The findings of this investigation, and of numerous others that followed, disclosed critical deficiencies with the U.S. effort.[74]

---

[72] Ibid., 6. The price of rice increased at a rate 50 percent faster than the cost of living in Saigon. See also "Vietnam Rice Situation," 1967(?), NSF, CF, VN, box 58, LBJL.

[73] *An Investigation*, 3–5.

[74] *Illicit Practices Affecting the U.S. Economic Program in Vietnam (Followup Investigation)*, Committee on Government Operations, Fourth Report, August 25, 1967. *The Port*

One of the most problematic elements of the overall aid package remained the CIP. This feature inundated southern Vietnam with such a volume of goods that it prevented home production and perpetuated dependence. The level of goods imported through the CIP had risen steadily over the previous few years. From around $98 million in 1962, the level climbed to $114 million for 1964, to $153 million for 1965, then to $399 million for fiscal year 1966.[75] Up to June 1966, Vietnamese importers paid for these goods at the effective exchange rate of sixty piasters to the dollar. That month, the effective rate changed to 118 to 1. And although the new rate, recommended by an International Monetary Fund (IMF) delegation to Vietnam in May, immediately sent retail prices up by 25 percent, it also brought in considerably more piasters for the regime and took them out of the money supply, thereby producing the desired anti-inflationary effect. As an anti-inflationary tool, however, the exchange rate was only a small and relatively unimportant measure.

The major anti-inflationary device of the entire program remained the CIP itself. Consumer goods brought into Vietnam via this channel amounted to 70 percent of all nonmilitary aid. Aside from keeping inflation tamped down by soaking up excess spending capacity, the increased volume of CIP goods created serious economic distortions and opportunities for windfall profits. Furthermore, goods entered southern Vietnam without a clearly established need and without any determination that they could be absorbed into the economy.[76] Iron and steel products, industrial machinery, machine parts, cement, chemicals, and pharmaceuticals, for example, all entered Vietnam in excessive quantities. So great was the fear of runaway inflation that the level of CIP imports swelled with little regard for many of the consequences. Among officials of the Johnson administration, inflation had become one of the principal preoccupations. As part of the effort to offset the effects of the massive buildup, Secretary McNamara, Ambassador Lodge, and others urged a sharp reduction in spending levels by the U.S. military and American

---

Situation in Vietnam (Followup Investigation), Committee on Government Operations, Sixth Report, August 25, 1967. A Review of the Inequitable Monetary Rate of Exchange in Vietnam, Committee on Government Operations, Twenty-sixth Report, June 25, 1970.

[75] U.S. Congress, Improper Practices, Commodity Import Program, U.S. Foreign Aid, Vietnam, Hearings before the Subcommittee on Investigations of the Committee on Government Operations, 90th Cong., 1st sess., 1967, 3.

[76] "Imports of Aid Supplies to Vietnam Outpace Control by US," New York Times, May 10, 1966.

contractor personnel. American military personnel alone spent an estimated $150 million to $200 million into the fragile economy and thus drove up prices for all those Vietnamese on fixed incomes working for the regime.[77] Secretary McNamara warned in late 1966 that "runaway inflation can undo what our military operations accomplish." "Unless we rigidly control inflation," McNamara wrote, "the Vietnamese Army desertion rate will increase further and effectiveness will decline, thus at least partially canceling the effects of increased U.S. deployments."[78] The specter of inflation was at least one of the factors leading to the construction of the giant U.S. military base at Long Binh.

The system did not contain checks and assurances that the goods would be used as intended, that they would not be diverted into the black market, or that they would not be hoarded to drive up prices. CIP imports entered Vietnam without a clear understanding of the disposition of similar goods imported earlier through the CIP or an assessment of stocks on hand to prevent excessive quantities piling up. One of the consequences of this lack of oversight was rampant speculation in American goods.

During the whole of the war, the black marketing of American goods created a substantial underground economy. One of the most visible manifestations of this economy could be found by visiting what was tellingly termed *PX Alley* (post exchange). PX Alley consisted of a several-block area of Saigon devoted to dozens of individual stalls or kiosks lining both sides of the street and selling American consumer goods such as Lucky Strike, Salem, Kent, and Winston cigarettes, radios, hair spray, razor blades, Styrofoam coolers, soap, U.S. Army K rations, blankets, and Campbell's Soup, among dozens of other well-known American goods. Though technically illegal, not to mention detrimental to larger objectives of American aid, this very visible and widespread phenomenon continued unabated for years. Nor was this market limited to PX Alley. The resale of American goods flourished, and they could easily be found all over Saigon and in other cities as well. In many instances, goods destined for the PX actually showed up on the black

[77] U.S. sector expenditures had increased from $31.6 million in 1964, to $210 million in 1965, then to $625 million in 1966. *USEASV*, I:113.

[78] Memorandum from Secretary of Defense McNamara to the Chairman, Joint Chiefs of Staff (Wheeler), November 11, 1966, *FRUS*, 1966, IV, Vietnam: 826–27.

market before they had been stocked on the shelves at the U.S. military facility. The exchange rate for these diverted black market goods ranged from 160 to 200 to 1.

The deputy director of the AID mission believed that "this is the most serious problem that exists for the U.S. Government in Vietnam today." The availability of American goods and the diversion of those goods into the black market economy created "a vast number of profiteers." Profiteers effectively obtained CIP goods at less than one-third their value and then sold them for more than their value on the black market. In the course of congressional investigations, officials discovered substantial diversion of goods and numerous warehouses full of tons of goods being hoarded to drive up local prices. Investigators found, for example, a back ally warehouse containing forty thousand tons of fertilizer. They discovered over eighty thousand metal files initially imported through the CIP that were then exported to Bangkok, Thailand, at substantial profit. The source of the diversion could not be determined because many different Vietnamese importers dealt with these items, and the AID kept few, if any, records of these transactions. Investigation also turned up a large camp that acted as a depot for receiving pilfered American aid goods. This camp contained, among other items, fifteen hundred tons of rice, six thousand pieces of galvanized sheet metal, and one thousand gallons of kerosene. Half a dozen times in six months, the U.S. military seized American pharmaceutical goods from the insurgents.[79]

Importers could bring in essentially anything they thought they could sell internally or easily export. These importers, licensed by the regime, enjoyed considerable advantages over domestic producers. As mentioned earlier, the domestic producer sold his goods within a much more rigid currency regime. The importer applied for a license, ordered goods, paid the piasters to the counterpart fund at the fixed rate, then sold those goods essentially to the highest bidder. Additionally, importers could avoid the competitive bidding process by simply applying for a license to import commodities valued at slightly under ten thousand dollars. Any import order for less than this amount did not have to go through the more rigorous and potentially competitive process, but was simply approved and the transaction moved through the pipeline. These transactions, which one congressman termed an "invitation to

---

[79] *An Investigation*, 17, 22, 26–37. See also Herring, *America's Longest War*, 196–98.

steal," could be simply handed out to friends and associates and were, by design, beyond the reach of the AID. For fiscal year 1966, approximately 85 percent, or twenty-five thousand transactions, of all licenses issued came in below $10,000, and a large number of them amounted to $9,900.[80] There were a little more than two thousand licensed importers in southern Vietnam. The privilege had been granted to them several years earlier. Investigators found that despite AID's knowledge of these importers and of the substantial diversion of commodities to the insurgency and the black market, there still existed no system to check on the honesty, the integrity, past patterns of good or bad behavior, or the political background of importers. The regime disqualified and blacklisted only twenty-three of the two thousand importers. For twenty of those twenty-three, officials only did so following the congressional investigation.[81]

On the import side, Vietnamese businessmen enjoyed, in fact, extraordinary latitude in their conduct of commercial activities. U.S. exporters, for example, often used agents or commissioners to handle the importation of their goods into Vietnam. These Vietnamese agents acted as the company's liaison, for which they earned a commission. In some cases, the agents themselves contacted the U.S. firms to offer their services and thus began the business relationship. Because the aid program lacked adequate controls and oversight, the agents could go well beyond this simple arrangement. U.S. firms sometimes paid agents fees greater than half the value of the goods to be imported simply to avoid the competition of an open bidding process. In a number of cases, the agents actually set up paper companies as appendages of the real company in the United States. The agents themselves would then head the dummy corporation. This peculiar arrangement allowed the agent to earn far greater commission than was otherwise permitted by simply billing the company back in the United States for the necessary "expenses" of running its Vietnam branch. For the U.S. company, it could thus avoid paying the taxes normally associated with such a relationship between countries. The payments to the subsidiary for "expenses" (actually payments to the agent for his services) went to Vietnam, then into a Swiss account that was shielded from the normal process of taxation, inspection, or

---

[80] U.S. Congress, *Improper Practices*, 2–4, 91. *USEASV*, II:461–62.
[81] *An Investigation*, 16. U.S. Congress, *Commodity Import Program*, 9.

audit. U.S. exporters funneled hundreds of thousands of dollars through this system. Vietnamese agents earned large commissions and succeeded in the real objective, removal of their money from the volatile economic conditions prevalent in Vietnam into a much safer European account. This kind of capital flight actually became commonplace, and accounts were discovered in Asia as well as in Europe for the express purpose of taking money out of Vietnam.[82]

For these and numerous other reasons, the Saigon regime simply could not generate any internal investment in the building of the new state. It still could not generate sufficient revenue through taxation to come close to paying for its constantly expanding budget costs. For fiscal year 1968, domestic taxes still accounted for only 16 percent of the total budget. Of these tax revenues, income taxes accounted for only a small fraction of the total. Revenue from excise taxes on such items as tobacco, beer, and beverages was substantially more important but still critically limited.[83] The regime generated more revenue through taxes on U.S. imports than through domestic taxes. This inability to collect sufficient taxes, or what the AID characterized as "the inelasticity of domestic tax revenues," was a burden created and perpetuated by the aid program itself. According to the AID's Rutherford Poats, the regime's "capacity to tax efficiently the Vietnamese businessman, the Vietnamese shop owner, and the Vietnamese cabaret operator, and so on, who is making a lot of money from the current military expenditures, is very limited." It not only lacked the resources and manpower to adequately collect taxes, it also lacked a tax base due in large measure to the effects of war. The Saigon regime, Poats explained in 1967, "has had a continued depletion of staff through war, through the draft, through diversion of people to more profitable business instead of working for the Government at the Government-fixed wage, and it has a very limited tax collection capacity."[84] Despite a critical lack of tax base and related

---

[82] U.S. Congress, *Improper Practices*, 91–209.

[83] Income taxes for the 1966–1969 period never exceeded 14 percent of the total domestic tax revenue. Domestic tax revenue for the period is as follows: 1966, $213 million (budget, $1 billion); 1967, $315 million (budget, $1.6 billion); 1968, $345 million (budget, $2.16 billion); 1969, $500 million (budget, $2.46 billion). I have calculated these figures based on an exchange rate of sixty to one. Dacy, *Foreign Aid*, 213, 215.

[84] *USEASV*, I:114. U.S. Congress, *Improper Practices*, 70. Telegram from Saigon to U.S. State Department, Subject: Economic Policy – 1968, December 1967, NSF, CF, VN, box 58, LBJL.

revenue, the regime nevertheless piled up over $300 million in foreign exchange reserves earned primarily through customs duties on American imports, a fact the AID called "embarrassing."[85] Southern Vietnam's, and, more specifically, Saigon's, dependence was thus nurtured by the aid program and the exigencies of war. Officials of the regime in Saigon could not themselves pay for their own existence. Nor could they pay for the police, the military, and related infrastructure necessary to protect that existence. For the entire period, the United States financed the vast majority of the regime's budget through the aid program. For its own part, the United States could not simply scale back the aid or reduce the level of warfare and the related American presence. Everyone recognized that doing so would mean the certain collapse of the whole project. During more than twelve years of American involvement in Vietnam, the situation had only grown more pronounced. The very structure of the state-building program prevented the United States from leaving Vietnam.

By the late 1960s, only the war itself received adequate attention and funding. Other initiatives and other features of the aid program touching on state building suffered. Some aspects of the larger program were in near-total disarray, such as the efforts to aid the refugees and alleviate social misery. Others simply were counterproductive, such as the CIP, the largest of the four major components of the aid package. The standard of living for a small number of Vietnamese rose at a rate of about 1.5 to 2.0 percent annually, which probably helped prevent a revolt among the people. Beyond this modest treading of water, American aid and assistance did little to develop an independent South Vietnam. Economist Douglas Dacy, who studied the economy of southern Vietnam for the Institute for Defense Analyses, concluded that "only a small share of the aid was directed toward long-run development."[86] The vast majority of aid went to support the military and military-related infrastructure, particularly after 1964.

Nonmilitary aid perpetuated southern Vietnam's dependence through massive imports, and an alarming portion was diverted away from

[85] *USEASV*, I:119. Memorandum for the President, June 30, 1967, NSF, CF, VN, box 58, LBJL.
[86] Dacy, *Foreign Aid*, 20.

people into the black market economy or to the insurgents. The AID concluded in its multivolume final report that "corruption was pervasive throughout the period of U.S. involvement at all levels." Countless officials scavenged the system from top to bottom for personal gain. "Vietnamese officials had more opportunities for gains by corrupt means – the U.S. presence itself assured that." Little oversight, a heightened sense of urgency to continually get things done, regardless of costs, and the sheer scope and complexity of the project created an atmosphere in which few questions were asked and much was taken for granted. Legitimate opportunities to work and to earn a living were limited, and much of Vietnam was wracked by war and politically and economically profoundly uncertain. Bribes, kickbacks, and petty theft became a common method to supplement one's income. Corruption characterized the system at every level, not just among civil servants and lower-level representatives of the regime, but among politicians, businessmen, and military officers as well. According to the AID, "there was an inordinate amount of corruption – by any standard." "The amount of corruption was far beyond that which could be tolerated under the grease-the-wheel theory." On the American side, too, corruption ran rampant in the black market, in currency manipulation scandals and theft. Corruption ate into the program's effectiveness, its legitimacy, its members' morale, and its ability to carry out the ultimate aims of the United States.[87]

There are many explanations for the high level of corruption. Ultimately, congressional investigators and others concluded that a psychology of abundance had emerged years earlier and continued to govern thinking on spending and oversight of the aid program. Because so much emphasis had been placed on accomplishing the military objectives in southern Vietnam, the costs of the project became at best secondary. As those costs soared, as inflation became a serious problem, as the

---

[87] The statement on corruption goes on, "There is little question that corruption ... was a critical factor in the deterioration of national morale which led ultimately to defeat." *USEASV*, I:224–26. For corruption within the U.S. mission, see U.S. Congress, *Fraud and Corruption in Management of Military Club Systems, Illegal Currency Manipulations Affecting South Vietnam, Hearings before the Permanent Subcommittee on Investigations of the Committee on Government Operations*, 91st–92nd Cong., 1969–1971, parts I–VIII.

economy hemorrhaged, and as criticism of the serious deficiencies built in to the program mounted, officials in Vietnam simply papered over the problems. Mission officials in Vietnam actively discouraged audits that might reflect poorly on the program. Either reports were shelved or records were discarded. Officials investigating the assistance program complained repeatedly that no paper trail existed to follow up on allegations of fraud, and that mission representatives simply could not provide answers to even the most basic questions. Illinois representative Donald Rumsfeld, a member of the House investigative team sent to Vietnam early in 1966, expressed his frustration over this problem:

I want this record and you gentlemen to know how disappointed I was at the discussions in Vietnam with AID personnel. Invariably the reason [our questions] could not be answered was because of the lack of records, the lack of audits, the lack of procedures whereby this information would be available.... I got the feeling... that the information is not available.... It is distressing for a... member of a subcommittee to be attempting to come to grips with these problems, and to be repeatedly told that necessary and basic information is not available.[88]

At the same time, those officials in Vietnam were themselves caught off guard.

The war expanded so rapidly, the economic, political, social, infrastructural, and military needs became so great so quickly, that everyone, the Vietnamese included, were quickly overwhelmed. The regime had been precariously held together for several years before the buildup only through substantial American effort. As a relatively limited assistance program mushroomed into large-scale war, massive destruction and dislocation, an immense public health crisis, a massive construction program to transform southern Vietnam, an unprecedented commodity import program, and serious economic disorders, the near-total lack of a state infrastructure was at last manifest.

CONCLUSION

Between 1966 and 1968, the United States prosecuted major war over much of Vietnam. The effort, however, was not aimed at creating a new,

[88] *An Investigation*, 56, 62–63.

independent Vietnam south of the seventeenth parallel, a still unrealized objective. The effort aimed instead at the defeat of enemies as part of a military campaign and, at the same time, at protecting American credibility. The failure of state building had been at least tacitly recognized by the administration through the massive construction program and major war. By the Tet Offensive of early 1968, the war had brought near-total disruption in both the countryside and the cities as well.

The war turned several million Vietnamese into refugees. Large numbers of them fled into already crowded cities and makeshift camps. City infrastructure proved woefully inadequate, and the added burden of hundreds of thousands of desperate and war-ravaged people only exasperated what were serious deficiencies. This large mobile population also created a grave public health crisis in southern Vietnam. The rate of infection, incidence of death from treatable illness, infant mortality, and amputations all increased with the war. Substandard medical facilities, too few doctors and nurses, outdated equipment, a lack of infrastructure to convey the war's victims into a medical aid system, and inadequate funding all contributed to and perpetuated the crisis. These millions of people adversely affected by the war, despite what the various pacification programs measured from time to time, became more estranged from the larger objectives of the project. Furthermore, as the countryside increasingly became the venue for massive war and destruction, agricultural production fell off and rice imports increased sharply, as did the commodity's price. In short, the war destroyed what had made the countryside coherent and cohesive and of potential value in the invention of the new state.[89]

At the same time, the Vietnam Builders and the U.S. Navy spent many hundreds of millions to hurriedly turn southern Vietnam into a defensible piece of territory. Because of the critical lack of modern communications and transportation infrastructure, the construction needs were enormous. In the short period from 1965 to 1968, the Builders put in place an impressive and modern network of military bases, state-of-the-art port facilities, jet airfields rivaling those in the United States, an upgraded road network, hundreds of millions of square feet of warehouse space, an electrical power grid, and hospitals, clinics, hotels, civic

[89] Goodman, *Causes and Consequences.*

buildings, houses, and other facilities and structures too numerous to list.[90] In the process, this "paradox of construction and destruction" did not yield an independent state. It instead facilitated the increasing destruction of the southern half of Vietnam. By 1968, the process was essentially complete: a modern military network of epic proportion made possible the defense of the territory, while the war itself wreaked havoc on much of the countryside, and the aid program perpetuated the regime's dependence.

The war also created stark contrasts in the urban environments, particularly in Saigon. The flood of American personnel, both military and civilian contractors, created a demand for an array of services from barbershops and restaurants to nightclubs and prostitutes. The level of consumer goods available in the city, in addition to feeding the black market, also brought to Vietnam American goods and, along with them, American consumer culture. Vietnamese children sported Batman T-shirts, men drank Miller and Budweiser beer; many wore American fashions, smoked American cigarettes, traded in American goods, and, for tens of thousands, found employment as part of the sprawling economy of servicing the American military. All of the best clubs, cabarets, and bars maintained ample stocks of American whiskey, wine, beer, and soda. Much of the urban population became a part of this service economy made possible by the war. The city of Saigon, in fact, contained over one thousand bars and more than one hundred nightclubs. The city garnered 14 percent of its total revenue from various taxes associated with the thriving nightlife. This nightlife employed twenty-five thousand bar girls, nine hundred orchestra personnel, twenty thousand club/bar employees, "and countless hangers-on and policemen who receive monthly tips for protection," according to a Central Intelligence Agency estimate of December 1968. Club owners actually lamented the removal of U.S. troops designed to alleviate the problem of inflation because it cut substantially into their profits.[91] Whatever wealth the

---

[90] For a survey of the construction program's accomplishments, see "The Construction Miracle of the Decade," *RMK-BRJ Papers. The Jones Centennial*, chap. 16. *Diary of a Contract.*

[91] Telegram from Saigon to Department of State, Subject: Saigon Night Life Faces an Evolution, December 21, 1967, NSF, CF, VN, box 61, LBJL. Gabriel Kolko, *Anatomy of a War: Vietnam, The United States, and the Modern Historical Experience* (New York: New Press, 1985), 203–207. Herring, *America's Longest War*, 196–98.

war created, however, would evaporate as soon as the United States pulled out of Vietnam. But like others benefiting from the aid economy, the club owners had not begun to plan for its end.

Ultimately, the period of major warfare in Vietnam can be seen as masking much larger problems with the whole range of U.S. policy objectives stretching back more than a decade by 1968. Years earlier, American policy makers and other officials had stopped talking about creating a new state below the seventeenth parallel. They had long since stopped talking about the need for land reform, for democracy and transparency, for an industrial base and an export economy. They had begun to talk instead of the need for greater security and greater military preparedness to put down the insurgency and to destroy its links with the communists above the seventeenth parallel. They had also come to refer to southern Vietnam exclusively as South Vietnam, a sovereign state in need of defense from its enemies beyond its borders. The utility of this ploy is not difficult to discern. Characterizing southern Vietnam as a separate state did, however, make it virtually impossible to speak honestly about problems with the whole project. It also made it nearly impossible to bring about conditions for an American withdrawal. At no time could the officials of the regime in Saigon survive without the enormous level of aid provided by the United States. By 1968, southern Vietnam was no better positioned to declare itself independent of American aid than in any previous year. If anything, it was less able to do so.

EPILOGUE: WAR, POLITICS, AND THE END IN VIETNAM

"After 17 years of total involvement in Vietnamese internal affairs, the United States has sanctified in power a polished and ruthless military Machiavellian, heading a one-party military regime, authoritarian, institutionalized in its corruption, and lacking support among the people." Thus Wesley Fishel made known his unabashed disapproval of U.S. policy in Vietnam in a 1971 *New York Times* op-ed.[1] Fishel had, since 1962, watched uneasily as U.S. policy drifted further from what he and his fellow Michigan State University Vietnam Advisory Group (MSUG) state builders had envisioned in the late 1950s. In his view, the United States had long since failed in the most important of its objectives: building a stable, independent state infrastructure in southern Vietnam. Looking back over the nine years since the official end of his role in building the state, the political science professor subsequently told an interviewer that the United States had "undermined . . . the very thing we set out to help achieve" through a penchant for overusing immense power on behalf of ill-fitting solutions. As he put it, "there is an American obsession that if 100 Americans can do a job well, 10,000 can do it better."[2] Fishel, and his MSUG colleagues as well, had for years issued repeated disapprovals of military escalation in Vietnam.

In the early 1970s, and having endured student protests around campus for his role in the failed U.S. policies in Southeast Asia, Michigan State University's (MSU) Fishel continued to believe the problem in Vietnam was a political one that defied military solutions and that U.S.

---

[1] Wesley Fishel, "Government by Force," *New York Times*, October 13, 1971.
[2] George J. Barmann, "Did Nixon Muff Chance in Vietnam?," *Plain Dealer*, November 14, 1971.

objectives could have otherwise been achieved. At the same time, he had long been deeply ambivalent regarding the U.S. role in Vietnam and its ultimate objectives. To be sure, he remained a committed state builder. Fishel still believed in the potential for victory in Vietnam; Johnson and Nixon had just got it all wrong. His critique of U.S. policy, however, did not adequately account for the contradictions and failings of his own efforts and their relationship to the militarization that accompanied them. An otherwise good and effective set of ideas was not simply overrun by those of more hawkish advisors. The efforts of the MSUG and of the U.S. Operations Mission in those early years relied on increasing police/military power; MSU advisors had been crucial in building that power as part of their state-building campaign. The former, in fact, made the latter necessary. As advisors and experts put in place many of the accoutrements of a modern state with Ngo Dinh Diem at its head, greater levels of force became necessary to centralize power in the president's hands, to maintain order through removing native opposition groups and individuals, and to impose a range of forced-draft economic and political transformations amid growing unrest and hostility. Greater levels of military aid and involvement, coupled with large-scale infrastructure projects, were an inherent part of the policy trajectory. Fishel articulated, if unknowingly, the larger ambivalence of U.S. Vietnam policy: at once championing the myriad changes he helped bring to southern Vietnam and criticizing the heavy-handedness, militarization, and eventual war that underwrote them.

By the late 1960s, the war itself had brought considerable destruction and disarray to the countryside and the cities of southern Vietnam. Major combat operations produced millions of refugees, untold civilian suffering, and a profound public health crisis; it disrupted the rural environment and agricultural production of southern Vietnam. The massive construction program that made possible large-scale warfare also transformed southern Vietnam into a defensible piece of territory by littering it with dozens of modern military installations, a modern port system, airfields, and an improved transportation grid. At the same time, the U.S. aid economy was rife with corruption, graft, waste, and outright fraud. The Commodity Import Program continued to more or less effectively prevent galloping inflation. It also prevented local production and created enormous opportunity for pilferage and piracy. Countless millions of tons of commodities and supplies of all kinds wound through the labyrinth of the black market, providing profit-taking opportunities for numerous clandestine operators. Local businessmen were shielded from punishment by the lack of effective records, audits, and investigations, among other protections. Even American GIs, many of them gone AWOL, found the opportunities too great to pass up. Just one such well-organized ring of fifty U.S. servicemen netted as much as a quarter million dollars a month in "one of the largest black market/currency manipulation rings in Saigon," according to one study. Theft in these cases involved illegally obtaining and then selling U.S. money orders and military pay certificates on the black market, often at astonishingly different exchange rates.[3] Congressional investigators could not even determine the precise level of corruption. They could only guess at the amount of capital being hurried out of Vietnam and into safer accounts elsewhere. Some suggested that the black market in currency manipulation was a billion-dollar business.[4] Whatever the precise volume of the theft, the economy of southern Vietnam continued to hemorrhage, as both Americans and Vietnamese bled the aid program dry.

By the late 1960s, the United States fought a major war in Vietnam with a much different, if more ambiguous, set of objectives. On the surface, U.S. officials repeatedly offered assurances that they wanted only peace and the preservation of an independent, noncommunist South Vietnam. Despite such assurances, the war itself really had more to do with the U.S. than with Vietnam. It had more to do with American credibility in the world. The initial goal of creating an independent, modern, noncommunist state out of southern Vietnam now seemed a distant and perhaps noble fantasy. Nevertheless, officials mouthed the now standard assumptions about the existence of the independent state of South Vietnam and its desperate need for defense from outside aggression.

The U.S. continued to use its overwhelming military power as a way to control events it had otherwise been unable to control. Warfare on a scale large enough to enable the United States to hold southern Vietnam involved another series of physical transformations. Even though that construction effort succeeded on its own terms, the war

---

[3] William Allison, "War for Sale: The Black Market, Currency Manipulation and Corruption in the American War in Vietnam," *War and Society* 21, no. 2 (2003): 146.

[4] U.S. Congress, Senate, "Fraud and Corruption in Management of Military Club Systems, Illegal Currency Manipulations Affecting South Vietnam," September 30, 1969, Part I, 91st Cong., 1st sess., 2.

it made possible had completely undermined the larger aims of U.S. policy. It had substantially disrupted southern Vietnam through heavy damage and destruction of much of the countryside; the turning out of millions of Vietnamese as refugees; the increased flood of capital, troops, and equipment into southern Vietnam; the continued manipulation of the economy; and the further alienation of many Vietnamese. By this time, too, revolutionary forces in the countryside, coupled with the insurgency, North Vietnamese regulars, and aid from China and the Soviet Union, waged an increasingly conventional war that soon arrived at a very costly stalemate.

The war had become far too costly for the United States to maintain. By 1967–1968, the war cost between $20 billion and $25 billion per annum. For years, the U.S. economy operated amid balance of payment (BOP) deficits. By the late 1960s, this deficit grew ominous and threatened to destabilize the Bretton Woods system that had gone a long way toward remedying serious global economic difficulties in the aftermath of World War II. Now, the BOP deficit soared, spurred on by the rising defense expenditures, and by the costs for war in Vietnam in particular. The dangerously high costs of the war made it near impossible to remedy the rising deficit, which experts warned would likely exceed the $15 billion range in fiscal years 1968 and 1969. As European allies, such as France and Great Britain, charged the United States with exporting the costs of its war in Southeast Asia through the Bretton Woods fixed exchange system, some took matters a step further and began cashing dollars for gold and drawing down American gold reserves, exacerbating America's economic troubles stemming from the war. This *gold drain* in the weeks following the Tet Offensive amounted to hundreds of millions of dollars, climbing to more than $1.2 billion in the first two weeks of March alone.[5]

---

[5] Robert Buzzanco, "Tet, Gold, and the Transformation of American Hegemony," unpublished manuscript, 5–9. Center for Strategic Studies, *Economic Impact of the Vietnam War* (Washington, DC: Georgetown University, 1967). *The National Economy and the Vietnam War: A Statement on National Policy by the Research and Policy Committee of the Committee for Economic Development* (New York: Committee for Economic Development, 1968), 21. At the same time, the war in Vietnam had been immensely valuable to Japan, South Korea, and Taiwan. One analysis concludes that the war propelled these emerging economies into the stratospheric export-led growth of the late 1970s and 1980s. See Richard Stubbs, "War and Economic Development: Export-Oriented Industrialization in East and Southeast Asia," *Comparative Politics* 31, no. 3 (April 1999): 337–55.

Coupled with these global economic problems, Lyndon Johnson also struggled against spiking inflation at home. By late 1965 and into 1966, the president's economic advisors were warning of large increases in new business investment, the drop in unemployment to just over 4 percent, and rising prices. Some business leaders seemed to interpret escalation in Vietnam as good times ahead.[6] The gross national product surged forward, threatening to overheat the economy. By the end of 1966, real growth amounted to a whopping 7 percent, while unemployment had fallen to 3.8 percent. Council of Economic Advisors chairman Gardner Ackley urged the president to consider a tax hike, however unpopular and unsavory that might be for domestic political reasons; budget director Charles Schultze suggested a hike on the order of $5 billion. The president steadfastly opposed such a move. Raising taxes would be akin to admitting the deeply flawed nature of the "guns and butter" policy and would open the door to Republican criticism and certain attacks on the Great Society programs. Johnson had earlier refused to make this trade-off between domestic programs and the war, saying, "If I left the woman I really loved – the Great Society – in order to get involved with that bitch of a war on the other side of the world, then I would lose everything at home."[7]

Politically, the latest poll numbers reflected the downward spiral of Johnson's fortunes both at home and abroad. A survey in early 1967 indicated only 16 percent "strongly approved" of the president's leadership, while still only 45 percent gave their approval overall. For his conduct of the war in Vietnam, Johnson received the approval of only 37 percent of those polled, an all-time low.[8] The movement against the

---

[6] The business press and the construction industry press in particular certainly interpreted escalation in this way. See, inter alia, "Leading Contractors Exploiting Industrial and Overseas Booms," *Engineering News-Record* (ENR), May 19, 1966. "War Slows Equipment Deliveries," ENR, February 17, 1966. "Guns vs Butter Poses a Budget Problem," ENR, January 6, 1966.

[7] Johnson was correct in his assessment, and he ended up doing precisely what he had sworn off: trading the Great Society for the war in Vietnam. Allen J. Matusow, *The Unraveling of America: A History of Liberalism in the 1960s* (New York: Harper & Row, 1984), 155–61. Stanley Karnow, *Vietnam: A History* (New York: Penguin Books, 1997), 336.

[8] Robert Dallek, *Flawed Giant: Lyndon Johnson and His Times, 1961–1973* (New York: Oxford University Press, 1998), 394. By December 1967, pollsters found 45 percent of respondents believed the war had been a mistake, yet only 10 percent recommended immediate U.S. withdrawal. This kind of ambivalence among most Americans grew more

war had also grown into a considerable force itself by the late 1960s. The war cost over ten thousand American lives every year, not to mention the far more numerous Vietnamese civilians killed. Generally, the human, social, and economic costs of waging war in Southeast Asia had become clear to millions of Americans. The administration's justifications for the war increasingly rang hollow. Tens of thousands signed petitions, refused to pay taxes, boycotted, marched, burned draft cards, went to teach-ins, refused induction into the armed services, wrote letters to political leaders, and engaged in guerrilla street theater to show their opposition to the war. Johnson was concerned enough with the movement that he ordered his Central Intelligence Agency director to find evidence that it had been communist infiltrated, and then refused to believe the director's conclusion that no such evidence existed.[9]

Criticism of Johnson's guns and butter policy mounted within Congress as well. Even the iron-clad liberal Cold War consensus showed signs of serious strain. Democrats began to question the administration's use of power to force itself upon an unwilling Vietnam. Many came to view the situation in Vietnam as unwinable. In January 1966, fifteen senators demonstrated their displeasure by signing a letter to the president that urged a continued bombing pause to bring about negotiations to end the war. In February, New York Senator Robert Kennedy even went as far as recommending the National Liberation Front be brought into a power-sharing arrangement as part of a negotiating strategy also aimed at ending the war. At the same time, the chairman of the Senate Foreign Relations Committee and for years the authoritative voice in the Senate on foreign policy matters, J. William Fulbright, began televised

pronounced during the mid- to late 1960s. See Melvin Small, *Johnson, Nixon, and the Doves* (New Brunswick, NJ: Rutgers University Press, 1988), 94–95.

[9] Lyndon Johnson's memoirs on this subject are at best ambiguous. The protests against the war are scarcely mentioned, and when they are, they are dismissed as foolish, short-sighted, and/or irrelevant. At the same time, Johnson praises dissent as vital to a free society. The former president, e.g., wrote, "My biggest worry was not Vietnam itself; it was the divisiveness and pessimism at home." And at another point, he wrote, "Debate and dissension are part of the fabric of a free society...but I am convinced that it [the opposition to the war] passed the bounds of reasonable debate and fair dissension. It became a self-inflicted wound of critical proportions. There is not the slightest doubt in my mind that this dissension prolonged the war, prevented a peaceful settlement on reasonable terms, encouraged our enemies, disheartened our friends, and weakened us as a nation." Lyndon Baines Johnson, *The Vantage Point: Perspectives of the Presidency, 1963–1969* (New York: Holt, Rinehart and Winston, 1971), 422, 530.

hearings on the war.[10] He, too, sharply criticized the administration's "arrogance of power." In a series of lectures published under that title, the Arkansas liberal portrayed the events in Vietnam in very different terms:

It is said that we are fighting against North Vietnam's aggression rather than its ideology and that the "other side" has only to "stop doing what it is doing" in order to restore peace. But what are the North Vietnamese doing, except participating in a civil war, not in a foreign country but on the other side of a demarcation line between two sectors of the same country, a civil war in which Americans from ten thousand miles across the ocean are also participating? What are they doing that is different from what the American North did to the American South a hundred years ago, with results that few of my fellow Southerners now regret?

In the same lecture, Fulbright decried what he termed an "Asian doctrine" that "represents a radical departure" in U.S. foreign policy because it was both "unilateral" and of "virtually...unlimited objectives."[11] The United States had dangerously and shortsightedly engaged in a war to impose solutions at odds with the realities on the ground in Vietnam. It was, the senator believed, the fact of the regime's considerable weaknesses that explained the failure so far to make southern Vietnam into a separate, sovereign, noncommunist state.[12] Fulbright's total break with his longtime friend and fellow southerner Lyndon Johnson over U.S. policy in Vietnam was a momentous political event. It was even more momentous because it emboldened others to dissent, and a number of fence-sitters in the Democratic Party would follow where Fulbright led. Democratic criticism of the war was soon no longer limited to Senators Wayne Morse and Ernest Gruening, the lone nay votes on the Gulf of Tonkin resolution in August 1964. It now involved a broad range of increasingly outspoken congressional leaders from Frank Church, George McGovern, and Eugene McCarthy to Joseph Clark, Mike Mansfield, and now such anticommunist Cold War stalwarts as Fulbright.

---

[10] J. William Fulbright, *The Vietnam Hearings: The Complete Statements of Dean Rusk, James M. Gavin, George F. Kennan, Maxwell D. Taylor* (New York: Vintage, 1996).

[11] J. William Fulbright, *The Arrogance of Power* (New York: Random House, 1966), 107, 109. Randall Bennett Woods, *Fulbright: A Biography* (New York: Cambridge University Press, 1995), chap. 21.

[12] Fulbright, *Arrogance of Power*, 118.

Republicans, too, rebuked the administration for what was seen as an unnecessarily costly, sloppy, and endless war, with no clear and immediate relevance to American national security. Representative Rumsfeld returned from his investigative trip to Vietnam in 1966 outraged by what he found. In addition to appending, along with Representative Robert Dole (R-KS), an official letter articulating his disquiet to the committee's comprehensive report,[13] Rumsfeld took to the floor of the House to roundly criticize the president's Vietnam policies and his related cozy relations with the private contractors working there, saying,

Under only one contract, between the U.S. Government and this combine [RMK-BRJ] it is officially estimated that obligations will reach at least $900 million by November 1967.... Why this huge contract has not been and is not now being adequately audited is beyond me. The potential for waste and profiteering under such a contract is substantial.

The Illinois representative charged the administration with letting contracts that "are illegal by statute" and at least implicitly offered that these immensely profitable deals resulted from the very close relationship between Johnson and the Brown brothers, extending back many years to the president's first foray into politics.[14] Rumsfeld, Senator Dole, House Republican leader Gerald Ford, and other congressional Republicans became increasingly critical of the war and its effect on the country.[15]

Republican and Democratic critics of Johnson policies were not radicals by any stretch; nor were they antiwar on principle. Most, if not all,

---

[13] See *An Investigation of the U.S. Economic and Military Assistance Programs in Vietnam, Additional Views of Hon. Donald Rumsfeld and Hon. Robert Dole*, U.S. House, Committee on Government Operations, 89th Cong., 2nd sess., 126–28.

[14] Rumsfeld quoted in *Congressional Record* 112 (August 30, 1966): 21,304. On Rumsfeld's criticism of Johnson's relationship with Brown and Root more generally, see *Congressional Record* 112 (August 18): 19,920–22 and Congressional Record 112 (August 31, 1966): 21,392. See also R. W. Apple Jr., "Vietnam Building Curtailed by United States – Pentagon Decides to Review Program of Consortium," *New York Times*, August 29, 1966. John Maffre, "U.S. Military Expected to Assume Vietnam Construction Program," *Washington Post*, August 30, 1966.

[15] William D. Smith, "Economy Held Election Key," *New York Times*, December 3, 1968. Representative Ford earlier told the *New York Times*, "Put bluntly, Americans must pay more and more to make powerful Saigon interests richer and richer and the Vietnamese people more completely dependent on us. This is just the opposite of our declared purpose of building a free and independent South Vietnam." Felix Belair Jr., "Rep. Ford Scores the 'Other War'," *New York Times*, October 8, 1967.

of them had for years supported U.S. policy in Vietnam and the larger aims of America's Cold War containment policy, in general. However, Republicans shared with congressional Democrats a deep and abiding concern that the war in Vietnam had acquired far greater import than it warranted and that it threatened greater economic and political distress both at home and abroad. Furthermore, many of them had also come to the realization that U.S. policy in Vietnam had reached a dead end and that the administration had no viable alternative.

THE TET OFFENSIVE

On January 30, 1968, a combination of northern regular soldiers and southern insurgents numbering perhaps seventy thousand launched concerted and near-simultaneous attacks over the whole of southern Vietnam. These forces attacked both urban and rural areas, even entering the U.S. embassy compound in Saigon. Over 100 cities, 36 of 44 provincial capitals, 64 of 242 district towns, and numerous smaller villages and hamlets came under direct attack. The offensive demonstrated, among other things, that the regime and the Americans could claim complete control over no area of southern Vietnam. The immediate gains of the attacks were beaten back within a few weeks in most cases, and the insurgents paid an immense price.[16] The Tet Offensive seemed to lay bare all the Johnson administration's claims of success in the war in Vietnam.

The violence unleashed by the offensive resulted in nearly 1 million new refugees, eight thousand to fifteen thousand civilians killed, and thirty thousand to forty thousand wounded. Most urban centers remained in a state of chaos for months following the attacks. The Agency for International Development (AID) reported that in many critical aspects having to do with relief to civilians, it did not recover from Tet until the end of the year. The economy was also hit hard by this latest round of attacks. Businesses were "frozen," according to journalist

---

[16] A very useful collection of essays on the offensive is Marc J. Gilbert and William Head, eds., *The Tet Offensive* (Westport, CT: Praeger, 1996). See also Tom Wicker, "Illusions and Deceptions," *Nation*, February 11, 1968. On the national press following Tet, see Min S. Yee, "The U.S. Press and Its Agony of Appraisal," *Boston Globe*, February 18, 1968.

accounts, by the shock and concomitant instability in the wake of the offensive. Goods remained in warehouses, and importers either reduced orders or stopped placing new orders altogether. Prices soared on such staples as rice, meat, and fish; the price of the latter increased by more than 300 percent immediately after January 30. Rice shipments from the delta to Saigon, normally on the order of 20,000–30,000 tons per month, shrank to just 456 tons in February. Theft and graft were also more pronounced, according to one U.S. official, who believed "the offensive by the Vietcong has unleashed a lot of people in the police who are hauling things out of trucks quite freely.... There has been theft and looting.... The businessmen also feel that they can't leave their inventory in place without getting looted.... Businessmen are not buying because they fear the Vietcong as well as the police."[17] In many ways, recovering from Tet occupied the U.S. mission and the officials of the regime for the remainder of the year.

The Tet Offensive has, for obvious reasons, figured largely in accounts of U.S. policy in Vietnam and of the Vietnam War more specifically. It occurred at a time when U.S. officials, General Westmoreland most notably, had forecast considerable progress for the coming year and had even spoken of seeing "light at the end of the tunnel" in Vietnam.[18] The numbers on pacification programs looked relatively positive as well. The offensive also occurred at a time of considerable exhaustion with a war that seemed to some observers to continue expanding, with little end in sight. It was a watershed moment and, in retrospect, a turning point in U.S. policy.[19] While Tet no doubt exposed serious problems of security and with the effort to attrite the enemy in the countryside, it did no more damage to this larger goal than had been done over the previous several years. As Lyndon Johnson removed himself from the presidential contest early in the year, U.S. policy in Vietnam floundered.

[17] Subcom on Refugee Hearings, May 9, 1968, 4. *U.S. Economic Assistance to South Vietnam* (*USEASV*), II:837–39. Agency for International Development, *USEASV*, I:130. Ray Richard, "Viet Corruption Incredible, Says Milton Man," *Boston Globe*, September 25, 1968. Bernard Weintraub, "South Vietnam's Economy Termed Battered by Enemy Offensive," *New York Times*, March 17, 1968.

[18] Westmoreland's own account is in William C. Westmoreland, *A Soldier Reports* (New York: Dell, 1976), 423–31.

[19] For this historical debate over the meaning of Tet, see Gilbert and Head, *Tet Offensive*.

Lyndon Johnson also seemed to grasp this. He spoke before a televised audience on March 31, 1968, to announce, among other things, the he was effectively quitting politics; he would not run for reelection. He did so amid this crumbling base of support for the war in Vietnam. Though the latest polls showed a majority of Americans still refusing to consider unconditional withdrawal from Vietnam, nearly 60 percent now viewed the war as a mistake. The base of support that made escalation possible a few years earlier was surely gone.[20] His own withdrawal from the election that year opened the contest to a range of candidates, from Vice President Hubert Humphrey and Senator Robert Kennedy on the Democratic side to former Vice President Richard Nixon on the Republican ticket and Alabama's rock-ribbed segregationist Governor George C. Wallace as an independent. The Democrat's campaign season, from April through the August convention in Chicago, only widened the seams in the New Deal liberal coalition that had dominated American political life for years. Richard Nixon capitalized on this political disarray, eking out the win with 43.4 percent to Democratic nominee Humphrey's 42.7 percent of the popular vote.[21] The former vice president under Dwight Eisenhower was savvy enough a politician to read the American political landscape: he could not continue the war in Vietnam along the same lines of the past several years.

LEAVING VIETNAM UNDONE

Development planning and aid continued in the years after 1968. Some continued to forecast and lay plans for the eventual birth of a modern, developed, and independent South Vietnam. Following the Honolulu Conference of 1966, the Johnson White House had charged longtime development expert David Lilienthal with planning for the development of a postwar South Vietnam. Lilienthal's 1967 recommendations flew in the face of then conventional wisdom on the internal circumstances of southern Vietnam when he suggested economic planning and development could not wait for the war's end. Development of agriculture, industry, and the economy in general had to proceed immediately,

---

[20] Small, *Johnson, Nixon, and the Doves*, 130–31.

[21] James T. Patterson, *Grand Expectations: The United States, 1945–1974* (New York: Oxford University Press, 1996), 685–704.

despite lack of security. He also believed "the economic damage of war is greatly exaggerated." Citing Germany and Japan following World War II, Lilienthal argued that wars were not necessarily the worst thing for a nation and that "in terms of wealth-producing capacity war is the best thing that happened to them in 100 years."[22] The Development and Resources Corporation, Lilienthal's private company under contract with the AID,[23] concluded in its final 1970 report that if the right kind of development plans were implemented sooner rather than later,

within a decade, systematic exploitation of the nation's economic potentials can at least increase per capita income by one-third and Gross National Product (GNP) by 50 percent. GNP will grow faster than per capita income but per capita consumption will also increase. For some time the nation will have to allocate an important portion of economic resources to national security and defense and an important portion of economic products to exports in order to finance imports. With an appropriate set of policies, it is believed that the termination of dependence on foreign aid can be achieved within ten years.

The report lauded certain "structural economic strengths" in southern Vietnam acquired during the war such as improved "port facilities, roads, and other infrastructure."[24] As former head of the Tennessee Valley Authority and, later, of the Atomic Energy Commission, Lilienthal embodied the kind of supreme national confidence and unshakable faith in the power of technology to solve big problems. He boldly claimed shortly following the Tet Offensive in early 1968 that "after five years [the people of southern Vietnam] will be on their own [as an independent nation]."[25]

---

[22] Lilienthal, contradicting nearly all available intelligence, believed southern Vietnam was "as secure as Central Park is right now." He went further, bizarrely suggesting a parallel between what he called "terrorists" in New York and New Jersey who represented only a "peripheral risk" at home and the insurgent threat in Vietnam. Tom Buckley, "Lilienthal Gives a Plan to Saigon," *New York Times*, November 16, 1967.

[23] For considerably more detail on this contractual arrangement, the conclusions of the group, the response of officials within the Saigon regime, and more, see *USEASV*, II:479–88.

[24] Joint Development Group, *The Postwar Development of the Republic of Vietnam: Policies and Programs* (New York: Praeger, 1970), 3. Albert P. Williams Jr., "South Viet-Nam's Development in a Postwar Era: A Commentary on the Thuc-Lilienthal Report," *Asian Survey* 11, no. 4 (1971): 352–70.

[25] "Lilienthal Hopeful on Saigon Economy," *New York Times*, May 13, 1968.

In many ways, these latest prognostications were not new at all. Nearly every word was in fact offered over the years since 1954 and amid the many different efforts to build the southern state. Most planners had considered these very elements of national development essential if they were to succeed in Vietnam. Furthermore, given the changed military, political, social, and economic climate then prevailing in Vietnam and the United States, they were far less likely to become either U.S. policy or the policy of the regime in Saigon, let alone to succeed in finally building the new Vietnam below the seventeenth parallel. What David Lilienthal and others did not consider was that possibilities related to economic development and state building for southern Vietnam had virtually disappeared by 1968. They had been overtaken by events years earlier. They seemed also to ignore or not grasp the contradictions of U.S. state-building programs over the years. The importance of development planning continued to fade over the next several years as the Nixon administration sought ways to decrease direct U.S. involvement in Vietnam, to quell domestic dissent related to an unpopular war, and to shore up America's global position vis-à-vis the Soviet Union and China.[26]

Like his predecessors and many of his contemporaries, Richard Nixon understood the war in Vietnam as communists attempting to impose themselves from without by taking advantage of a powerless population under weakened circumstances. He failed to recognize the organic nature of the insurgency or its substantial revolutionary component. Additionally, as a product of the previous ten years of U.S. policy, Nixon clung to the external aggression thesis explaining the war; the North continued its effort to conquer the South, and the whole thing was directed from the Soviet Union. It was from this vantage point that Nixon offered the policy of détente to America's Cold War adversaries as a way to change his nation's fortunes in Vietnam.[27] The new president's worldview explains his use of military force coupled with diplomatic efforts in the search for political victory in Vietnam.

---

[26] On decline in aid program, see *USEASV*, I:189–90. On global shifts in U.S. foreign aid, see Doug Bandow, *Intervention into the 1990s: U.S. Foreign Policy in the Third World* (Boulder, CO: L. Rienner Publishers, 1992), 79. Chen Jian, *Mao's China and the Cold War* (Chapel Hill: University of North Carolina Press, 2001), chap. 9.

[27] Jeffrey Kimball, *Nixon's Vietnam War* (Lawrence: University Press of Kansas, 1998), 47–51, 120–21.

Nixon viewed South Vietnam not as a failed state-building enterprise, but as a Cold War ally on which rested American credibility. In the few years following 1968, he and national security advisor Henry Kissinger determined to find a way to end large-scale American involvement (and casualties) in Vietnam. After vaguely campaigning on what some referred to as a "secret plan" to end the war, the president concluded, albeit grudgingly, that an exit from Vietnam could only be accomplished through the abandonment of the long-failed project. Simultaneously, Nixon viewed the preservation of the regime as vital. Despite the reality on the ground in Vietnam, Nixon still would not countenance a Cold War defeat. The administration settled on a policy dubbed "Vietnamization," which meant turning the war over to the Vietnamese and getting U.S. troops out. Circumstances no longer allowed for talk of substantial reforms. Neither the administration nor the regime in Saigon possessed the political will or the time required to implement major reforms anyway. By the end of 1969, just over 475,000 American troops remained in Vietnam; by the end of the following year, that number dropped to 334,600; it dropped again to 156,800 the next year. Understanding that the regime in Saigon could not stand on its own without a U.S. military presence and aid, the administration offered an increased volume of military aid and a continued air war to prevent the regime's demise.

Consequently, between 1968 and 1973, military aid increased from $1.2 billion to more than $3.3 billion, while economic aid went from $651 million to $531 million.[28] The forces supporting the regime of Nguyen Van Thieu climbed from 850,000 in 1968 to over 1 million. The administration also provided an enormous volume of military equipment, including twelve thousand M-60 machine guns, forty thousand M-79 grenade launchers, and more than 1 million M-16 rifles. The regime used this aid in part to increase the commitment to pacification of the countryside to five hundred thousand soldiers, each with an M-16. The administration also began or ramped up aerial bombardment of Cambodia, Laos, and Vietnam north of the seventeenth parallel, including Hanoi and the mining of Haiphong harbor. In a series of bombing campaigns collectively known as "Menu," B-52s flew 3,825 sorties

---

[28] Douglas C. Dacy, *Foreign Aid, War, and Economic Development: South Vietnam, 1955–1975* (New York: Cambridge University Press, 1986), 200.

and dropped more than one hundred thousand tons of bombs along the Vietnamese-Cambodian border in just over a year, extending from March 1969. By war's end, the United States had dropped more than 210,000 tons of bombs on neutral Cambodia, profoundly destabilizing that country. Above the seventeenth parallel, bombers dropped more than 155,000 tons of bombs in the seven months from April 1972, in a series of raids termed "Linebacker." Linebacker II followed in December, with bombers unleashing more than fifteen thousand tons of bombs in just over ten days around Hanoi. As part of operation Lam Son 719, the U.S. Air Force dropped another forty-eight thousand tons of bombs on Laos in support of the regime's effort to interdict supplies along the Ho Chi Minh Trail.[29] This renewed and expanded carpet bombing was not designed to bring about a military victory as such. Rather, Nixon and Kissinger viewed massive bombing as a diplomatic tool to demonstrate both U.S. power and resolve and to bring about a more favorable end to the war.

Direct U.S. involvement in the Vietnam War finally ended in January 1973 with the signing of the Paris Agreement on Ending the War and Restoring Peace in Vietnam. The settlement promised continued American support, although for domestic political and economic reasons, that would soon end as well. The long, drawn out, frustrating, and even infuriating negotiations yielded only what the realities on the ground would allow. The state below the seventeenth parallel had never been put in place sufficiently to stand on its own, and consequently, it could not now be preserved in the absence of direct American involvement. As Kissinger and aide Alexander Haig explained to Nguyen Van Thieu, toward the end of 1972, only "brutal U.S. retaliation" via air strikes could maintain the existence of the regime once the United States had withdrawn. Despite such promises, however, the United States could not and would not sustain its crumbling client below the seventeenth parallel indefinitely.[30] With large numbers of northern troops and southern

---

[29] Mark Clodfelter, *The Limits of Airpower: The American Bombing of North Vietnam* (New York: Free Press, 1989), 158–76, 194–95. George C. Herring, *America's Longest War: The United States and Vietnam, 1950–1975*, 4th ed. (New York: McGraw-Hill, 2002), 286–93, 298.

[30] Larry Berman, *No Peace, No Honor: Nixon, Kissinger, and Betrayal in Vietnam* (New York: Free Press, 2001), 210–11, 218.

15. Aerial view of Binh Loi Highway bridge under construction, spanning Saigon River, 1972.

insurgents spread out over the whole of southern Vietnam, the regime's days were certainly numbered once the United States pulled out. The long-failed effort in southern Vietnam came to an ignominious end as northern tanks rolled into Saigon a little over a year following the signing of the Paris Agreement.

On preparing to leave Vietnam in 1972, the Vietnam Builders' contract sponsor Morrison-Knudsen (MK) had taken stock of all the consortium's accomplishments over the previous decade. Through much hard work, the engineers had substantially transformed southern Vietnam. It was now blanketed with large air bases, deep-draft ports, primary and secondary roads of high quality, hundreds of buildings and structures, and countless military bases and related infrastructure. Only weeks earlier, the consortium had completed work on six major highway bridges totaling more than two miles in length as part of its "Lines of Communication" project aimed at renovating the highway system. Reflecting on all of this, MK general manager John Kirkpatrick wrote, "There are no more pyramids to build. We have just about completed the largest construction effort in history."[31] The contradictions present during all the years of effort in southern Vietnam also characterized the U.S. exit

[31] John B. Kirkpatrick, "End of Viet Nam Construction," *The Em-Kayan*, 1, June 1972. Also, "Building Bridges in South Viet Nam," *The Em-Kayan*, 10–11, April 1972.

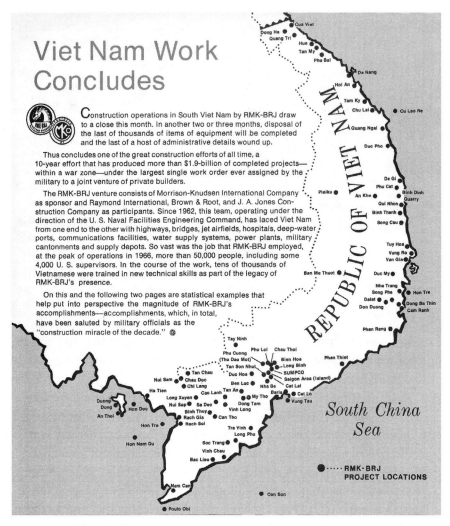

Viet Nam Work Concludes

Construction operations in South Viet Nam by RMK-BRJ draw to a close this month. In another two or three months, disposal of the last of thousands of items of equipment will be completed and the last of a host of administrative details wound up.

Thus concludes one of the great construction efforts of all time, a 10-year effort that has produced more than $1.9-billion of completed projects—within a war zone—under the largest single work order ever assigned by the military to a joint venture of private builders.

The RMK-BRJ venture consists of Morrison-Knudsen International Company as sponsor and Raymond International, Brown & Root, and J. A. Jones Construction Company as participants. Since 1962, this team, operating under the direction of the U. S. Naval Facilities Engineering Command, has laced Viet Nam from one end to the other with highways, bridges, jet airfields, hospitals, deep-water ports, communications facilities, water supply systems, power plants, military cantonments and supply depots. So vast was the job that RMK-BRJ employed, at the peak of operations in 1966, more than 50,000 people, including some 4,000 U. S. supervisors. In the course of the work, tens of thousands of Vietnamese were trained in new technical skills as part of the legacy of RMK-BRJ's presence.

On this and the following two pages are statistical examples that help put into perspective the magnitude of RMK-BRJ's accomplishments—accomplishments, which, in total, have been saluted by military officials as the "construction miracle of the decade."

REPUBLIC OF VIET NAM

Cua Viet
Dong Ha · Quang Tri
Hue
Tan My
Phu Bai
Da Nang
Hoi An
Tam Ky
Chu Lai · Cu Lao Re
Quang Ngai
Duc Pho
De Gi
Phu Cat
Pleiku · An Khe · Binh Dinh Quarry
Qui Nhon
Binh Thanh
Song Cau
Tuy Hoa
Vung Ro
Van Gia
Ban Me Thuot · Duc My
Nha Trang
Song Pha · Hon Tre
Dalat · Dong Ba Thin
Don Duong · Cam Ranh
Phan Rang

Tay Ninh
Phu Loi · Chau Thoi
Phu Cuong (Thu Dau Mot) · Bien Hoa · Long Binh · Phan Thiet
Tan Son Nhut
Tan Chau · Duc Hoa · SUMPCO
Nui Sam · Chau Doc · Ben Luc · Nha Be · Cat Lai · Saigon Area (Island)
Ha Tien · Chi Lang · Tan An · Baria · Cat Lo
Cao Lanh · My Tho · Vung Tau
Duong Dong · Long Xuyen · Dong Tam
An Thoi · Hon Doc · Nui Sap · Sa Dec · Vinh Long
Binh Thuy · Can Tho
Hon Tre · Rach Gia
Rach Soi · Tra Vinh
Hon Nam Du · Long Phu
Soc Trang
Vinh Chau
Bac Lieu

Nam Can

Con Son

Poulo Obi

South China Sea

● ·····RMK-BRJ
PROJECT LOCATIONS

16. This image was published in *The Em-Kayan* in June 1972, detailing the work accomplished at the end of the contract period.

from Southeast Asia: as the Builders put the finishing touches on a massive highway renovation project, Washington cemented plans to exit Vietnam and to retain its relationship with Saigon through military aid and massive bombardment.

BIBLIOGRAPHY

PRIMARY SOURCES

Michigan State University, University Archives and Historical Collections

The Papers of John Hannah
The Papers of Wesley Fishel
The Vietnam Project Papers

The National Archives

Record Group 59

The John F. Kennedy Library

National Security Files
Oral History Collection, Roger Hilsman
Oral History Collection, Walt W. Rostow
The Papers of Bernard Fall, 1946–1967
President's Office Files
White House Central Files
White House Staff Files 1961, Walt Rostow

The Lyndon B. Johnson Library

Administrative Histories, Agency for International Development
Administrative Histories, Council of Economic Advisors
Komer-Leonhart Files
Meeting Notes File
Memoranda to the President File
National Security Files
Office Files of the White House Aides, Fred Panzer
Oral History Collection, Walt W. Rostow
Oral History Collection, William Colby
The Papers of Clark Clifford
The Papers of McGeorge Bundy

The Papers of Robert Komer
Statements of LBJ File
Tom Johnson's Meeting Notes File
White House Central Files

J. A. Jones Construction Corporation
Records Department
Charlotte, NC

Washington Group International Inc. (formerly Morrison-Knudsen)
720 Park Blvd.
Boise, ID 83712

Washington Group International Inc.
Bruce Walters
Boise Records Center
P.O. Box 73
Boise, ID 83729

Boise State University
Albertson's Library
Mary Carter, Special Collections
1910 University Drive
Boise, ID 83725

The Military History Institute
Carlisle, PA

GOVERNMENT DOCUMENTS AND DOCUMENT COLLECTIONS

Brown, William Adams, Jr. *American Foreign Assistance*. Washington, DC: Brookings Institution, 1953.
Center for Strategic Studies. *Economic Impact of the Vietnam War*. Washington, DC: Georgetown University, 1967.
The Comptroller General of the United States. *United States Construction Activities in the Republic of Viet Nam, 1965–1966*, May 1967.
The National Economy and the Vietnam War: A Statement on National Policy by the Research and Policy Committee of the Committee for Economic Development. New York: Committee for Economic Development, 1968.
The Pentagon Papers: The Defense Department History of Decisionmaking on Vietnam. Senator Gravel ed. 5 vols. Boston: Beacon Press, 1971–1972.
Public Papers of the Presidents of the United States, Dwight Eisenhower
Public Papers of the Presidents of the United States, Lyndon B. Johnson
Public Papers of the Presidents of the United States, John F. Kennedy
Public Papers of the Presidents of the United States, Harry S. Truman
United Nations. Department of Economic Affairs. *United Nations, Economic Development in Selected Countries: Plans, Programmes and Agencies*. Lake Success, NY: United Nations, 1947.

United Nations. Department of Economic Affairs. *United Nations, World Economic Report, 1948.* Lake Success, NY: United Nations, 1949.

United Nations. Department of Economic Affairs. *United Nations, World Economic Report, 1949–1950.* Lake Success, NY: United Nations, 1951.

U.S. Air Force Project. *The Vietnamese "Strategic Hamlets": A Preliminary Report.* Santa Monica, CA: Rand Corporation, 1962.

U.S. Department of State. *Foreign Relations of the United States, 1950, Indochina.* Vol. IV. Washington, DC: GPO, 1950.

U.S. Department of State. *Foreign Relations of the United States, 1952–1954.* Vols. XIII–XVI. Washington, DC: GPO, 1954.

U.S. Department of State. *Foreign Relations of the United States, 1955–1957, Vietnam.* Washington, DC: GPO, 1957.

U.S. Department of State. *Foreign Relations of the United States, 1958–1960, Vietnam.* Washington, DC: GPO, 1960.

U.S. Department of State. *Foreign Relations of the United States, 1960–1963, Vietnam.* Vols. I–IV. Washington, DC: GPO, 1963.

U.S. Department of State. *Foreign Relations of the United States, 1964–1968, Vietnam.* Vols. I–VI. Washington, DC: GPO, 1968.

Williams, William A., Thomas McCormick, Lloyd Gardner, and Walter LaFeber. *America in Vietnam: A Documentary History.* New York: Anchor Books, 1985.

THE U.S. CONGRESS: HOUSE OF REPRESENTATIVES

U.S. Congress. House. *Report of Special Subcommittee to South Vietnam,* following an inspection tour, 89th Cong., 1st sess., June 10–21, 1965.

U.S. Congress. House. Committee on Government Operations. *An Investigation of the U.S. Economic and Military Assistance Programs in Vietnam.* 89th Cong., 2nd sess., 1966.

U.S. Congress. House. *Report of Special Subcommittee Following Visit to Southeast Asia, April 7–19, 1966.* 89th Cong., 2nd sess., 1966.

U.S. Congress. House. Committee on Government Operations. *Illicit Practices Affecting the U.S. Economic Program in Vietnam (Followup Investigation).* 90th Cong., 1st sess., 1967.

U.S. Congress. House. Committee on Government Operations. *The Port Situation in Vietnam (Followup Investigation).* 90th Cong., 1st sess., 1967.

U.S. Congress. House. Committee on Government Operations. *A Review of the Inequitable Monetary Rate of Exchange in Vietnam.* 91st Cong., 2nd sess., 1970.

U.S. Congress. House. Committee on Government Operations. *Commercial (Commodity) Import Program for Vietnam (Followup Investigation).* 91st Cong., 2nd sess., 1970.

U.S. Congress. House. Committee on Government Operations. *A Review of Steel Purchased for the Commercial Barge Construction Program in Vietnam.* 91st Cong., 2nd sess., 1970.

U.S. Congress. House. Committee on Armed Services. *United States–Vietnam Relations, 1945–1967: Study Prepared by the Department of Defense.* 12 vols. Washington, DC: GPO, 1971.

THE U.S. CONGRESS: SENATE

U.S. Congress. Senate. *Report on Indochina: Report of Senator Mike Mansfield on a Study Mission to Vietnam, Cambodia, Laos.* 83rd Cong., 2nd sess., 1954.

U.S. Congress. Senate. Special Committee to Study the Foreign Aid Program. *The Objectives of the United States Economic Assistance Programs,* by the Center for International Studies, Massachusetts Institute of Technology. 85th Cong., 1st sess., 1957.

U.S. Congress. Senate. Committee of Foreign Relations. *Situation in Vietnam: Hearings before the Subcommittee on State Department Organizations and Public Affairs of the Committee of Foreign Relations.* 86th Cong., 1st sess., 1959.

U.S. Congress. Senate. Committee on Foreign Relations. *United States Aid Program in Vietnam.* 86th Cong., 2nd sess., 1960.

U.S. Congress. Senate. *Viet Nam and Southeast Asia: Report of Senator Mike Mansfield, et al., to the Committee on Foreign Relations.* 88th Cong., 1st sess., 1962.

U.S. Congress. Senate. *Refugee Problems in South Vietnam and Laos: Hearings before the Subcommittee on Refugees and Escapees of the Committee on the Judiciary.* 89th Cong., 1st sess., 1965.

U.S. Congress. Senate. *Report No. 2, Viet Nam: The Situation and Outlook, Report to the President of the United States by Senator Mike Mansfield.* 1965.

U.S. Congress. Senate. *Supplemental Military Procurement and Construction Authorizations, Fiscal Year 1966, Hearings before the Committee on Armed Services and the Subcommittee on Department of Defense of the Committee on Appropriations.* 89th Cong., 2nd sess., 1966.

U.S. Congress. Senate. *U.S. Apparatus of Assistance to Refugees throughout the World, Hearings before the Subcommittee to Investigate Problems Connected with Refugees and Escapees of the Committee on the Judiciary.* 89th Cong., 2nd sess., 1966.

U.S. Congress. Senate. *Improper Practices, Commodity Import Program, U.S. Foreign Aid, Vietnam, Hearings before the Permanent Subcommittee on Investigations of the Committee on Government Operations.* 90th Cong., 1st sess., 1967.

U.S. Congress. Senate. *Civilian Casualty and Refugee Problems in South Vietnam, Findings and Recommendations of the Subcommittee to Investigate Problems Connected with Refugees and Escapees of the Committee on the Judiciary.* 90th Cong., 2nd sess., 1968.

U.S. Congress. Senate. *Civilian Casualty, Social Welfare and Refugee Problems in South Vietnam, Hearings before the Subcommittee to Investigate Problems Connected with Refugees and Escapees of the Committee on the Judiciary.* 91st Cong., 1st sess., 1969.

U.S. Congress. Senate. *Fraud and Corruption in Management of Military Club Systems, Illegal Currency Manipulations Affecting South Vietnam, Hearings before the Permanent Subcommittee on Investigations of the Committee on Government Operations, Part I.* 91st Cong., 1st sess., 1969.

U.S. Congress. Senate. *Fraud and Corruption in Management of Military Club Systems, Illegal Currency Manipulations Affecting South Vietnam, Hearings before the Permanent Subcommittee on Investigations of the Committee on Government Operations, Part II.* 91st Cong., 1st sess., 1969.

U.S. Congress. Senate. *Fraud and Corruption in Management of Military Club Systems, Illegal Currency Manipulations Affecting South Vietnam, Hearings before the Permanent Subcommittee on Investigations of the Committee on Government Operations, Part III.* 91st Cong., 1st sess., 1969.

U.S. Congress. Senate. *Fraud and Corruption in Management of Military Club Systems, Illegal Currency Manipulations Affecting South Vietnam, Hearings before the Permanent Subcommittee on Investigations of the Committee on Government Operations, Part IV.* 92nd Cong., 1st sess., 1970–1971.

U.S. Congress. Senate. *Fraud and Corruption in Management of Military Club Systems, Illegal Currency Manipulations Affecting South Vietnam, Hearings before the Permanent Subcommittee on Investigations of the Committee on Government Operations, Part V.* 92nd Cong., 1st sess., 1971.

U.S. Congress. Senate. *Fraud and Corruption in Management of Military Club Systems, Illegal Currency Manipulations Affecting South Vietnam, Hearings before the Permanent Subcommittee on Investigations of the Committee on Government Operations, Part VI.* 92nd Cong., 1st sess., 1971.

U.S. Congress. Senate. *Fraud and Corruption in Management of Military Club Systems, Illegal Currency Manipulations Affecting South Vietnam, Hearings before the Permanent Subcommittee on Investigations of the Committee on Government Operations, Part VII.* 92nd Cong., 1st sess., 1971.

U.S. Congress. Senate. *Fraud and Corruption in Management of Military Club Systems, Illegal Currency Manipulations Affecting South Vietnam, Hearings before the Permanent Subcommittee on Investigations of the Committee on Government Operations, Part VIII.* 92nd Cong., 1st sess., 1971.

THE AGENCY FOR INTERNATIONAL DEVELOPMENT

U.S. Agency for International Development. *United States Economic Assistance to South Vietnam, 1945–1975.* Vols. I and II. Washington, DC: U.S. Agency for International Development, 1975.

U.S. Agency for International Development. *United States Economic Assistance to South Viet Nam, 1954–1975, Terminal Report.* Prepared by the Asian Bureau, Office of Viet Nam Affairs. Washington, DC: U.S. Agency for International Development, 1975.

U.S. Agency for International Development. *United States Operations Mission, Operational Report 1963–1964.* Vietnam: U.S. Agency for International Development, 1964.

THE U.S. OPERATIONS MISSION

Annual Statistical Bulletin of the United States Operations Mission to Viet Nam, data through 1957.

Gittinger, J. Price. *Studies on Land Tenure in Vietnam: Terminal Report.* 1959: Division of Agriculture and National Resources, U.S. Operations Mission to Viet Nam, 1959.

U.S. Operations Mission to Viet Nam. *Vietnam Moves Ahead: Annual Report for Fiscal Year 1960.* Washington, DC: U.S. Operations Mission to Viet Nam, 1960.

U.S. Operations Mission to Viet Nam. *Vietnam Meets Its Challenge: USOM Annual Report for Fiscal Year 1961.* Washington, DC: U.S. Operations Mission to Viet Nam, 1961.

U.S. Operations Mission to Viet Nam. *Annual Report for Fiscal Year 1962.* Vietnam: U.S. Operations Mission to Viet Nam, 1962.

NEWSPAPERS/JOURNALS/MAGAZINES

Washington Post
New York Times
Boston Globe
New York Herald Tribune
Christian Science Monitor
Vietnam Builders
Baltimore Sun
Times of Viet Nam

Asian Survey
International Affairs
Diplomatic History
Development and Change
Cultural Anthropology
Economic Development and Cultural Change
Journal of American History
International History Review
Pacific Affairs
Political Science Quarterly
Foreign Affairs
Pacific Historical Review
Far Eastern Survey

The Em-Kayan
Jones Journal
Construction Equipment and Materials
Engineering News-Record
Fortune
New Republic
Life
Parameters
Power Parade
All Hands
U.S. Naval Institute Proceedings
Ramparts

BIBLIOGRAPHY

BOOKS/MEMOIRS/ARTICLES

Acheson, Dean. *Power and Diplomacy*. New York: Atheneum, 1966.

———. *Present at the Creation: My Years in the State Department*. New York: W. W. Norton, 1969.

Adas, Michael. *Dominance by Design: Technological Imperatives and America's Civilizing Mission*. Cambridge, MA: Harvard University Press, 2006.

Allen, George W. *None So Blind: A Personal Account of the Intelligence Failure in Vietnam*. Chicago: Ivan R. Dee, 2001.

Allison, William. "War for Sale: The Black Market, Currency Manipulation and Corruption in the American War in Vietnam." *War & Society* 21, no. 2 (2003): 135–64.

Ambrose, Stephen E. *Eisenhower: Soldier and President*. New York: Simon & Schuster, 1990.

Anderson, David. *Trapped by Success: The Eisenhower Administration and Vietnam, 1953–1961*. New York: Columbia University Press, 1991.

Arndt, H. W. *Economic Development: The History of an Idea*. Chicago: University of Chicago Press, 1989.

Ball, George. *The Past Has Another Pattern*. New York: W. W. Norton, 1982.

Baritz, Loren. *Backfire: How American Culture Led Us into the Vietnam War and Made Us Fight the Way We Did*. New York: Morrow, 1985.

Bergureud, Eric. *The Dynamics of Defeat: The Vietnam War in Hau Nghia Province*. Boulder, CO: Westview Press, 1991.

Berman, Larry. *Planning a Tragedy: The Americanization of the War in Vietnam*. New York: W. W. Norton, 1982.

———. *Lyndon Johnson's War: The Road to Stalemate in Vietnam*. New York: W. W. Norton, 1989.

———. *No Peace, No Honor: Nixon, Kissinger, and Betrayal in Vietnam*. New York: Free Press, 2001.

Blaufarb, Douglas. *The Counterinsurgency Era: U.S. Doctrine and Performance*. New York: Free Press, 1977.

Blum, John M. *Years of Discord: American Politics and Society, 1961–1974*. New York: W. W. Norton, 1991.

Bradley, Mark P. *Imagining Vietnam and America: The Making of Postcolonial Vietnam, 1919–1950*. Chapel Hill: University of North Carolina Press, 2000.

Brigham, Robert. *Guerrilla Diplomacy: The NLF's Foreign Relations and the Vietnam War*. Ithaca, NY: Cornell University Press, 1999.

Brown, William A., Jr., and Opie Redvers. *American Foreign Assistance*. Washington, DC: Brookings Institution, 1953.

Burdick, Eugene, and William J. Lederer. *The Ugly American*. New York: W. W. Norton, 1958.

Buzzanco, Robert. *Masters of War: Military Dissent & Politics in the Vietnam Era*. New York: Cambridge University Press, 1996.

———. *Vietnam and the Transformation of American Life*. Malden, MA: Blackwell, 1999.

Cable, Larry. *Unholy Grail: The U.S. and the Wars in Vietnam, 1965–8*. New York: Routledge, 1991.

Catton, Philip E. "Counter-Insurgency and Nation Building: The Strategic Hamlet Programme in South Vietnam, 1961–1963." *International History Review* 21 (December 1999): 918–40.

———. *Diem's Final Failure: Prelude to America's War in Vietnam.* Lawrence: University Press of Kansas, 2002.

Chomsky, Noam. *Rethinking Camelot: JFK, the Vietnam War, and US Political Culture.* Boston: South End Press, 1993.

Chomsky, Noam, Ira Katznelson, R. C. Lewontin, David Montgomery, Laura Nader, Richard Ohmann, Ray Siever, Immanuel Wallerstein, and Howard Zinn. *The Cold War and the University: Toward an Intellectual History of the Postwar Years.* New York: New Press, 1996.

Cooper, Chester. *The Lost Crusade: America in Vietnam.* New York: Dodd, Mead, 1970.

Cullather, Nick. "Development? Its History." *Diplomatic History* 24 (Fall 2000): 641–53.

Dacy, Douglas C. *Foreign Aid, War, and Economic Development: South Vietnam, 1955–1975.* New York: Cambridge University Press, 1986.

Dallek, Robert. *Flawed Giant: Lyndon Johnson and His Times, 1961–1973.* New York: Oxford University Press, 1998.

Diamond, Sigmund. *Compromised Campus: The Collaboration of Universities with the Intelligence Community, 1945–1955.* New York: Oxford University Press, 1992.

Dieu, Nguyen Thi. *The Mekong River and the Struggle for Indochina: Water, War, and Peace.* Westport, CT: Praeger, 1999.

Donald, Aïda D., ed. *John F. Kennedy and the New Frontier.* New York: Hill and Wang, 1966.

Draper, Theodore. *Abuse of Power.* New York: Viking Press, 1966.

Duiker, William J. *Sacred War: Nationalism and Revolution in a Divided Vietnam.* New York: McGraw-Hill, 1995.

———. *The Communist Road to Power in Vietnam.* 2nd ed. Boulder, CO: Westview Press, 1996.

———. *Ho Chi Minh: A Life.* New York: Hyperion, 2000.

Dunn, Carroll H. *Base Development in South Vietnam, 1965–1970.* Washington, DC: Department of the Army, 1972.

Eisenstadt, S. N. "Sociological Aspects of Political Development in Underdeveloped Countries." *Economic Development and Cultural Change* 5, no. 4 (1957): 289–98.

Elliott, David W. P. *The Vietnamese War: Revolution and Social Change in the Mekong Delta, 1930–1975.* New York: M. E. Sharpe, 2002.

Ellsberg, Daniel. *Secrets: A Memoir of Vietnam and the Pentagon Papers.* New York: Viking/Penguin, 2002.

Engerman, David C., Nils Gilman, Mark H. Haefele, and Michael E. Latham. *Staging Growth: Modernization, Development, and the Global Cold War.* Amherst: University of Massachusetts Press, 2003.

Ernst, John. *Forging a Fateful Alliance: Michigan State University and the Vietnam War.* East Lansing: Michigan State University Press, 1998.

Escobar, Arturo. "Power and Visibility: Development and the Invention and Management of the Third World." *Cultural Anthropology* 3, no. 4 (1988): 428–43.

————. *Encountering Development: The Making and Unmaking of the Third World*. Princeton, NJ: Princeton University Press, 1994.

Fall, Bernard B. *The Two Viet-Nams: A Political and Military Analysis*. Rev. ed. New York: Praeger, 1964.

————. *Viet-Nam Witness, 1953–1966*. New York: Praeger, 1966.

————. *Hell in a Very Small Place: The Siege of Dien Bien Phu*. New York: J. B. Lippincott, 1967.

Fitzgerald, Francis. *Fire in the Lake: The Vietnamese and the Americans in Vietnam*. New York: Vintage Books, 1972.

Fulbright, J. William. *The Arrogance of Power*. New York: Random House, 1966.

Gardner, Lloyd C. *Approaching Vietnam: From World War II through Dienbienphu*. New York: W. W. Norton, 1988.

————. *Pay Any Price: Lyndon Johnson and the Wars for Vietnam*. Chicago: Ivan R. Dee, 1995.

Gendzier, Irene. *Managing Political Change: Social Scientists and the Third World*. Boulder, CO: Westview Press, 1985.

Giglio, James N. *The Presidency of John F. Kennedy*. Lawrence: University Press of Kansas, 1991.

Gilman, Nils. *The Mandarins of the Future: Modernization Theory in Cold War America*. Baltimore, MD: Johns Hopkins University Press, 2003.

Goodman, Allan E. *The Causes and Consequences of Migration to Saigon, Vietnam*. New York: Southeast Asia Development Advisory Group, 1973.

Greene, Graham. *The Quiet American*. New York: Viking Press, 1955.

Halberstam, David. *Ho*. New York: Vintage Books, 1971.

————. *The Best and the Brightest*. Greenwich, CT: Fawcett, 1972.

————. *The Making of a Quagmire: America and Vietnam during the Kennedy Era*. Rev. ed. New York: McGraw-Hill, 1988.

Hammer, Ellen. *A Death in November: America in Vietnam, 1963*. New York: E. P. Dutton, 1987.

Hendry, James B. "American Aid in Vietnam: The View from a Village." *Pacific Affairs* 33 (December 1960): 389–90.

————. "Land Tenure in South Viet Nam." *Economic Development and Cultural Change* 9 (October 1960): 27–44.

————. *The Small World of Khanh Hau*. Chicago: Aldine, 1964.

Herring, George C. "'Peoples Quite Apart': Americans, South Vietnamese, and the War in Vietnam." *Diplomatic History* 14 (Winter 1990): 1–23.

————. *America's Longest War: The United States and Vietnam, 1950–1975*. 4th ed. New York: McGraw-Hill, 2002.

Hersh, Seymour M. *The Price of Power: Kissinger in the Nixon White House*. New York: Summit Books, 1983.

Hess, Gary R. "The Unending Debate: Historians and the Vietnam War." *Diplomatic History* 18 (Spring 1994): 239–64.

Hickey, Gerald C. *Village in Vietnam*. New Haven, CT: Yale University Press, 1964.

Hilsman, Roger. *To Move a Nation: The Politics of Foreign Policy in the Administration of John F. Kennedy*. New York: Doubleday, 1967.

Hogan, Michael J. *America in the World: The Historiography of American Foreign Relations since 1941*. Cambridge: Cambridge University Press, 1995.

Hunt, Richard A. *Pacification: The American Struggle for Vietnam's Hearts and Minds.* Boulder, CO: Westview Press, 1995.

Immerman, Richard H. "Confessions of an Eisenhower Revisionist: An Agonizing Reappraisal." *Diplomatic History* 14 (Summer 1990): 319–42.

———, ed. *John Foster Dulles and the Diplomacy of the Cold War.* Princeton, NJ: Princeton University Press, 1990.

Immerman, Richard, and Fred L. Greestein. "What Did Eisenhower Tell Kennedy about Indochina? The Politics of Misperception." *Journal of American History* 79 (September 1992): 568–87.

Jacobs, Seth. "'Our System Demands the Supreme Being': The U.S. Religious Revival and the 'Diem Experiment,' 1954–1955." *Diplomatic History* 25 (Fall 2001): 589–624.

Jamieson, Neil L. *Understanding Vietnam.* Berkeley: University of California Press, 1993.

Jian, Chen. *Mao's China and the Cold War.* Chapel Hill: University of North Carolina Press, 2001.

Johnson, Lyndon Baines. *The Vantage Point: Perspectives of the Presidency, 1963–1969.* New York: Holt, Rinehart and Winston, 1971.

Johnson, Robert David. "The Origins of Dissent: Senate Liberals and Vietnam, 1959–1964." *Pacific Historical Review* 65, no. 2 (1996): 249–74.

Kahin, George M. *Intervention: How America Became Involved in Vietnam.* New York: Anchor Books, 1987.

———. *Subversion as Foreign Policy: The Secret Eisenhower and Dulles Debacle in Indonesia.* New York: New Press, 1995.

Kahin, George M., and John W. Lewis. *The United States in Vietnam.* New York: Delta Press, 1969.

Kaiser, David. *American Tragedy: Kennedy, Johnson, and the Origins of the Vietnam War.* Cambridge, MA: Harvard University Press, 2000.

Karnow, Stanley. *Vietnam: A History.* New York: Penguin Books, 1997.

Kennedy, John F. "A Democrat Looks at Foreign Policy." *Foreign Affairs* 36, no. 1 (1957): 44–59.

Kimball, Jeffrey. *Nixon's Vietnam War.* Lawrence: University Press of Kansas, 1998.

Kolko, Gabriel. *Anatomy of a War: Vietnam, the United States, and the Modern Historical Experience.* New York: New Press, 1985.

Lacouture, Jean. *Ho Chi Minh: A Political Biography.* New York: Vintage Books, 1968.

LaFeber, Walter. *America, Russia, and the Cold War, 1945–2000.* 9th ed. New York: McGraw-Hill, 2002.

Lansdale, Edward G. *In the Midst of Wars: An American's Mission to Southeast Asia.* New York: Fordham University Press, 1991.

Latham, Michael E. "Ideology, Social Science, and Destiny: Modernization and the Kennedy Era Alliance for Progress." *Diplomatic History* 22 (Spring 1998): 199–229.

———. *Modernization as Ideology: American Social Science and "Nation Building" in the Kennedy Era.* Chapel Hill: University of North Carolina Press, 2000.

Leffler, Melvyn P. *A Preponderance of Power: National Security, the Truman Administration, and the Cold War*. Stanford, CA: Stanford University Press, 1992.

Lerner, Daniel. *The Passing of Traditional Society: Modernizing the Middle East*. London: Free Press of Glencoe, 1958.

Lewy, Guenter. *American in Vietnam*. Oxford: Oxford University Press, 1978.

Logevall, Fredrik. *Choosing War: The Lost Chance for Peace and the Escalation of War in Vietnam*. Berkeley: University of California Press, 1999.

Long, Ngô Viñh. *Before the Revolution: The Vietnamese Peasants under the French*. New York: Columbia University Press, 1973.

Lummis, C. Douglas. *Radical Democracy*. Ithaca, NY: Cornell University Press, 1996.

Marquis, Jefferson P. "The Other Warriors: American Social Science and Nation Building in Vietnam." *Diplomatic History* 24 (Winter 2000): 79–104.

Marr, David G. *Vietnamese Tradition on Trial, 1920–1945*. Berkeley: University of California Press, 1981.

———. *Vietnam 1945: The Quest for Power*. Los Angeles: University of California Press, 1995.

Matusow, Allen J. *The Unraveling of America: A History of Liberalism in the 1960s*. New York: Harper & Row, 1984.

McCormick, Thomas J. *America's Half-Century: United States Foreign Policy in the Cold War*. Baltimore, MD: Johns Hopkins University Press, 1989.

McHale, Shawn F. *Print and Power: Confucianism, Communism, and Buddhism in the Making of Modern Vietnam*. Honolulu: University of Hawaii Press, 2004.

McMahon, Robert J. "Eisenhower and Third World Nationalism: A Critique of the Revisionists." *Political Science Quarterly* 101 (1986): 453–73.

———. *The Limits of Empire: The United States and Southeast Asia since World War II*. New York: Columbia University Press, 1999.

Montgomery, John D. *The Politics of Foreign Aid: American Experience in Southeast Asia*. New York: Praeger, 1962.

Morely, Morris H. *Imperial State and Revolution: The United States and Cuba, 1952–1986*. New York: Cambridge University Press, 1987.

Morgan, Joseph. *The Vietnam Lobby: The American Friends of Vietnam, 1955–1975*. Chapel Hill: University of North Carolina Press, 1997.

Murray, Martin J. *The Development of Capitalism in Colonial Indochina, 1870–1940*. Berkeley: University of California Press, 1980.

Olson, Gregory A. *Mansfield and Vietnam: A Study in Rhetorical Adaptation*. East Lansing: Michigan State University Press, 1995.

Osanka, Franklin M., ed. *Modern Guerrilla Warfare: Fighting Communist Guerrilla Movements, 1941–1961*. New York: Free Press, 1962.

Palmer, Bruce. *The Twenty-five Year War: America's Military Role in Vietnam*. Lexington: University Press of Kentucky, 1984.

Parsons, Talcott, and Edward Shils. *Toward a General Theory of Action*. Cambridge, MA: Harvard University Press, 1951.

Paterson, Thomas G. *On Every Front: The Making of the Cold War*. New York: W. W. Norton, 1979.

———, ed. *Kennedy's Quest for Victory: American Foreign Policy, 1961–1963*. New York: Oxford University Press, 1989.

———. *Contesting Castro: The United States and the Triumph of the Cuban Revolution*. New York: Oxford University Press, 1994.

Patterson, James T. *Grand Expectations: The United States, 1945–1974*. New York: Oxford University Press, 1996.

Patti, Archimedes. *Why Viet Nam? Prelude to America's Albatross*. Berkeley: University of California Press, 1980.

Peet, Richard. *Theories of Development*. With Elaine Hartwick. New York: Guilford Press, 1999.

Perez, Louis A. *Cuba and the United States: Ties of Singular Intimacy*. Athens: University of Georgia Press, 1997.

Popkin, Samuel L. *The Rational Peasant: The Political Economy of Rural Society in Vietnam*. Berkeley: University of California Press, 1979.

Prados, John. *The Hidden History of the Vietnam War*. Chicago: Ivan R. Dee, 1995.

———. *The Blood Road: The Ho Chi Minh Trail and the Vietnam War*. New York: John Wiley, 1999.

Rabe, Stephen. *Eisenhower and Latin America: The Foreign Policy of Anti-Communism*. Chapel Hill: University of North Carolina Press, 1988.

———. *The Most Dangerous Area in the World: John F. Kennedy Confronts Communist Revolution in Latin America*. Chapel Hill: University of North Carolina Press, 1999.

Race, Jeffrey. *War Comes to Long An: Revolutionary Conflict in a Vietnamese Province*. Berkeley: University of California Press, 1972.

Reeves, Richard. *President Kennedy: Profile of Power*. New York: Simon & Schuster, 1993.

Robequain, Charles. *The Economic Development of French Indochina*. London: Oxford University Press, 1944.

Rosenstein-Rodan, P. N. "The International Development of Economically Backward Areas." *International Affairs* 20, no. 2 (1944): 157–65.

Rostow, Walt W. *The Process of Economic Growth*. New York: W. W. Norton, 1952.

———. *The Stages of Economic Growth: A Non-communist Manifesto*. New York: Cambridge University Press, 1960.

———. *Eisenhower, Kennedy, and Foreign Aid*. Austin: University of Texas Press, 1985.

Rostow, Walt W., and Max Millikan. *A Proposal: Key to an Effective Foreign Policy*. New York: Harper & Brothers, 1957.

Rotter, Andrew J. *The Path to Vietnam: Origins of the American Commitment to Southeast Asia*. Ithaca, NY: Cornell University Press, 1987.

Rust, William J. *Kennedy in Vietnam: American Vietnam Policy, 1960–1963*. New York: Charles Scribner's Sons, 1985.

Schlesinger, Arthur M., Jr. *A Thousand Days: John F. Kennedy in the White House*. Boston: Houghton Mifflin, 1965.

Schmitz, David. *Thank God They're on Our Side: The United States & Right-Wing Dictatorships, 1921–1965*. Chapel Hill: University of North Carolina Press, 1999.

Schraeder, Peter J., ed. *Intervention into the 1990s: U.S. Foreign Policy in the Third World.* 2nd ed. Boulder, CO: Lynne Rienner, 1992.

Schulzinger, Robert D. *A Time for War: The United States and Vietnam, 1941–1975.* New York: Oxford University Press, 1997.

Scigliano, Robert. "Political Parties in South Vietnam under the Republic." *Pacific Affairs* 33 (December 1960): 327–47.

———. *South Vietnam: Nation under Stress.* Boston: Houghton Mifflin, 1963.

Scigliano, Robert, and Guy Fox. *Technical Assistance in Vietnam: The Michigan State University Experience.* New York: Praeger, 1965.

Scott, James C. *The Moral Economy of the Peasant: Rebellion and Subsistence in Southeast Asia.* New Haven, CT: Yale University Press, 1977.

———. *Seeing Like a State: How Certain Schemes to Improve the Human Conditions Have Failed.* New Haven, CT: Yale University Press, 1998.

Sears, Dudley. "The Birth, Life and Death of Development Economics." *Development and Change* 10 (1979): 707–19.

Shaplen, Robert. *The Lost Revolution: The Story of Twenty Years of Neglected Opportunities in Vietnam and of America's Failure to Foster Democracy There.* New York: Harper & Row, 1966.

Sheehan, Neil. *A Bright Shining Lie: John Paul Vann and America in Vietnam.* New York: Random House, 1988.

Simpson, Christopher. *Universities and Empire: Money and Politics in the Social Sciences during the Cold War.* New York: New Press, 1999.

Small, Melvin. *Johnson, Nixon, and the Doves.* New Brunswick, NJ: Rutgers University Press, 1988.

———. *Antiwarriors: The Vietnam War and the Battle for America's Hearts and Minds.* Wilmington, DE: Scholarly Resources, 2002.

Spector, Ronald. *Advice and Support: The Early Years – The U.S. Army in Vietnam.* Washington, DC: Center of Military History, 1983.

Steinberg, David Joel, ed. *In Search of Southeast Asia: A Modern History.* Rev. ed. Honolulu: University of Hawaii Press, 1987.

Summers, Harry G. *On Strategy: A Critical Analysis of the Vietnam War.* Novato, CA: Presidio Press, 1982.

Taylor, Keith W. *The Birth of Vietnam.* Berkeley: University of California Press, 1983.

Taylor, Leonard B. *Financial Management of the Vietnam Conflict, 1962–1972.* Washington, DC: Department of the Army, 1974.

Taylor, Milton C. "South Viet-Nam: Lavish Aid, Limited Progress." *Pacific Affairs* 34, no. 23 (1961): 242–56.

Trued, M. N. "South Viet-Nam's Industrial Development Center." *Pacific Affairs* 33, (1960): 250–67.

Trullinger, James W. *Village at War: An Account of Conflict in Vietnam.* Stanford, CA: Stanford University Press, 1994.

Truman, Harry S. *Years of Trial and Hope.* New York: Doubleday, 1956.

Wehrle, Edmund F. "'A Good, Bad Deal': John F. Kennedy, W. Averell Harriman, and the Neutralization of Laos, 1961–1962." *Pacific Historical Review* 67 (1998): 349–59.

Westad, Odd Arne. *The Global Cold War: Third World Interventions and the Making of Our Times.* New York: Cambridge University Press, 2005.

Wiesner, Louis A. *Victims and Survivors: Displaced Persons and Other War Victims in Viet-Nam, 1954–1975*. New York: Greenwood Press, 1988.

Williams, Albert P., Jr. "South Viet-Nam's Development in a Postwar Era: A Commentary on the Thuc-Lilienthal Report." *Asian Survey* 11, no. 4 (1971): 352–70.

Williams, William Appleman. *The Tragedy of American Diplomacy*. 3rd ed. New York: W. W. Norton, 1972.

———. *The Contours of American History*. New York: W. W. Norton, 1988.

Winters, Francis. *The Year of the Hare: America in Vietnam, January 25, 1963–February 15, 1964*. Athens: University of Georgia Press, 1997.

Woods, Randall Bennett. *Fulbright: A Biography*. New York: Cambridge University Press, 1995.

Wurfel, David. "Agrarian Reform in the Republic of Vietnam." *Far Eastern Survey* 26 (June 1957): 81–92.

Young, Marilyn B. *The Vietnam Wars, 1945–1990*. New York: Harper Perennial, 1991.

Zasloff, Joseph J. "Rural Resettlement in South Viet Nam: The Agroville Program." *Pacific Affairs* 34, no. 4 (Winter 1962): 327–40.

Zeiler, Thomas W. *Dean Rusk: Defending the American Mission Abroad*. Wilmington, DE: Scholarly Resources, 2000.

Zhai, Qiang. *China and the Vietnam Wars, 1950–1975*. Chapel Hill: University of North Carolina Press, 2000.

Zinoman, Peter. *The Colonial Bastille: A History of Imprisonment in Vietnam, 1862–1940*. Los Angeles: University of California Press, 2001.

INDEX

INDEX